WWII Blackouts

Britain and Germany

Benjamin Bachmeier

Abstract

The impact of air raid precautions in Britain and Germany has received little scholarly attention since the end of the Second World War. Of the protective measures brought about as a result of the invention of the bomber, the blackout was by far the most intrusive and extensive form of civil defence. Yet the historiography of the home front and the bombing war in Britain and Germany has tended to sideline the blackout, or else ignore it entirely.

The lack of study given to the blackout is at odds with the scale of its impact across wartime society. This thesis furthers understanding of the blackout and the social history of the British and German home fronts by contextualising the blackout within the development of aviation, and its social and economic effects. It also examines the impact technology could have on the relationship between state and citizens, and addresses the lack of comparative research on Britain and Germany during the Second World War.

The thesis draws on extensive research conducted in local and national government archives in Britain and Germany, as well as a wide range of secondary literature on the war and inter-war period. It argues that the blackout was a profound expansion of the state into the lives of each nation's citizens, and though it was set within two politically very different states, it brought with it similar practical and social problems. The blackout, as the most social' form of civil defence, is an ideal aspect of the war by which to compare the British and German home fronts. Ultimately, the differences between the two countries were less important than the shared sense of obligation that the blackout principle was intended to foster within the wartime community.

Table of Contents

Abbreviations

ARP	Air Raid Precautions
BA Berlin	Bundesarchiv Berlin (Federal Archives, Berlin)
BA-MA	Bundes Militärarchiv Freiburg (Federal Military Archives, Freiburg)
BAYHSTA	Bayerische Staatsarchiv (Bavarian State Archives)
BBC	British Broadcasting Corporation
BRO	Bristol Records Office
IR	Infrared
IWM	Imperial War Museum
MO	Mass Observation
MOA	Mass Observation Archive
NAS	National Archive of Scotland
NSKK	Nationalsozialistisches Kraftfahrkorps (National Socialist Motor Corps)
RAF	Royal Air Force
RDI	Reichsverband der Deutschen Industrie (Association of German Industry)
RLB	Reichsluftschutzbund (National Air Raid Protection League)
SA	Sturmabteilung (Stormtroopers)
SD	Sicherheitsdienst (SS Security Service)
SPD	Sozialdemokratische Partei Deutschlands (German Social Democratic Party)
TNA	The National Archives
USAAF	United States Army Air Forces

Chapter One – Introduction

On the evening of 1 September 1939, the people of Glasgow watched their city darken under the first night of the wartime blackout. People arrived from the suburbs to see the city centre in the gloom, with the mood of the crowd varying between nervous excitement and happy-go-lucky abandon.[1] From the roof of *The Glasgow Herald*'s offices the view was less ambiguous; in its words, the city stretched to the horizon black and forbidding'.[2] To the south, a severe electrical storm was building. The city would not be lit up again for another six years.

Across the cities, towns and villages of Britain and Germany the lights were dowsed, covering them with a dark that seemed at odds with the pace of modernity that had been so fast and transformative since the turn of the century. Civilised nations were once again at war; those of a philosophical mind could not help but wonder if the darkened cities and towns were a symbol of technology's capacity for ruining, rather than building civilization. The preceding six years in Germany had seen an unprecedented mobilisation of civilians into a permanent readiness for war and, most notably, the potential devastation of air war. Across the country, bombs on plinths had advertised air defence exhibitions and branches of the local air raid precaution organization. These strange menhirs of the air age, which always stood as though primed, only an instant away from striking ground, were evidence of a profound shift in the German public's knowledge of space and of the militarization of it. By comparison, British preparations for air raid precautions during the inter-war years were far less evident. Moves towards international disarmament by the British government had come

---

[1] 'First Blackout of the War', *The Glasgow Herald*, 4 September 1939, p.7.
[2] Ibid.

to little, and with a domestic political climate that was unfavourable for militarisation, ARP was given very little profile before the Munich crisis.[3] Yet despite their apparent differences, both countries were to experience the most complete blackout in Europe over the course of the war. It would be maintained for every day of the war in every house and office block, every factory and shipyard, and on every vehicle on land and water. Where light shone in the dark it had to be extinguished. Because of this, the impact of the blackout on both countries was profound and unprecedented. This study is an attempt to describe how the blackout was organised in both countries, and investigate its impact on civilian life. While the civilian experience of bombing and the war in general is often filtered through the perspective of a single nation, this study makes an explicit attempt to broaden the narrative of the war past national borders. In trying to discover what was common and what was different under the blackout, it is hoped that a new perspective on the home fronts of Britain and Germany can be found. This chapter begins by establishing the methodological framework of the study, and moves on to setting out its place within the historiography of the Second World War, the bombing war, and the social history of both countries.

Methodology

This section establishes the methodological framework for the analysis of this research, and discusses the selection of sources. First, it explains the validity of using the comparative method, drawing on current theoretical literature. This then forms the basis for outlining and qualifying the sources used in this study. Though reading histories of the war will show there are a number of ways of spelling it, for the purposes of this thesis the blackout' will be spelled as it sounds when spoken, rather than

---

[3] On this see Carolyn Kitching, *Britain and the Problem of International Disarmament, 1919-1934* (London: Routledge, 1999). David Edgerton argues that the British military-industrial complex was far better supported during these years than is generally acknowledged. Despite this, it is still the case that the government was not inclined to promote civil defence publicly, in case it was seen as militarisation. See David Edgerton, *Warfare State: Britain, 1920-1970* (Cambridge: Cambridge University Press, 2006), pp.15-58.

hyphenated or separated. Air Raid Precautions will be referred to as ARP, under which I will also draw the German system of civil defence, *Luftschutz*, and which was generally maintained by members of the *Reichsluftschutzbund* (RLB). ARP therefore corresponds to the system of civil defence in both countries.

Comparative history

What is the use of comparative history when studying the home front, and what can be learned in this approach that is absent from nationally based studies? The lack of any previous comparative study of the British and German home fronts might indicate that the approach is not in fact that useful, or of interest. However, what the following discussion demonstrates is that comparative analysis is a necessary corrective to histories of the home front that are rooted in a single nation.

Though generally absent from treatments of the home front, theoretical work on the uses of comparative analysis in history is nevertheless well established. An early turn towards comparison can be found within the French Annales School of the 1930s. For Marc Bloch, the comparative method was a way to test the explanations and hypotheses of historians, in much the same way as the scientist would test hypotheses through experimentation. As Sewell writes, for Bloch the comparative method, like the experimental method, is a means of systematically gathering evidence to test the validity of our explanations'.[4] In this case, general explanations given to the experience of one region or country can be interrogated by comparing it with another. Doing so allows the study to identify similarities and contradictions, so that existing knowledge can be developed or discounted. Given the rather narrow focus of national histories of the home front, this approach is invaluable for determining wider transnational patterns

---

[4] William H. Sewell, 'Marc Bloch and the Logic of Comparative History', *History and Theory*, 6/2 (1967), p.209.

in European history. Jürgen Kocka, one of the leading contemporary writers on comparative history, agrees with this in principle. He writes:

> Comparison opens the door to seeing other possibilities, it sharpens the historian's sense for possibilities, and allows to discern the observed case as one possibility among several. It helps to relativize one's own record in the light of others.[5]

In this regard, comparative history can become political. Choosing to relativize national histories within the context of other nations alters the tenor of both; it is a *deliberate* attempt to re-cast their explanations in a regional, transnational or international setting, in order to critique existing knowledge. The importance of selecting the comparative bodies is paramount here. Choosing one body over another may alter the tenor and findings of research. Similarly, an asymmetry in how sources are treated or understood could also distort the results of any comparison. Kocka is forthright on the dangers of this. Drawing on the critiques of the *Sonderweg* thesis of German history advanced by David Blackbourn and Geoff Eley, Kocka argues that the *Sonderweg's* comparative core presumes that Germany diverged in its development from other European nations only by omitting any real analysis of those other nations. *Sonderweg* scholarship defines modernization in a way that is too prescriptive and normative; Germany cannot be judged to have ‗diverted' from a true path to modernization without assuming that there is only one defined way to it. This superficial, asymmetric treatment provides the basis for the ideas of the *Sonderweg*.[6] While it has remained resilient within German historiography, displaying what Sheehan calls ‗remarkable persistence' despite its critics, the refinement of its comparative basis has been necessary.[7] Indeed, some scholars have sought to move beyond it entirely. Konrad Hugo Jarausch and Michael Geyer argue that the problem of what modernity means in the context of German history can only be understood by removing from the term its usual baggage. For them:

---

[5] Jürgen Kocka, 'Comparative History: Methodology and Ethos', *East Central Europe,* 36 (2009), p.15.
[6] Jürgen Kocka, 'Asymmetrical Historical Comparison: The Case of the German Sonderweg', *History and Theory,* 38/1 (1999), pp.43-50.
[7] James J. Sheehan, 'Paradigm Lost? The "Sonderweg" Revisited', in Sebastian Conrad Gunilla-Friederike Budde, Oliver Janz (ed.), *Transnationale Geschichte: Themen, Tendenzen und Theorien* (Göttingen: Vandenhoeck & Ruprecht, 2006).

A post-Sonderweg history ought not to view modernity as an obvious end in itself but rather as a Janus-faced problem that needs to be historicized... the Holocaust debate, the peace movement, and ecological criticism have produced shocking evidence of the pathologies of modernity in the misuse of science for killing or the abuse of technology for environmental degradation... Only a less deterministic and sanguine understanding of the meanings of 'modern' can come to terms with the profoundly ambivalent consequences of the industrial era.[8]

In this context, the blackout becomes a useful point around which to examine German modernity and the peculiarities of the German state against its British neighbour. Both were modern states with advanced aviation industries, and both had a cultural heritage of flight that permeated through the public sphere. This cultural aspect of aviation was important in the development of the ARP, and of the blackout in particular. There were two levels at which air defence was organized. The first tier lay within government itself, and the associated bodies attached to it such as the military, the air forces and aviation industry. Though public opinion played a factor, development of air defence at this first tier could proceed without the need to mobilize citizens. The second tier corresponded with the measures needed to secure civil defence in peacetime, and this did indeed involve the mobilisation of the public. This is level at which ARP, and the blackout, were developed. Though planning for both could be handled within national and local government, their successful operation required the involvement of large numbers of civilians in organisations dedicated to defending the country against bombing, and public understanding of what required of them in the event of a large scale bombing war. This was especially true of the blackout, as it was an entirely social form of civil defence. It was, effectively, a response to militarised aviation. The political climate and structure in which this response was organised by the German and British state, and the extent to which their populations were mobilized before and after the outbreak of war, provides a useful focus for relativizing their approach to preparations for bombing, and for discerning what was unique and what was common in them.

---

[8] Michael Geyer Konrad Hugo Jarausch, *Shattered Past: Reconstructing German Histories* (Princeton: Princeton University Press, 2003), pp.104-105.

Owing to their entirely different political complexion by 1939, choosing Britain and Germany may at first glance seem odd. Before 1939 neither had a comparable public sphere, nor was official policy on rearmament and civil defence remotely similar. These factors alone could militate against any comparative evaluations. Yet despite their differences, the fact that Britain and Germany held the most complete blackout observed by pilots during the war marks it as a valid point of comparison. They were also the only two countries that fought for the entire length of the European war, from September 1939 to May 1945. This is not to say that no comparisons between Britain and Germany exist, and there are indeed comparative studies that identify common cultural and political ground during the pre-war years, as the literature review will later establish. But it is perhaps strange that the British and German home fronts have yet to be compared. Given the focus on explaining the home front as a nationally unifying phenomenon, this is perhaps more a quirk of that particular historiography than a reason for not undertaking it. The problem of relying solely on histories that are traditionally bound to the national experience is that they lack a point of comparison that might identify behaviours as particular to systems or technology, rather than as specifically _national' behaviours. We might presuppose that German civil defence was more thoroughly organised in Germany owing to its increasingly higher profile during the inter-war period, compared with its lower status in Britain until the late 1930s. But how can we be certain if we do not compare them? Likewise, is there anything particularly British about the traditional blackout narrative – irritating wardens, fear of crime, and an enormous increase in road casualties? This study's comparative focus allows it to analyse and, if necessary, correct the narrative of the wartime blackout, and the public's experience of the war more generally.

However, there are of course limitations to this study. Only two countries are analysed here. A third country might refine the analysis and throw into relief aspects of the blackout that are otherwise absent in this study. As detailed in the literature review, comparative studies of fascist and communist societies during the war are more prevalent than studies of fascist and democratic systems. Yet studies of the Italian experience of bombing suggest that the blackout was altogether weaker, and much less effective there.[9] This alone suggests that thoroughness in mobilising ARP owed more to other aspects of states than simply their political systems. The conclusions drawn from this research are therefore specific to both nations; no more generalised conclusions should be deduced from the thesis, though the potential is certainly there for developing its conclusions beyond Britain and Germany. These issues will be explored more fully in the concluding chapter of the thesis.

The theoretical weight of comparative history in the period which concerns this research is inclined towards Germany. This is due, in part at least, to a reflexive need amongst some scholars of German history to redefine what it is about it that is unique, and to problematize those aspects attributed as specific to the German experience. As seen in the previous discussion of *Sonderweg* historiography, analysing the traumas of recent German history against the histories of other nations, and of other transnational trends, provides some measure for gauging what was unique about the origins of the Third Reich. However, the methodology of comparative history is not without its critics, and mapping it across British and German approaches brings out some differences in interpretation. While this is not the space to develop these arguments in detail, a sketch of them is necessary in order to justify not only the choice of countries and sources for this study, but also the validity of a comparative approach.

---

[9] On this see Marco Fincardi Claudia Baldoli, 'Italian Society under Anglo-American bombs: Propaganda, Experience, and Legend, 1940-1945', *The Historical Journal, 52/4* (2009).

Despite the efforts of some scholars, the distinction between comparative and transnational history is still rather murky.[10] Transnational history has lately established a higher profile in Anglo-American academia. The problems of comparative history as described in the troubles of the *Sonderweg* – that the method itself can end up producing ideas of national difference as much as any national study – are drawn on by some scholars to justify attempts to move towards a more transnational frame of comparison. They see the comparative method as related to the more traditional form of international history, which transnational history works explicitly against. Where international history's focus lies in how states interact with other states, transnational history instead examines multi-directional flows of history, focussing on the units that spill over and seep through national borders, units both greater and smaller than the nation-state'.[11] Again, there is no space in this thesis to develop these arguments more fully. The methodological ambitions of this study are very modest, namely to demonstrate the use of comparative history in studying the British and German home fronts. Investigating the subtle differences between transitional and comparative history is therefore outside its scope. However, reflecting on methodology does have its use in this study for developing a nuanced comparative framework. The charge that the comparative method may, in Seigel's words, discourage attention to exchange between the two [units]' is well taken.[12] This research attempts to mitigate this by retaining a focus on both nations as modern powers, adapting to a process of technological change that is not bounded by national borders. Without wanting to delve too far into abstraction, in the context of this thesis the invention of flight creates, firstly, a network of knowledge that extends across the borders of the developed world, and secondly, a problem of knowledge in how flight and its militarisation affects the internal

---

[10] See Sven Beckert C. A. Bayly, Matthew Connelly, Isabel Hofmeyr, Wendy Kozol, Patricia Seed, 'AHR Conversation: On Transnational History', *American Historical Review*, 111/5 (2006); Patricia Clavin, 'Defining Transnationalism', *Contemporary European History*, 14/4 (2005).
[11] Micol Seigel, 'Beyond Compare: Comparative Method after the Transnational Turn', *Radical History Review*, 91 (2005), p.63.
[12] Ibid., p.65.

politics of nation states. This is integral to how the blackout was legitimated in both countries, and will be set out over the next two chapters of this thesis.

Sources

This section discusses the sources drawn on in this research. In the absence of comprehensive treatments of the blackout, this study uses a wide range of original documents, supplemented by a range of secondary literature, which is discussed more fully in the literature review.

The selection of archives for this research was dictated by the need to examine a broad spread of city records in both countries. The study focuses on cities with differing sizes and levels of bombardment. While some measure of depth must be sacrificed to accommodate research over two countries, the breadth of material drawn on here is sufficient to draw reliable distinctions. In the main, this material is collated from national and local archives. This study also draws on the vast array of contemporary published sources, particularly newspapers and journals, alongside some of the literary and artistic responses to the blackout. Finally, of substantial importance in filling out the civilian experience are the wartime diaries and letters of civilians, both published and unpublished. The cities and archives selected are detailed in the following tables.

Table 1.1 – Cities selected

Britain	Germany
Bristol	Berlin
Exeter	Dortmund
Glasgow	Hamburg
London	Munich
Manchester	Soest

Table 1.2 - Major archives accessed

Britain	Germany
Bristol Record Office	Bayerisches Hauptstaatsarchiv
Glasgow Record Office	Bundesarchiv Berlin
Imperial War Museum Archives	Bundesarchiv-Militärarchiv Freiburg
London Metropolitan Records Office	Landesarchiv Berlin
Manchester City Archives	Staatsarchiv München
Mass Observation Archive	Stadtarchiv Dortmund
National Archives	Stadtarchiv Hamburg
National Archives of Scotland	Stadtarchiv Soest
	Tagebucharchiv Emmendingen

Most of these archives provide narratives of the administrative and political development of the blackout. These in turn provide indications of how well it was followed through reports in the minutes of meetings, statements issued to local authorities from central government, statements made by government to the wider community, as well as legal cases. Three archives in particular – the Mass Observation Archive, the archives of the Imperial War Museum, and the Tagebucharchiv Emmendingen - deal with the public's response through diaries and letters. Private material from this period is treated carefully because there was a distinct asymmetry in the degree of free speech allowed in Britain and Germany. Criticisms of the blackout are therefore more often found in Britain, and their tenor is different. Any comparisons between the two countries are tempered by this. Critical consideration is also given to the manner in which diarists and respondents presented their experience. Helen Jones writes that some diarists are more conscious of presenting their private experience to a third party, adjusting their mode of address and perhaps also their level of candour. The degree of selection and editing that occurred before observers wrote up their reports is therefore kept in mind.[13] This also extends to official reports on the mood of the population. In Germany, the reports of the *Sicherheitsdienst* (SD) remain one the key sources for tracking the opinion of the German public over the course of the war.

---

[13] Helen Jones, *British Civilians in the Front Line: Air Raids, Productivity and Wartime Culture, 1939-45* (Manchester: Manchester University Press, 2006), pp.12-17.

But though invaluable, they are also problematic. Ian Kershaw, who uses the reports extensively in his study of popular opinion in Nazi Germany, writes:

> Reconstruction of opinion in the Third Reich has to rely on reported opinion, in sources moreover which were compiled for particular administrative and political purposes and contain their own heavy internal biases and colouring... Conclusions must remain, for the most part, tentative and suggestive.[14]

Neil Gregor writes that SD reports on the mood of the population after bombing used the imagery of the *Schicksalsgemeinschaft* in its reports, referring to the alleged sense of community and resolve of the German civilian population created by the allied air raids'.[15] British sources will also have to be measured against any internal bias. As Jones writes of the composition of Ministry of Information reports:

> Two assessors produced abstracts and summaries and compiled a report from the material they received. The assessors then wrote a final report, in consultation with Adams [Director of Home Intelligence at the Ministry of Information, 1939-1941]. Public opinion was thus interpreted and reinterpreted. Sometimes the views of the compilers came across strongly, although it is not always easy to tell at what point interpretation is overlaying original comments.[16]

The degree of filtering that occurs across all public sources used in this study is conditioned by the fact that both countries were at war. Reporting or commenting on the blackout was never a neutral act as it was an integral and invasive part of the civil defence system. The thesis will acknowledge these factors and reflect on how they impact on its findings.

Literature Review

As a comparative piece of research, this study attempts to synthesize a wide range of reading and sources into a coherent body of work. The following section outlines the

---

[14] Ian Kershaw, *Popular Opinion and Political Dissent in the Third Reich* (Oxford: Clarendon Press, 1983), p.6.
[15] Neil Gregor, 'A Schicksalsgemeinschaft? Allied Bombing, Civilian Morale and Social Dissolution in Nuremberg, 1942-1945', *The Historical Journal*, 43/4 (2000), p.1053.
[16] Jones, *British Civilians in the Front Line: Air Raids, Productivity and Wartime Culture, 1939-45*, p.12.

comparative literature relevant to this study. However, as there are few such studies, the review will also deal with texts that focus on each nation separately. As will be seen, the scale of the blackout's impact requires a synthesis of a wide range of texts that address the home front.

There has been no single study of the blackout since the war ended. Where it has been mentioned in studies of the war it has generally been in the context of home front life, or else wider defence preparations. However, few of these studies have attempted to describe the scale on which the blackout affected the home front. Richard Evans' final book in his trilogy on Germany under Nazi rule, *The Third Reich at War*, is a case in point. In nearly 800 pages describing life in Germany during the war the blackout receives no more than a few mentions, and any sense of the scale of its cumulative impact is absent.[17] Juliet Gardiner's book on the British home front, *Wartime: Britain 1939-1945*, devotes more attention to it, with an entire chapter on the blackout that outlines some of its main features.[18] Andrew Thorpe's study of British political organization during the war mentions the blackout in several instances, and its impact on their ability to organize and maintain their membership.[19] No detailed discussion of the blackout's effect on industry, on cultural life, on transportation or crime is attempted in these or any of the works given here. The only two exceptions are ageing studies of the civil defence preparations in Britain and Germany, neither of which has the scope for examining the social impact of the blackout.[20] Terence O'Brien's *Civil Defence*, published in 1955, is instead an extensive study of the administrative development of ARP. Erich Hampe's *Der Zivile Luftschutz im Zweiten Weltkrieg*, published in 1963, is again largely confined to the administrative development of ARP, though his generally

---

[17] For these see Richard J. Evans, *The Third Reich at War* (London: Penguin, 2009), p.72; 249; 437; 458; 513; 732.

[18] Juliet Gardiner, *Wartime: Britain 1939-1945* (London: Review, 2004), pp.53-64.

[19] Andrew Thorpe, *Parties at War: Political Organization in Second World War Britain* (Oxford: Oxford University Press, 2009).

[20] See Erich Hampe, *Der Zivile Luftschutz im Zweiten Weltkrieg* (Frankfurt am Main: Bernard & Graefe Verlag für Wehrwesen, 1963); T.H. O'Brien, *Civil Defence* (London: HMSO, 1955).

positive assessment of German preparations is coloured by his position within the German military, and as deputy leader of the *Technische Nothilfe* (Technical Emergency Corps). Despite its absence in the literature of home front and civil defence, the blackout had a substantial impact on all facets of the wartime home front. As will be shown in this study, its absence is perhaps due to its mundaneness. After the drama of the war's first few months the blackout became part of the of its backcloth, a nightly presence that was irritating yet ultimately predictable. As an event in the daily lives of citizens, it was rather boring. Yet this study contends that the blackout forms one of the most extraordinary and wide-ranging impositions on the daily lives of citizens during the twentieth century. As a programme for re-directing the behaviour of citizens in both countries it has few parallels. How can its domestic mundaneness be reconciled with its impact on the infrastructure and society of both countries?

Comparative work on the wartime nation has tended towards studying the differences across fascist and communist regimes.[21] Where comparative work between Britain and Germany exists it has instead tended to focus on the First World War, though this is again rather limited. Richard Wall and Jay Winter's study *The Upheaval of War: Family, Work and Welfare in Europe, 1914-1918* and Winter's and Jean-Louis Robert's *Capital Cities at War: Paris, London, Berlin, 1914-1919* are the only two comparative studies of social history, with the latter focussing on the city rather than the nation as its analytical unit.[22] The absence of comparative work is generally a result of the fact that Soviet Russia, Italy and Germany, as totalitarian systems, are seen to have more in common with each other than with liberal democracies. Richard Overy notes that earlier studies on these totalitarian states favoured an emphasis on national peculiarities, while more

---

[21] It should be noted here that Dietmar Süß' extensive comparative study of the German and British population under the bombs was unfortunately published too late to be incorporated into this thesis. See Dietmar Süß, *Tod aus der Luft* (München: Siedler, 2011).
[22] Jean-Louis Robert Jay Winter, *Capital Cities at War: Paris, London, Berlin, 1914-1919, Volume 1* (Cambridge: Cambridge University Press, 1999); Jay Winter Richard Wall (ed.), *The Upheaval of War: Family, Work and Welfare in Europe, 1914-1918* (Cambridge: Cambridge University Press, 2005).

recent work has allowed for a more nuanced view that begins to reconcile their differences with their common totalitarian make-up.[23] Indeed, Payne notes that the Nazi state had more in common with its Communist antagonist than its Fascist counterpart Italy.[24]

Where then is the space, or indeed the reason, for a comparison between fascist Germany and liberal democratic Britain within the context of the blackout? Some indication is given by the fact that extant comparative work examining these two countries is generally interested in their shared political, technical and administrative histories. In this context, comparative work on civil defence does exist. Bernd Lemke's study of the preparations for civil defence in Germany and Britain supposes that the manner by which a state organises itself for an existentially devastating threat – in this case bombing – allows for an insight into its fundamental political structure.[25] For the purposes of this thesis Lemke's study is limited by its pre-war timeframe. While it is strong on the political and administrative planning of civil defence – which in the absence of war is all that can generally be studied in this period – there is a lingering question; when war was declared, how did each state's planning actually turn out? This study attempts to answer that question by examining not only the blackout during the war, but the political context in which it was planned during the inter-war years. Doing this makes particular sense for the blackout since it remained largely settled in both countries after its first six months.

---

[23] Richard Overy, *The Dictators* (London: Penguin, 2005), p.xxxii.
[24] Stanley G. Payne, *A History of Fascism, 1914-1945* (Oxford: Routledge, 1995), pp.208-211. Further recent comparative studies between Russia and Germany can be found in Moshe Lewin Ian Kershaw (ed.), *Stalinism and Nazism: Dictatorships in Comparison* (Cambridge: Cambridge University Press, 1997); Sheila Fitzpatrick Michael Geyer (ed.), *Beyond Totalitarianism: Stalinism and Nazism Compared* (Cambridge: Cambridge University Press, 2009).
[25] Bernd Lemke, *Luftschutz in Großbritannien und Deutschland 1923 – 1939* (Freiburg i.Br: Albert-Ludwigs-Universität, 2001), p.563.

As part of the focus on the technological heritage of both nations, Bernhard Rieger's

book *Technology and the culture of modernity in Britain and Germany 1890-1945*, is a

signal text. Rieger sees Britain and Germany as ideal comparators for considering the

manifestations of how the public understood and adapted to new technologies. In his

words:

> The British and German publics often reacted towards new technologies in
> similar ways, which highlights transnational *cultural* patterns that promoted
> innovation in a politically heterogeneous Europe. Their shared cultural traits
> existed alongside divergent, primarily *political* evaluations of technology's
> significance for each nation that, while becoming most pronounced after 1933,
> pre-dated National Socialism's ascent to power.[26]

In Rieger's study, modernity is used as a locus for discussing the similarities of both

nations as technologic states, and allows for considering their own national

peculiarities. As a framework, this is somewhat analogous to the comparisons of

German and Soviet totalitarianism. But instead of examining the blackout solely in a

comparison of Britain and Germany's political systems, it is also useful to draw on the

transnational effects of militarised aviation. As outlined above, this approach allows for

a more nuanced approach to the comparative method. This is of particular use for this

study. In his conclusion, Rieger notes that a lessening of national technological

aggrandizement in post-war Britain and Germany can, in part, be attributed to fears of

nuclear annihilation. This fear of an existential threat from advanced military technology

was not new, and indeed existed before the war. In the discourses of ARP and civil

defence, annihilation from the air was ultimately the driving force for preparation in both

countries, and presented a significant problem of knowledge for both governments and

the public. Rieger focuses instead on the ‚idea' of aviation and aviators, rather than the

existential problem of bombing. He suggests that the risks of technology in the pre-war

period were aggregated across both societies, producing a nascent climate of risk. But

the aerial threat was in fact a very explicit manifestation of the risks of technology

before the Second World War. In particular, Germany mobilised a vision of aviation that

---

[26] Bernhard Rieger, *Technology and the Culture of Modernity in Britain and Germany 1890-1945* (Cambridge: Cambridge University Press, 2005), p.12.

was civic, as well as military and defensive, through the early establishment of gliding clubs, ARP organisations, and the high visibility given to civil defence after 1933. Peter Fritzsche's excellent study of this German airmindedness provides a substantial analysis of the extent to which aviation permeated the German public sphere.[27] His treatment of civil defence is excellent but rather brief, and reflects more on the efforts the Nazi state put into mobilising the population's airmindedness, rather than its effectiveness. He writes that:

> Air-readiness meant nothing less than massive mobilization and militarization, which were the distinctive ability of the nation state... It was this hazardous but survivable air future, this permanent condition of watchfulness, that the modern authoritarian state and particularly Nazi Germany claimed it could best manage.[28]

Fritzsche's analysis of German and Nazi airmindedness is convincing, though it closes with the above statement without asking just how successful the Nazi state actually was in preparing itself for the threat of bombing. Claims that totalitarian states were better equipped to survive it were nothing new; newspapers in Britain were asking just this question in the first few months of the war. But Fritzsche's study lacks any comparator for assessing the extent to which German airmindedness was novel, and to what extent its prevalence carried over into people's behaviour under the bombs. To an extent, this research attempts to bridge both Rieger's and Fritzsche's approaches. Analysing the effectiveness and prevalence of discourses of airmindedness within a comparative framework allows for a fuller discussion of the attempts by the totalitarian Nazi state to mobilise its population. Equivalent studies of British airmindedness are less comprehensive than Fritzsche's, and none cover the same time span. There are, however, standard texts on the development of British aviation and its relationship with the state and public – Gollin's *The Impact of Air Power on the British People and Their Government, 1909-14* being a key work here, though it is rather more comfortable in

---

[27] Peter Fritzsche, *A Nation of Fliers: German Aviation and the Popular Imagination* (Cambridge, Mass.: Harvard University Press, 1992). See also Peter Fritzsche, 'Machine Dreams: Airmindedness and the Reinvention of Germany', *The American Historical Review*, 98/3 (June 1993).
[28] Fritzsche, *A Nation of Fliers: German Aviation and the Popular Imagination*, p.219.

dealing with government than it is with the wider impact of aviation on the public.[29]

David Edgerton's *England and the Aeroplane* is also a key text, and deconstructs the misconception of Britain as a nation that was less technologically inclined than others. Aviation was instead actively encouraged by the state, with a culture of scientific and technological development of aircraft that was sustained in Britain during the interwar period.[30] More recently, Liz Millward has examined British airmindedness and gender, describing how the gendering of airspace as a masculine environment was contested in the years before the war by women aviators. Again, though useful in its definition of the cultural and discursive function of airmindedness, Millward's study is limited to a specific, elite group of women.[31] As yet, there are no studies that have linked airmindedness to the mass-mobilisation of civil defence in Britain as understood in the German case. That is this has remained the case so far reflects the markedly different character of discourses surrounding ARP before the war. Mass mobilisation of ARP, with its inevitable associations of militarisation and conflict, had a propagandistic use in Germany that was largely absent in Britain for just those reasons. Identifying the prevalent discourses of airmindedness before the war is therefore necessary for any study of ARP or the blackout. The relationship between the state's aviation and civil defence policy, and the airmindedness of its citizens, was every bit as important as the external relationship of the state to its neighbours. In contrast with the more domestic technology of automobiles, trains and radios, airmindedness rested on an appreciation of a technology that few had any direct experience of, beyond the spectacle of air shows and fly-bys. Because of its distance from the experience of most people's lives, aviation was primarily represented as an idea. This abstraction of technology had an effect on how it was understood. Hobsbawm wrote of the scientific revolution in the twentieth century that

---

[29] Alfred Gollin, *The Impact of Air Power on the British People and Their Government, 1909-14* (London: Macmillan, 1989).
[30] David Edgerton, *England and the Aeroplane: an Essay on a Militant and Technological nation* (London: Macmillan, 1991).
[31] Liz Millward, *Women in British Imperial Airspace, 1922-1937* (Quebec: McGill-Queens University Press, 2007).

though all of us today live by and with a technology which rests on the new scientific revolution, in a world whose visual appearance has been transformed by it, and one in which educated lay discourse may echo its concepts and vocabulary, it is far from clear to what extent this revolution has been absorbed into the common processes of thought of the lay public even today. One might say that it has been existentially rather than intellectually absorbed.[32]

The idea that knowledge of technology can be existential rather than intellectual is key to understanding the development of airmindedness before 1939. The disconnect between public experience and ARP meant that the political and social context in which it was legitimated was of fundamental importance. This explains why the greatest difference between Britain and Germany was not in how well their blackout was followed, but in how visible the blackout and ARP were during the inter-war period.

ARP by its nature was invasive, and savoured of war. In no aspect of ARP was this more apparent to the public than the blackout. More than other ARP measures of this period, it was a form of social control. Bunkers, flak batteries and decoy sites were defences that could be constructed from raw materials. But the blackout had to be constructed through the public's assent, and where that was not forthcoming, through the machinery of the state instead, and through the law. It necessitated a mobilisation of the public into a ready state of awareness of bombing, and in its language and ethic it imagined a ‚community‘ of citizens cooperating in their own defence. In Germany attempts at mobilisation were developed with increasing success from 1930, towards the end of Weimar Republic, and after 1933 with all the purpose a totalitarian state could muster. The British government, however, was far more reticent about trying to engage the public with ARP in any meaningful way. O'Brien's study of civil defence in Britain during this period shows a generally unfavourable climate in which to mobilise the population for peacetime preparations.[33] Rather than developing it systematically, British development of ARP reacted instead to the perceived threat from Germany, and

---

[32] Eric Hobsbawm, *The Age of Empire, 1875-1914* (London: Abacus, 1987), pp.244-245.
[33] O'Brien, *Civil Defence*, p.5.

the deterioration of the political situation on the continent. This explicit link between the two countries' development of ARP underscores their use as comparators. With little written on the importance of this dynamic in mobilising civil defence, this study fills a gap in the literature on the understanding of the development of aviation and civil defence.

Many surveys of bombing's effectiveness have been published since the end of the war, and while this study concentrates on the social history of the blackout, the operational context is also of value. The largest assessment remains the United States Strategic Bombing Survey which, in over 200 volumes, meticulously assesses the impact of the Allied bombing strategy. However, the survey's own opinion of the blackout is confined to a short paragraph.

> England and Germany both had extensive blackout systems. A question for the future is, 'How much protection does a black-out give?' The German results showed that for night-bombing it was only a slightly delaying factor. New detection devices make it doubtful that a city or even a large structure can be long concealed in the most perfect of black-outs. Flares and incendiaries vitiate its value. The usefulness of black-outs needs a critical appraisal.[34]

This appraisal was never forthcoming. The low profile of the blackout's impact is typical amongst operational studies. As with nearly all surveys of the war, it is reduced to a side issue or else not mentioned at all.[35] Civil defence lies in that liminal zone between the military and civilian spheres, and because of this it may be that operational surveys have tended to ignore the blackout, concentrating on the more physical attrition of fighter defence and flak batteries. To a large extent, this is mirrored in histories of the home front, and the next section reviews the place of this research within that context.

---

[34] *United States Strategic Bombing Survey - Overall Report (European War), Volume 2* (Washington, 1945), p.103.
[35] Sebastian Cox British Bombing Survey Unit, *The Strategic Air War Against Germany, 1939-1945: Report of the British Bombing Survey Unit* (London: Routledge, 1998); Alan J. Levine, *The Strategic Bombing of Germany, 1940-1945* (Westport: Praeger, 1992); Richard Overy, *The Air War, 1939-1945* (London: Europa, 1980).

Comparative studies of the German and British home fronts may have been hindered for want of a reasonable analytical framework. Individual treatments of both countries are, however, far more common. Within Britain, Richard Titmuss' now aging study *Problems of Social Policy* remains a touchstone, but there is a growing literature on the British home front that has sought to redefine and re-examine the experience of the war.[36] Angus Calder's work remains a key reference point for later studies of bombing and the British home front.[37] Calder began the process of turning over the received narratives of the war – of the people standing united, fighting as one, pulling victory from the jaws of defeat. Calder's work criticised the bland and populist histories of the war, whose roots lay in the officially sanctioned narratives produced during it, which had brushed aside tensions and differences within the wartime community.

Perhaps of most relevance to this research are Sonya O. Rose's *Which People's War* and Helen Jones' *British Civilians in the Front Line*.[38] Rose's research examines how the British _nation' was constructed during the war, framed through class, gender, and regional identities. Drawing on several approaches to understanding the concept of _community' within the context of the wartime nation, Rose's discussion of the cultural construction of the nation as a community also retains some space for the contributing structural factors, such as the law and work. Nationhood, as an _abstraction that produces the pull of unity', was a consequence not of automatic processes, but of _ideological work', framed the cultural and social context that generated them.[39] The arguments of this thesis contend that blackout's system of obligations played an important and little remarked upon role in generating the ideological discourses that constructed the idea of a unified home front. The blackout activated an idea of

---

[36] Richard Titmuss, *Problems of Social Policy* (London: HMSO, 1950).
[37] Angus Calder, *The People's War: Britain, 1939-1945* (London: Pantheon Books, 1969); Angus Calder, *The Myth of the Blitz* (London: Johnathan Cape, 1991).
[38] Jones, *British Civilians in the Front Line: Air Raids, Productivity and Wartime Culture, 1939-45*; Sonya O. Rose, *Which People's War? National Identity and Citizenship in Britain, 1939-1945* (Oxford: Oxford University Press, 2003).
[39] Rose, *Which People's War? National Identity and Citizenship in Britain, 1939-1945*, pp.13-14.

community that magnified the responsibilities of the individual to others; to show a light was to endanger one's street or town as much as oneself. In this case, the blackout can also been seen as a vector in how national unity is constructed and, to a large extent, legitimated. This is particularly important when considering that though the entirety of both countries was subject to the universal blackout restrictions, the experience of bombing itself was not a universal phenomenon. Some cities were bombed heavily for days, then left in ruins, and in peace, for the rest of the war. Other major centres were the sustained focus of bombing attacks over the course of the war. Yet there were areas of both countries where bombing never directly impacted on the environment. For people living in these areas, bombing' was a distant reality. Rose also elaborates on the concept of citizenship in wartime, whose discursive framework creates legal and political' subjects with certain rights and duties.[40] Falling outside of the boundaries of good citizenship meant public and legal censure. Rose writes that citizenship was predominantly understood to be a moral of ethical practice that was deemed crucial for national survival.'[41] The blackout was the only physical manifestation of the bombing war that was experienced by everyone, and for which every citizen was responsible for. With it came specific ideas of community obligation and the relationship between the state and citizen. By drawing on Rose's work, this study helps to re-orient the blackout and civil defence as more than simply a nuisance. It was also an aspect of the war that contributed to public understanding of nation, class, power, and the priorities of the wartime state, and made them more problematic. For the purposes of this research, the national community can be understood in the way that Rose defines it in the following extract.

> Understanding nationhood as an ideological discourse that produces a common belief that the national community is one people and creates subjects who understand or experience themselves as national beings suggest why it is that war can so powerfully activate and make central national identity. As the external frontiers' of the nation are threatened, so too, are the internal frontiers' of individuals... As the bombs rained down on British soil, destroying British houses, British monuments, factories and ports, citizens of Britain understood at

---

[40] Ibid., p.17.
[41] {Rose, 2003 #56@p.22}

some very deep level that their personal lives and well-being were at risk only because of the national belonging.[42]

This definition, although written for a study of Britain, can nevertheless be mapped onto understandings of how the German wartime nation was constructed. In both countries, the blackout's universality operated on a similar basis, and for a long time with markedly similar effects. Rose writes that representations of the British nation were an abstraction that produced the pull of unity'.[43] These abstractions could be found in the discursive frameworks surrounding gender, community, race, and geographical location. The blackout contributed to these frameworks, by providing a structural system of obligations that emphasised the community above the individual. As a consequence, both Germany and Britain relied to a certain extent on the framework of the blackout to engender a spirit of national unity. Though the profile of pre-war preparations and the mobilisation a sense of airmindedness for the purposes of civil defence favoured Germany, the imposition of the blackout and its obligations is one of the few areas in which the British and German home fronts were structurally similar.

Jones' work examines the impact of air-raids on the wartime working culture of Britain and its productivity. Surveying the impact of ARP across the entirety of industry, her study is excellent in marshalling detail and drawing out the key problems that ARP caused. Chapter seven of this thesis, which focuses on labour and transport, draws on Jones' work in particular. Her focus on behaviour is of particular relevance to this study. Where Rose's work looks at the ambiguous construction of the nation, Jones' focus lies in how the war affected the behaviour of the citizens who lived through it. As she notes, studies of consensus in wartime Britain have tended to analyse it primarily in terms of party politics and attitudes towards welfare reforms, rather than in relation to wartime

---

[42] Ibid., p.11.
[43] Ibid., p.13.

behaviour.'[44] Her study is a step towards redressing this gap. However, as a work that focuses exclusively on Britain, there is some lack of distinction between what might be ascribed to national behaviours, and what might termed more systemic ones attributable to the condition of war. This thesis develops Jones' work by limiting analysis to the blackout alone, rather than the myriad effects of ARP and bombing, and expanding the source base to include two countries. That Britain and Germany had the most complete blackouts in Europe indicates some behavioural similarities, both in how it was constructed and how it was monitored. Examining the blackout as a system that engendered certain behaviours and ideals shifts the analysis of the home front out of the limits of individual nations, and towards a study of people's wartime behaviour under particular systems.

However, the literature on the home fronts of both countries is nevertheless not immediately comparable. As such, it requires some level of re-interpretation. Writing in 2000, Gregor noted the disparities between British and German studies of the home front.

> [W]hile the last two decades have seen a growing body of literature examining both the history and the construction of the memory of the British experience of the war, centring on a critical reappraisal of the `myth of the Blitz ', a corresponding examination of the impact of the bombing on German society has failed to take place on anything like the same scale.[45]

Though the literature on bombing has been growing over the last ten years in Germany, it has taken a particular turn. High profile studies such as Jörg Friedrich's *Der Brand* and W.G. Sebald's *Luftkrieg und Literatur* sought to articulate what was seen by them and others as an absence of public discussion of German casualties

---

[44] Jones, *British Civilians in the Front Line: Air Raids, Productivity and Wartime Culture, 1939-45*, p.4.
[45] Gregor, 'A Schicksalsgemeinschaft? Allied Bombing, Civilian Morale and Social Dissolution in Nuremberg, 1942-1945', p.1051.

under the bombs; an almost deliberate forgetting of German suffering.[46] This was not in itself uncontroversial; in particular, Friedrich's polemical tone throughout *Der Brand* arguably distances it from more academic literature on bombing, and towards a populism which some have found discomforting. Arpaci argues that *Der Brand* explicitly constructs a version of German victimhood that, for some on the extreme right, makes the bombing war comparable with the holocaust.[47] Attempts to critically engage with both Friedrich's and Sebald's theses have sought to question their use of the language of victimhood', and the central tenet that the air war was ever forgotten in the first place.[48] Certainly, the literature on bombing in Germany is by no means sparse; local and national studies of the devastation the Allied attacks wrought on the German people are many. Groehler's *Bombenkrieg* and Beck's *Under the Bombs* are both excellent, though again rather limited in their consideration of the blackout.[49] There is a difference though between the academic study of the bombing war and the popular perception and discussion of it. While the last ten years have seen renewed interest in the impact of bombing on Germany, simply reading it alongside its British comparator is not enough. The framework of this thesis provides a way through which both can be filtered and re-interpreted, and given some measure of equivalence.

The impetus since the late 1960s towards unpicking the dominant narrative of the British home front has not been without its critics. Robert Mackay's recent study, *Half*

---

[46] Jörg Friedrich, *Der Brand: Deutschland im Bombenkrieg 1940-1945* (Ullstein Taschenbuchvlg, 2004); W.G. Sebald, *Luftkrieg und Literatur* (Frankfurt am Main: Fischer, 2001).

[47] Annette Seidel Arpaci, 'Lost in Translations? The Discourse of 'German Suffering' and W.G. Sebald's Luftkrieg und Literatur', in Helmut Schmitz (ed.), *A Nation of Victims?: Representations of German Wartime Suffering from 1945 to the Present* (New York: Rodopi, 2007), p.162.

[48] On this see Bill Niven (ed.), *Germans as Victims: Remembering the Past in Contemporary Germany* (London: Palgrave Macmillan, 2006); William Rasch (ed.), *Bombs Away!: Representing the Air War over Europe and Japan* (Amsterdam: Rodopi, 2006); Karina Berger Stuart Taberner (ed.), *Germans as Victims in the Literary Fiction of the Berlin Republic* (New York: Camden House, 2009); Susanne Vees-Gulani, *Trauma and Guilt: Literature of Wartime Bombing in Germany* (Berlin: Walter de Gruyter, 2003).

[49] Earl Beck, *Under the Bombs: the German Home Front 1942-1945* (Lexington: University of Kentucky, 1986); Olaf Groehler, *Bombenkrieg gegen Deutschland* (Berlin: Akademie-Verlag Berlin, 1990).

the Battle: Civilian Morale in Britain during the Second World War, was an attempt to check the revision of the traditional narrative to see if the new received version taking root was as overdrawn as that it sought to replace.[50] That this has occurred is partly a result of the very narrow, national focus that has predominated in studies of the home front. An absence of comparators can make national narratives of transnational events a hothouse of conjecture when examining the behaviour of citizens; if A does such a thing, how can we know if it is particular or general without looking at what B does? While this thesis does not claim to map out the behaviours of either nation in explicit detail, it does begin to analyse what made them similar, under the peculiar conditions of a well organised blackout.

Structure

Rather than a chronological treatment, this study breaks down the impact of the blackout into thematic chapters. Chapter two details the development of air raid precautions from the turn of the century until 1939. This allows for a contextualization of the development of airmindedness' in Britain and Germany, and its impact on the operation and development of the blackout. The advent of militarized aviation moved war from the limits of public experience to being a fundamental part of it. The slow crystallization of civil defence within the public sphere between the wars – indeed slower in Britain's case – formed the discursive foundation on which the legitimacy of the blackout and the function of ARP were built.

Chapter two establishes the early development of ARP and blackout during the first world war, and examines the development of ARP during the interwar period. It argues that the major distinction between the British and German development of the blackout was the extent to which ARP and the importance of the blackout was mobilised in the public sphere. For ARP to be successful, it had to be sufficiently well established

---

[50] Robert Mackay, *Half the Battle: Civilian Morale in Britain During the Second World War* (Manchester: Manchester University Press, 2002), p.9.

amongst the population in peacetime to mitigate the consequences of a surprise enemy bombardment. Because of this, when the Nazis came to power in Germany ARP had the useful political function of militarising the public during peacetime. Conversely, it was for these reasons that ARP in Britain did not really reach a mass public until fairly late in the 1930s; whereas the German state could after 1933 propagandise a national emergency for legitimating ARP trials, Britain had to wait until the security situation on the continent allowed for a public mandate to overcome the disruption of ARP and blackout practices.

Chapter three examines the practical development of the blackout within government during the interwar, and argues that despite the differences in the militarisation of their publics, development of the blackout was hindered in Britain and Germany because of the inevitably disruptive effect any peacetime trial would have. Large scale exercises, limited to a short period over several nights, were the most that could be hoped for. Even here neither country managed to hold more than a few before the war began. The idea that people could be made familiar with the difficulties of living under a blackout before the war was thus compromised from the start. A rolling blackout of indefinite length was not something that could be adequately prepared for in advance. Indeed, the hasty development of civil defence in Britain after Munich was enough to result in both countries' blackouts being the most secure in Europe when war broke out. Thus it is possible that little material advantage was gained by early German development, beyond the propagandistic uses of ARP.

Chapter four argues that adherence to the blackout during the war played an important part in the construction of a unified home front. The obligations of the blackout restrictions elevated the safety of the community above the individual; a light in the blackout endangered not only your home, but your neighbours' and, by extension, the nation's potential to fight the war. A secure blackout became a visible manifestation of the ability of the nation to fight a war. Beyond the obligations of individual citizens, the universality of the blackout also meant that sites of state power became sensitive points in maintaining blackout discipline. Poorly blacked out official and military buildings compromised the integrity of the blackout not simply through their emitting light, but also because they reflected badly on the state's management of the war, and on the fairness of the restrictions. The chapter also argues that fairness was important in the sentencing of blackout offences in both countries, and the at times widely differing level of punishments served to undermine the blackout, and the community cohesion. This was also evident in how the blackout was policed, which for the purposes of the blackout was formed by representatives of the state, and the citizenry themselves. The blackout was a system of civil defence that each day fore-grounded citizenship and community.

The fifth chapter examines crime and sex under the blackout, and argues that the crime of leaving a light exposed was of an entirely different quality to those offences where people sought to exploit the blackout for personal advantage. These offences were treated with severity in both countries as a consequence of the blackout's universality, and the demands it made on the behaviour of the individual and the community. This chapter also argues that the relationship between the blackout and crime during the war is nuanced. It draws on post-war criminological studies of the relationship between light and the perception of crime, and shows that despite a heightened awareness personal safety brought about by the absence of light on the streets, the levels of crime in both countries did not rise dramatically as might have been expected. Indeed, only in juvenile crime was there any dramatic increase. It also argues that the general perception that crime greatly increased during the war in Britain, as is indeed inferred in the statistics for offences, needs to be seen in context with the higher profile of wrongdoing at a time of national emergency, with the liberties the blackout were thought to afford lawbreaking, and the effect this had on stricter policing and more regular reporting of certain offences.

Chapter six surveys the cultural impact of the blackout, and argues that the perception of the blackout was as important as its immediate reality. Yet how this manifested itself across both countries was by no means uniform. Existing discourses of light and darkness were heightened under the blackout, the darkness of the streets becoming a symbol for the darkness of the times. What was also heightened as a result of the blackout was the division between the public and private worlds. The chapter argues that while the function of the blackout was to accentuate the public over the private, it could also cause people to withdraw into themselves, and with the trouble of navigating the darkened towns and cities, from public life in general. Mitigating this effect of the blackout through the control and promotion of public culture, including broadcasting, became a concern in both Britain and Germany.

Chapter seven examines the impact of the blackout on the economic and transport infrastructures of both countries. It argues that the impact of the blackout on working conditions and productivity has been given little consideration in the existing home front literature. Poor lighting and ventilation as a consequence of blackout measures had substantial implications for worker safety and productivity. Despite earlier mobilisation of structural ARP preparations in German industry, little material benefit appears to have been gained in comparison with Britain; both continued to be as well blacked out as the other, and similar problems in blacking out large industrial sites and processes were faced in both countries. Against a generally steadfast line against reducing the blackout for the public's sake, productivity and the blackout's effect on the war effort were the only two areas of compromise in Britain and Germany. Relaxations were always measured against these two criteria, and there were inevitable tensions between these factors and the safety of the public. This chapter also argues that in Britain especially, the dramatic rise in road accidents at the beginning of the war was a real test of the state's handling of the blackout, and a major obstacle in establishing the blackout's legitimacy.

The final chapter presents the conclusions of this research. The successful operation of the blackout relied on two central features. Firstly, an existing discourse of aviation and civil defence that created a progressive attitude towards aviation and shaped the responsibilities of the individual to the community. Secondly, the blackout required a strong administrative backbone for its successful operation. This extended from the warden in the street to the law and its interpretation in the courts, to the systems of baffling industrial light. In a perfect system, there would of course be a perfect blackout. Yet there is no evidence to suggest that the political systems of either country had an effect on how successful the blackout was; both were comparably well attended to. This is not to say that the German totalitarian state was not advantaged through the restrictions in the public sphere and its greater control over individual thought and action. But the totalizing character of the war was borne out by the blackout. Though there were of course key differences, the scale on which it permeated the life of the nation meant that the differences between how Britain and Germany organized and legitimated their systems of civil defence narrowed. By the time the first air raids began it was difficult to see what advantage Germany might have gained from the previous ten years of high profile mobilisation.

We may speculate on what impact sudden devastating air raids of the kind seen in 1943 would have had on 1 September 1939 when the blackout began. It is rarely acknowledged just how fortunate Britain was that the devastating raids imagined during the inter-war years did not materialise on that first night. Submitted to a terrifying campaign by German forces from land and air on 1 September, the experience of the Poles was of the bomber's dreadful efficiency in harrying, bombing and breaking the Polish resistance.[51] Such was the effectiveness of the German military's advance and their aircraft that within the first months of the war the SD were picking up misgivings within the German populace over the effectiveness of the principle of ARP, with returning soldiers bringing home stories of what they had seen wrought by their forces on the German frontlines.[52] These first few months in both countries were invaluable in consolidating the principle of ARP, as well as familiarising the population with its practicalities. In Britain, the rate at which civil defence developed over the war's first winter and the next sixth months formed the basis of the blackout for the rest of the war. Likewise in Germany, the tweaking that could be done over these few months of relative peace meant that inefficiencies could be fixed, and the legitimacy of the blackout strengthened. The Phoney War allowed for the bedding down of wartime civilian behaviour and was invaluable in shaping the way the wartime population coped with bombing later on.

---

[51] Evans, *The Third Reich at War*, pp.3-9.
[52] BA Berlin, R58/146, SD mood report, 27 December 1939.

Chapter Two – Pre-war Air Raid Precautions and Airmindedness

Introduction

This chapter provides an overview of the development of ARP during the course of the First World War in both Germany and Britain, and its consequent development throughout the inter-war period. It argues that the key distinction between Britain and Germany during the interwar period in ARP was the extent to which it was mobilised within the public sphere. As a system of defence, it required the public to be made familiar with the tasks and responsibilities of ARP in peacetime. This distinguished it from more formal systems of air defence, such as fighters and flak emplacements, which though responsive to public opinion did not require their active participation. Early experience of air raids and blackouts in the first world war had shown planners in Britain and Germany that for ARP to work successfully, it required that national defence be moved from the edges of the public's experience during peacetime and more towards the centre of it. This chapter makes clear that whether in a dictatorship or a democracy, the public mandate for ARP was contingent on the perception of national security. After 1933, ARP in Germany was developed as much for its propaganda value as it was its utility in the event of war. With complete control over the terms of debate on ARP, the Nazi government could propagandise for a national emergency that made the development of ARP far easier to mobilise than in Britain, and on a larger scale. Development of ARP in Britain was as in Germany based on the perception of security. Yet because of its far more open political culture, resistance and indifference were more common, and this affected the scale on which interwar trials of ARP could be mobilised. As chapter three later makes clear, it was only after the events at Munich in 1938 that a public mandate for larger scale exercises could be relied upon.

38

Airmindedness and the nation

The advent of flight brought with it a new realm in which nations could imagine themselves, and constitute their political identities. For as much as airspace was now an element of the politics of the state, it was also a space in which the social and cultural politics of the nation could be altered and refashioned. Before the advent of flight, Britons' sense of security rested on the strength of the navy in policing the waters of the British Empire, and maintaining the nation's ability to import and export goods. This was tied to a concomitant sense of national prestige in naval supremacy that was gradually chipped away by the ambitions of Imperial Germany and the advent of powered flight. Redford suggests that the navy's decline in importance may be inferred from the dramatic collapse in branches of the Navy League, which was formed as a public organisation to campaign for the supremacy of the navy in the hierarchy of the defence services. From a peak in the First World War it had, by the 1930s, been reduced by more than two-thirds.[53] The public's appreciation of the navy dimmed with its apparent loss of advantage in an aerial age, and with it the security of the nation's maritime space. Flight, and the threat from it, was a far surer menace than a foreign navy. The key difference between them was that the frontlines of war were now drawn at the limit of a bomber's range, rather than the shelling distance of a battleship.

The relationship between the state and the airmindedness of its citizens was therefore every bit as important as the external relationship of the state to its neighbours. But if airmindedness can be commonly defined as an affirmation of the benefits of aviation, it is by no means straightforward. Millward, in her work on women and imperial aviation, defines airspace as part of a conceptualization of space; ...it is the processes and

---

[53] On this see Duncan Redford, 'Does the Navy Matter? Aspects of National Identity and the Navy's Vulnerability to Future Budget Cuts', *Royal United Services Institute* <http://www.rusi.org/analysis/commentary/ref:C4AB3833A02178/>, accessed 20 December 2009.

actions of developing the technology, infrastructure, training, finances, legislation, goals, and so forth that together produce what is then conceptualized as airspace.'[54] This conceptualization, while often constructed as a reiteration of existing power structures, is also open to debate and change. Where a nation is described as airminded, it is often within the narrow limits of a positive, progressive attitude to the benefits of aviation. In this sense, airspace is not a politically neutral space. To be against aviation, or to be fearful of its consequences, is to *not* be airminded. This is more than simply luddism. In his discussion of airmindedness in Germany, Peter Fritzsche links it to a specific combination of nationalism and technology.[55] As an aspect of the modern state, aviation was inseparable from national chauvinism. Its impact on the nation state destabilised its frontiers and sense of security. A recovery of both could only be found in expressing a progressive attitude to it. While this is perhaps self-evident, its consequences were complex. In Germany especially, the combination of the romantic ideas of the nation state and technology led to what Herf called the paradox of reactionary modernism'; the exploitation of technology while rejecting the rationalism of the Enlightenment that produced it.[56] It is how Hitler could both decry the speed of modern life where, in his words, restlessness and haste mark the thinking of our people', yet promote aviation – that most modern and potentially disruptive of technologies – as a means of strengthening both the state and national community.[57] Airmindedness was similarly susceptible to political ideology within Britain. Competition existed over its definition, broadly defined as that of a pacific internationalism against an imperialistic nationalism.[58] Holman and Zaidi have also shown that after the First World War, efforts at forming some sort of international control of aviation, and in particular military aviation, gained favour amongst politicians in Britain, France and the

---

[54] Millward, *Women in British Imperial Airspace, 1922-1937*, p.18.
[55] Fritzsche, *A Nation of Fliers: German Aviation and the Popular Imagination*, p.6.
[56] See Jeffrey Herf, *Reactionary Modernism: Technology, Culture and Politics in Weimar and the Third Reich* (Cambridge: Cambridge University Press, 1984).
[57] Cited in Richard Overy, *The Inter-war Crisis 1919-1939* (2nd edn.; London: Pearson Education, 2007), p.25.
[58] Millward, *Women in British Imperial Airspace, 1922-1937*, p.20-28.

United States.[59] Though they faltered, the attempts by liberal internationalists to restrain national sovereignty over air forces and air policy indicated the transformative potential of aviation. International control was about securing a framework that maintained the existing security and imperial interests of leading nations; Zaidi writes that International control would undoubtedly have found little purchase in Britain, France and the USA if it had been imagined that internationalized aviation would have been used against these countries themselves.'[60]

But of course, being airminded was not the only way of understanding aviation. For much of the twentieth century aviation remained outside the experience of the majority of the population, being the privilege of the wealthy and the elite.[61] Aviation in the years before cheap air travel was for most a spectacle, whether of the heroics of pilots or of the destruction wrought from bombing. Both embodied ideas of airmindedness that taken together were dissonant and contradictory. Yet it is the latter that had the most profound impact on the politics and consciousness of both countries. The invention of flight brought with it the invention of aerial bombardment, and with it the fear of bombing. This provided a powerful counter-discourse to the progressive tenets of airmindedness. The response was to construct airmindedness to be as much about steeling the civilian population for a bombing war as about eulogising its benefits. In both countries it promoted unity and collective responsibility in the face of aerial warfare. How these conceptions of airmindedness were shaped and altered, and how they functioned to condition the public's reception and understanding of ARP and by extension the blackout, is the subject of the rest of this chapter.

---

[59] Brett Holman, 'World Police for World Peace: British Internationalism and the Threat of a Knock-out Blow from the Air, 1919–1945', War in History, 17/3 (2010); Waqar H. Zaidi, "Aviation Will Either Destroy or Save Our Civilization': Proposals for the International Control of Aviation, 1920-45', Journal of Contemporary History, 46/1 (2011).
[60] Zaidi, "Aviation Will Either Destroy or Save Our Civilization': Proposals for the International Control of Aviation, 1920-45', p.177.
[61] On this see Marc Dierikx, Clipping the Clouds: How Air Travel Changed the World (Westport: Praeger, 2008).

Air war and the advent of flight

The possibilities of aircraft in war had been speculated on for many decades prior to the First World War.[62] While the air-war literature of both nations during this period was more often than not rather fanciful, it had as a common thread the belief in the importance of aircraft to a future war.[63] The German experience of ground based air warfare had already begun as early as 1870-71, against French attempts to escape the siege of Paris by balloon during the Franco-Prussian war. Of the sixty-six balloons that floated free of the city, only one was destroyed by the German military, using a 36mm cannon hastily commissioned and built by the Krupp armament works.[64] The illustration below from 1895 shows the difficulties this new form of warfare presented to armies, with Prussian hussars chasing after a drifting balloon.

---

[62] See Richard P. Hallion, *Taking Flight: Inventing the Aerial Age from Antiquity Through the First World War* (Oxford: Oxford University Press, 2003).
[63] See Tami Davis Biddle, *Rhetoric and Reality in Air Warfare* (Princeton, NJ: Princeton University Press, 2004), pp.11-20; I.F. Clarke, *The Great War with Germany, 1890-1914* (Liverpool: Liverpool University Press, 1997), pp.1-27.
[64] Edward B. Westermann, 'Fighting for the Heavens from the Ground: German Ground-Based Air Defenses in the Great War, 1914-1918', *The Journal of Military History*, 65/3 (2001), pp.641-642.

Prussian Hussars chase a balloon escaping the Siege of Paris. Taken from Julius von Pflugk-Harttung, *Krieg und Sieg 1870-1871: Ein Gedenkbuch* (Berlin: Schall & Grund, 1895), p.276.

The difficulties of coping with air warfare on the ground coloured the fiction and the political debate surrounding it, and as aircraft technology advanced into the new century it became ever more present in the public mind. Speculation on air warfare was frequently tied to national chauvinisms, and groups were formed to influence government into investing in aircraft production. In Britain, at a meeting at Mansion House in 1909 organised by the newly established Aerial League of the British Empire, the Lord Mayor was heard to say that Britain was justly proud of having taught other nations how best to navigate the sea and how to build the best ships; consequently he hoped that we would not be behind in the matter of navigating the air.'[65] The mayor's words belied the concerns some had in Britain's capability for aerial defence. Where Germany and France had by this time begun to build up their air industries, the Germans with Zeppelins and the French with airplanes, the idea that Britain had fallen

---

[65] 'The Mansion House Meeting and its Lessons', *Flight*, 1/15 (10 April 1909).

behind other nations, and in particular imperial Germany, was a motivating force behind calls for a greater focus on air defence.[66]

Powered flight had developed rapidly from the turn of the century. In Germany, the hope for the future lay in Count Ferdinand von Zeppelin's lighter-than-air dirigibles, which had so galvanised the German political and public imagination. Large crowds gathered to watch the flight of *Luftschiff Zeppelin* – or LZ4 – on 4 August 1908. Those who couldn't attend and were too impatient to await the reports of the newspapers' evening editions would pester editorial staff to hear the latest news of its journey. When the ship's motor failed and was forced to halt its flight at Oppenheim, crowds gathered around the stricken ship to sing the national anthem.[67] The following day problems with docking the ship after its flight caused it to collide with the ground, and the resultant fireball destroyed the ship entirely. In the wake of the disaster funds were quickly established to pay for the building of a replacement, and this national subscription, gathered from the German public, rose to 5 million marks, dwarfing earlier efforts and doubling the amount that had been offered by the German army.[68] The success of this populist campaign for funds, cast at the time as an appeal to patriotism and national unity, underlines the increasing significance that flight held on the public and the political imagination in Germany and the public's burgeoning airmindedness. Peter Fritzsche details the enthusiasm that Germans held for Graf Zeppelin and his namesakes.

> ...in marketplaces and carnival fairs, hundreds of cigars, pencils, spoons, suspenders, firecrackers, cheeses, cleaning agents, and even cans of boot polish bearing Zeppelin's name and displaying Zeppelin's face were hawked and sold... It was to this sort of Zeppelin kitsch that one appalled art critic pointed to indict Wilhemine Germany for its bad taste, but Germans – street hawkers, trinket buyers, and carnivalgoers – claimed the airship as their own.[69]

---

[66] For a detailed overview of this period see Gollin, *The Impact of Air Power on the British People and Their Government, 1909-14.*
[67] Fritzsche, *A Nation of Fliers: German Aviation and the Popular Imagination*, pp.9-11.
[68] Ibid., p.16.
[69] Ibid., p.18.

For Germany the Zeppelin had become a talisman not simply for the nation's technical prowess, but for its imperial ambitions as well, and an affirmation of the nation's strength. As the technology matured, flight and the exploitation of it for national advantage was intimately bound with the modernity of the nation.[70] Seen in this light, the modest position flight had so far held in the public and political imagination in Britain must have seemed unnerving when compared with the fervour of Germans for their airships. HG Wells, in his 1908 novel *The War in the Air*, envisioned German Zeppelins as at once admirable and terrible objects, laying waste to New York:

> [they] came to rest over Jersey City in a position that dominated lower New York. There the monsters hung, large and wonderful in the evening light, serenely regardless of the occasional rocket explosions and flashing shell-bursts in the lower air.[71]

This imagery, despite the repeated rejection of Zeppelins by the German military as viable weapons of war, would colour the British view of Zeppelins and the air threat in the years before 1914.[72] The mayor's words at that meeting in 1909 were at once nostalgic for the now vanishing security of the seas, and fearful of the loss of imperial strength that flight might now bring. That year also brought with it the phantom airship scares that gripped the nation. Amidst the paranoia of a German invasion, and fears of the nation's naval and imperial decline, 1909 saw Britain experience a wave of phantom' airships, apparently drifting across the country unchallenged and menacing the citizenry.[73] The reports of these sightings in the popular press so vexed the newspaper magnate Lord Northcliffe that he felt compelled to chastise the nation in print. For Northcliffe, who was visiting Berlin at the time, this apparent spasm of paranoia was nothing less than a national embarrassment. Cabling the *Daily Mail*, the

---

[70] For an extensive discussion of technology, the nation state and modernity see Rieger, *Technology and the Culture of Modernity in Britain and Germany 1890-1945*.
[71] H.G. Wells, *The War in the Air* (Project Gutenberg, 1908).
[72] For a discussion of Zeppelin fiction before and during the First World War see Ariela Freedman, 'Zeppelin Fictions and the British Home Front', *The Journal of Modern Literature*, 27/3 (2004).
[73] Gollin, *The Impact of Air Power on the British People and Their Government, 1909-14*, pp.49-63.

paper ran an article by him decrying his fellow countrymen's skittishness, and which ended with:

> Germans, who have so long been accustomed to regard Great Britain as a model of national deportment, poise, and cool-headed men, are beginning to believe that England is becoming the home of mere nervous degenerates.[74]

The threat of air warfare, and what was assumed to be the febrile character of the public in the face of it, was in the years leading up the war of great concern to those who advocated a greater emphasis on aviation in Britain. In the discourses that would develop around airmindedness in the inter-war years, public discipline was to be one of the key virtues. But though pre-war skittishness was the product of a genuine fear of the consequences of air warfare, it was also symptomatic of a concern at being outmatched in the air by foreign powers. The debate in newspapers and journals during this period was often concerned with Britain's apparent lack of capability to match its continental neighbours in aviation. But the period leading up to war found an accelerating British aviation industry that was perhaps more vigorous than believed. David Edgerton's study of the beginnings of aviation in Britain illustrates the momentum that aircraft production gradually acquired. Between 1908 and 1914 numerous aircraft manufacturers were established, each designing civilian and military aircraft to varying levels of success. Though British air strength was lower than that of either France or Germany on the outbreak of the war, Edgerton argues that seen as a ratio to the overall strength of each nation's military and naval force, Britain emerges as the more aeronautically inclined power.[75] So while the number of planes fielded by the three countries – 113, 120 and 232 for Britain, France and Germany respectively – might indicate their material strength, it is perhaps another thing to assert that Britain was not actively pursuing an aviation policy. This feeling was also present at the time, as an editorial published in the journal *Flight* on 5 June 1914 makes clear.

---

[74] Cited in Ibid., p.60.
[75] Edgerton, *England and the Aeroplane: an Essay on a Militant and Technological nation*, p.10.

The present concentration of the Royal Flying Corps at Netheravon should set at rest the minds of those who still will have it that we are doing nothing—or next to nothing—to bring our aerial defences into line with modern requirements. Seventy machines, over a hundred flying officers, 150 transport vehicles, and a staff of 650 air-mechanics, makes a fairly respectable showing for a small army like our own. In fact, so far as the records are there to show, it is the largest concentration of aerial strength that has been seen in any army, large or small. On this much we are justified in priding ourselves, and the more so because we felt that our personnel is at least equal to, and probably better than, that of any other of the Great Powers.[76]

Despite this, there was nevertheless a large gap between the ardour of German Zeppelin mania and the British public's fancy for aerial adventure, which never found expression in quite the same way. That concern existed amongst those with an interest in promoting aviation before the war is symptomatic of this gap.

Yet while both countries pursued the development of aircraft, defence against them was very much a secondary concern. In his analysis of German ground-based air defence prior to the First World War, Westermann attributes the failure to develop adequate air defences to the short amount of time the Germans envisaged the next war would take. The Schlieffen Plan was designed to avoid a two-front war by quickly defeating France, then concentrating German resources on defeating the Russians to the east. Such a plan left little time or indeed cause for aerial defence, and in anticipating a mobile front German military planners did not feel the need to develop extensive schemes of aerial defence.[77] In Britain, there were efforts to develop some system of aerial defence, but it was again rather piecemeal. Efforts began with the Admiralty in 1910, concerned that parts of the naval infrastructure, such as magazine and cordite factories, would be under particular threat from enemy aircraft. Yet despite agreements made and recommendations put forward within the ministries, no comprehensive solution to aerial defences was formed before the war. As Gollin writes,

---

[76] 'Editorial Comment - the Army Air Manoeuvres', *Flight*, 6/23 (5 June 1914).
[77] Westermann, 'Fighting for the Heavens from the Ground: German Ground-Based Air Defenses in the Great War, 1914-1918', pp.650-651.

Liberal Ministers were attempting to shore up the aeronautical defences of the country but little could be done in the direction in a short space of time. The provision of adequate funds for the purpose was not the only problem. The technical difficulties were immense... Men began to say that if war came and if it then turned out that the home air defences had been neglected, those responsible would be hanged from lamp-posts in Whitehall.[78]

If a general theme of unpreparedness is common to both nations' air defence at this time, then it is particularly so as regards the blackout. Neither country held any form of blackout preparation prior to the war. The sorts of trials that would take place in the inter-war period in Germany and Britain were entirely absent, and neither public would have been familiar with the idea of blacking out. When war did finally come, the blackout was an entirely novel experience for both countries.

The blackout in the First World War

Despite the advances made in aviation technology, air power as an instrument of military force was still in its infancy on the eve of the First World War, with its practical application more limited in comparison with the ideas of air power theory and literature.[79] Throughout the course of the war, military use of aircraft and their impact was overall negligible when compared with the battles on land and at sea. Nevertheless, the war formed the crucible in which air power was tested and evaluated for the first time in a large-scale conflict. By the war's end the major European powers had begun to assemble their airborne military capabilities, and to fashion the strategies they would later employ in the Second World War.[80] What is clear from this period is that the advent of long range strategic bombing shifted the home front's relationship to war. This was perhaps more marked in Britain than in Germany, where its island status had afforded it a certain immunity from invasion that the continental powers did not have. But the extension of the front that long range bombing now brought was a

---

[78] Gollin, *The Impact of Air Power on the British People and Their Government, 1909-14*, p.227.
[79] Richard Overy, 'Introduction', in Sebastian Cox and Peter Gray (ed.), *Air power history: turning points from Kitty Hawk to Kosovo* (London: Frank Cass, 2002), pp.ix-xix, p.ix.
[80] Raymond H. Fredette, *The Sky on Fire: the First Battle of Britain 1917-1918* (Washington D.C.: Smithsonian, 1991), pp.231-241.

problem common to both countries. Where the public's knowledge of previous wars on

foreign soil was at the edge of public experience, the bombing raids of the First World

War fundamentally altered this dynamic. The public's direct experience of the war

would become a major factor in how governments planned and managed the war

effort. The blackout was an extension of this new relationship, and its emergence as a

state phenomenon began with the first night raids by enemy aircraft.

As previously discussed, pre-war air defences were not as great a priority for

government as building aircraft, and civilians in both Britain and Germany were not

drilled in blackout practice as they would later be in the years before the Second World

War. However, though the use of aircraft in the war was quite limited when compared

with the raids experienced in 1940-45, those that did occur were sufficient enough to

rattle the population and the political establishment.[81] Casualty figures over the course

of the war help to illustrate the development of bombing and the strategies of both

sides. For both tables, the casualties as a result of night raids are far greater.

Table 2.1 - Total German bombing casualties from French and British raids, 1914-1918[82]

Year	By day	By night	Estimated number of bombs
1915	44	7	940
1916	21	75	917
1917	45	130	5234
1918	119	234	7117
Total	229	446	14208

[81] Tami Davis Biddle, 'Learning in Real-time: the Development and Implementation of Air Power in the First World War', in Sebastian Cox and Peter Gray (ed.), Air Power History: Turning Points from Kitty Hawk to Kosovo (London: Frank Cass, 2002), pp.3-20, pp.8-14.
[82] H.A. Jones, The War in the Air, vol.6 (Oxford: Oxford University Press, 1937), p.152.

Table 2.2 - Total British bombing casualties from German raids[83]

Year	By day	By night	Estimated number of bombs
1914	-	-	3
1915	-	208	1535
1916	17	296	3699
1917	401	294	2754
1918	-	198	587
Total	418	996	8578

Analysis of the material and strategic effects of bombing after the war showed that it was rather inefficient, when compared with the outlay and resources devoted to it.[84] However, the disruption and demoralization of the home front caused by bombing were notable indirect successes. As a result of bombing the quality of life under the bombs in the First World War in both countries was greatly diminished, not least by the introduction of night time blackouts to counter air raids.

The security of night bombing for a raiding force enabled them to drop a greater amount of explosive with a greater chance of their survival and return. Just how effective this was during the war is summed up by a memorandum titled ‚Night Air Raids on London' and written in 1917 by the South African Lieutenant-General Jan C. Smuts, who had joined the British War Cabinet earlier that year.

> The enemy has now at last resorted to the form of attack which our air commanders have long anticipated, and which it is most difficult to meet – viz. night attacks by aeroplanes. This form of attack we have for a long time now been carrying out with comparative impunity against his aerodromes, depots, bases, and lines of communication in France and Belgium. Almost every night tons of explosives are dropped by our aeroplanes on these objectives, and the enemy has as yet developed no means of meeting this attack.[85]

Smuts emphasised the effectiveness of bombing at night with aeroplanes rather than more fragile airships. Though these had menaced Britain during 1915 to 1916 using the

---

[83] Compiled from H.A. Jones, *The War in the Air, vol.3* (Oxford: Oxford University Press, 1931), pp.382-383; H.A. Jones, *The War in the Air, vol.5* (Oxford: Oxford University Press, 1935), pp.474-475.
[84] See Jones, *The War in the Air, vol.6*, pp.152-155.
[85] Cited in Jones, *The War in the Air, vol.5*, p.491.

cover of darkness, their shortcomings were evident; slow, prone to attack by faster, smaller and more aerodynamic aircraft, and more dependent on the weather for making their way. By 1917, the preference in Germany had switched to fixed wing aircraft, following the lead of their French and British enemies. As part of the scheme of passive aerial defence, the blackout was its most all-encompassing measure and for the public the most wearisome. By the end of the First World War parts of Britain had been under blackout conditions for over four years. Though it proved limited in comparison with the blackout experience in the Second World War, it nevertheless exhibited the majority of the issues that were to face both countries in that conflict.

The strategic intention of the blackout in the First World War, as defined in a Home Office briefing in 1929, was:

> a) to conceal particular premises or localities which might otherwise be exposed to enemy attack from the sea or from the air,
>
> b) to disguise them so that they might not afford navigational data to the enemy.[86]

The first orders for blackouts in Britain were made on 12 August 1914 and issued by the Secretary of State under Defence of the Realm regulation no. 11. Already prepared in 1913 by Winston Churchill as First Lord of the Admiralty, this first order was intended to darken ports and harbours so that their light would not throw shipping into relief for the benefit of marauding German submarines. The first general order for inland areas soon followed, and was issued the following month on 17 September 1914. The order only applied to the Metropolitan Police District and the City of London, and was intended to pre-empt possible raids by German airships on the capital. In the absence of the kind of ARP organisation that would be developed for the next war, the orders were enforced entirely by the police. London had already been surveyed from the air by naval airships, the results of which had made it clear that only complete darkness could

---

[86] TNA, HO 45/18132, memorandum by Robinson for the Police War Duties Committee, February 1929.

obscure the city from the air on a clear night. Mindful of the restrictions on life it would entail, the authorities were reluctant to pursue a complete blackout in the absence of any clear threat, and instead arranged for a partial blackout that would obscure the more strategic areas of the city.[87] While this first general restriction was imposed only on London, further orders were made as German air attacks on the country progressed. By 16 February 1916 the blackout had been extended to the whole of England. At the end of the First World War, the civilian population and the government were already used to the blackout, or at least one in keeping with the nascent air technology of the period. Compromises between security and the life of the nation were easier to make during the First World War, as a memorandum written for the Police War Duties Commission in 1929 illustrates:

> Though complete darkness might have been the ideal during the late war as a protective measure, its adoption as a permanent condition was obviously impossible having regard to the resulting interference with industrial and other essential activities. The method adopted therefore was to arrange for unessential lighting to be extinguished or effectively obscured; to reduce the remainder to the minimum that was tolerable without unduly interfering with essential activities; and to rely on emergency extinctions for further reduction when an attack was thought to be imminent.[88]

Despite the Zeppelin and aeroplane raids, this concern with minimising the problems for the population in blacking out could be afforded when considering the overall scale and frequency of the raids conducted. The political and public clamour for them varied with the frequency of the attacks. With the frequency and success of their raids rather diminished by the end of 1916, there was a feeling that German airships no longer posed a serious threat to the nation. But the restrictions remained. The coal controller, in calling for greater efficiency in coal consumption, was against any easing of the restrictions, and the Chief Constables were wary of allowing any increase in illumination in case there was competition between towns and cities over which had

---

[87] Jones, *The War in the Air, vol.3*, pp.83-84.
[88] TNA, HO 45/18132, memorandum by Robinson for the Police War Duties Committee, February 1929.

more light.[89] The lighting restrictions, though regarded as a nuisance, had been deemed by officials to be effective. German raiders had in previous sorties mistakenly identified whole cities and parts of the country, and this was partly attributed to the blackout.[90] The experience of the blackout in Germany was altogether less comprehensive, confined as it was to the western part of the country.[91] Blacked out zones were restricted to a strip of land of roughly 150 kilometres in length behind the western front lines, which at its greatest extent stretched south from Trier to Freiburg. Here, lights were reduced to as little as possible, and were extinguished entirely in the event of a raid.[92]

The restrictions in both countries were in keeping with the technology of the period. The years between the wars would see the refining of the capabilities of air forces to a degree that would inevitably pose a far greater threat to, and a greater burden on, the population. Comparing the blackouts of the two wars, the novelist and poet Thomas Burke wrote in 1941:

> The war of 1914 did not interfere with the night-life of our towns as the present war has done. There was a blackout of a sort, but only of a sort. All street lamps were alight at night, with their glasses painted a dark-blue, so that each street seemed full of police stations. Buses and cabs retained their lamps, just slightly dimmed, and one could get about quite easily. Shop-blinds and house-blinds had to be drawn, but not so rigidly as now, when not a half-inch gleam of the faintest glow must be seen. Shop-doors were not shrouded in maze-like contraptions of black-boarding through which one has to turn and turn; if the doors were of glass they just had a little curtain to them. It was such a black-out that if the young could see it in these days they would think all the lights had gone on.[93]

The problems the blackout presented to authorities were early signs of what was to come. In Britain, there were difficulties in deciding how best to prosecute offenders. The zealousness of some local officials caused the government to issue a notice

---

[89] Jones, *The War in the Air, vol.5*, pp.1-4.
[90] See Jones, *The War in the Air, vol.3*, pp.69-152.
[91] Hampe, *Der Zivile Luftschutz im Zweiten Weltkrieg*, p.546.
[92] Ibid., pp.7-8.
[93] Thomas Burke, *English Night-life: from Norman Curfew to Present Black-out* (London: Batsford, 1941), p.136.

advising against trivial prosecutions, which had a negative impact on the morale of the population. Nevertheless, the fear of air attack became such that there was popular clamour for a blackout even in those areas of the country that were exempted from lighting orders by dint of their remoteness, or lack of strategic importance. This was heard most strongly in the districts of provincial cities such as Cardiff, Exeter and Plymouth, in the wake of the Zeppelin raids on the West Midlands which had brought about an extension of the blackout restrictions there.[94] The belief in the security that the blackout afforded caused some to take matters into their own hands and forcibly extinguish lights. The journal *Flight* reported in 1915:

> One [defendant] had had his house newly painted, and the light helped to single out his abode as an especially fine mark for Zeppeliners. So he and his neighbours held council, and decided that the light should be extinguished... Another defendant, who failed to see why the only light in his street should be the brilliant one outside his house, parted with 5s., and a similar sum settled the cases of two others who protested in this manner against the undue brilliancy.[95]

The journal remarked of the sentencing that although little harm has been done... it is to be hoped that a good moral effect will have been produced, as without doubt such illicit attempts to further reduce the illumination of our streets can only be harmful, as it carries with it far more danger than if the lights are left burning'.[96] The tension - and contradiction - of managing a blackout that could be more dangerous than the threat it was intended to ward off, was one familiar to the authorities in Germany too. In the southern German town of Freiburg im Breisgau, the novelty of the blackout quickly gave way to weariness. Roger Chickering's study of the town during the war illustrates the effect of the blackout on the city's population, and their sometimes ambivalent opinion on it.

> Nocturnal paralysis set in. Whether between pedestrians on the sidewalks or between vehicles in the street, collisions became frequent. Travellers were reluctant to stray from the vicinity of the railway station in search of hotels in the inner city. Liability claims against the city increased, as did protests from

---

[94] Jones, *The War in the Air*, vol.3, pp.144-146.
[95] 'Air-raidism', *Flight*, 7/27 (2 June 1915), p.466.
[96] Ibid.

darkened neighbourhoods. Other residents, however, welcomed the dark for the protection it offered.[97]

Local government had to manage the needs of securing the town from bombing alongside the needs of military and civilian traffic. Managing this tension – and perhaps more importantly for the next war, legitimating it - would form the backbone of inter-war blackout development. Under the less draconian restrictions of the First World War, the life of both nations had been relatively free to carry on as normal. The period between the wars saw the British and German governments attempt to develop schemes that could cope with the advancing science of aviation, and the increased potential for destruction that it brought with it.

Inter-war airmindedness, politics and the blackout

The development of ARP in Germany and Britain was conditioned by the political atmosphere of the time. In Germany, ARP development in the period before Nazi rule had already become synonymous with the national humiliation of Versailles. In Britain, the government's focus on ARP drifted with the political situation in Europe. Britain's pre-war development of ARP was summarised in O'Brien's official history of civil defence as consisting of two distinct phases; the first period leading up to the creation of the Home Office's ARP department in 1935, the second period between then and the outbreak of war.[98] With some consideration of the Munich crisis, it is possible to adapt this to three distinct phases; the shivers that Munich sent through a panicked Home Office and the local authorities brought a new seriousness to preparations. The escalation of ARP resources and the attention paid to it were a reaction to the gradually deteriorating international climate. The Home Office and Air Ministry spent the years leading up to war attempting to develop a system sensitive to the needs of both the population and industry, worried about the debilitating effects a blackout would have on

---

[97] Roger Chickering, *The Great War and Urban Life in Germany: Freiburg, 1914-1918* (Cambridge: Cambridge University Press, 2007), p.301.
[98] See O'Brien, *Civil Defence*, p.5.

the morale of the nation and its industrial capacity. Despite much work trying to avoid it, the choice in 1939 was polarised between either leaving the lights on, in the belief a blackout would have little effect, or imposing the severest lighting restrictions possible.

After the First World War, Germany was left without a military air force. What airships that had not been destroyed by the German military were parcelled out amongst the victorious powers. The Versailles treaty, in addition to limiting the size of the German military, forbade it from having an air force. However, civilian aviation was allowed, and it was perhaps inevitable that the spectacles and successes of German aviation in the period before the Nazi takeover of power should foster a resentment against the terms of Versailles, which had left the prestigious and technically advanced German aviation industry almost crippled by its conditions. Articles 198 and 201 forbade the establishment of an air force and prohibited the import and manufacture of aircraft and aircraft parts for six months after the treaty came into force in 1920. But after a relaxation of the conditions of the treaty, Germany soon began to send Zeppelins around the world once more, and during the 1920s also began to establish a worldwide network of civilian air routes. This happened despite the absence of a military infrastructure to underpin the development of aircraft, as had been the case before the First World War, and indeed was the case in other European countries after it.[99] Disused airfields gradually became hives of industry, sending gliders and aircraft once more into the sky.[100] Zeppelins became pacific objects, their military careers now finished in the wake of their indifferent performance during the First World War and the development of faster aerodynamic craft. The first to be built after the war, the ZR 126, was purchased by the American government as recompense for the scuttling of the German fleet at Scapa Flow. Later renamed the *Los Angeles*, its flight across the

[99] See Hans Fabian, 'The Difficult Situation of Aeronautical Research and the Aeronautical Industry during the Weimar Republic, 1919-1932', in Horst Prem Ernst-Heinrich Hirschel, Gero Madelung (ed.), *Aeronautical Research in Germany: from Lillenthal until Today* (Berlin: Springer, 2004), pp.55-70.
[100] Fritzsche, *A Nation of Fliers: German Aviation and the Popular Imagination*, pp.135-137.

Atlantic in October 1924 heralded the revival in Germany's fortunes. Once again, the connection between flight and the state of the nation was invoked in the press and popular literature.[101] Yet though those on the right and left could agree on the national importance of the ZR 126's flight, Weimar Germany remained deeply divided, not least on what the politics of an airminded Germany should be. But the talismanic properties of the Zeppelin were still powerful in Germany. Another public subscription, similar to that gathered in the wake of the crash of the LZ4, generated fewer funds than in 1908 but, together with financial backing from the American newspaper magnate Randolph Hearst which made up the shortfall, it gave *Luftschiffbau Zepppelin's* manager Hugo Eckener enough capital to begin construction of another airship. The LZ 127, or *Graf Zeppelin*, was the largest yet built, and its flight across the Atlantic at the end of 1928 again captivated the nation. To the world outside its journey was no less important, and it was remarked upon in the journal *Flight*, if a little awkwardly, that its intent appeared to be a flight that would draw the eyes of the world to impress upon that world the fact that the time for Germany's resurrection in the air is at hand.'[102] The sight of the Graf Zeppelin drifting low over the FA Cup final in 1930 to an ambivalent crowd – some jeering, others waving to and cheering this immense and deafening manifestation of German aviation – could only have underscored this.

It was at this moment in Germany's renaissance in the air that ARP began to be seriously organised within Germany. Chapter three deals with the specifics of how the blackout was organised during the inter-war period, but it is no coincidence that Germany's re-discovery of itself as an aerial power should also be the time at which it became increasingly concerned with its exposure to the aerial threat. While there had been some lessening of the restrictions of the Versailles treaty, and in 1927 some allowance made for the organisation of ground-based defences against air raids,

---

[101] Ibid., pp.139-142.
[102] 'Editorial Comment - Nine Years After', *Flight*, 20/43 (18 October 1928).

Germany's right to military aviation was not one of them. Discussions within government regarding ARP had already begun in the wake of the occupation of the Ruhr by the French in 1923. Bernd Lemke, in his study on the state and preparations for war in the inter-war period in Britain and Germany, notes that the tone of discussions on ARP at this period would last until the rebuilt German Luftwaffe was dramatically revealed in 1935.[103] In the immediate aftermath of the First World War it was acknowledged within the German government that, given the weakness of the military, they would not be able to protect the population from enemy aircraft as they had done in the previous war. A memorandum from the Reich's Defence Ministry from 1923, outlining the requirements for ARP in the aftermath of the war, argued that the focus therefore had to be shifted towards a more elaborate system of civilian defence.[104] It stated that the occupation of the Ruhr in 1923 and the acquiescence of the major powers during it meant that a militarily neutered Germany now had to reckon with its more militarised and significantly more powerful neighbours. The nation would have to organise for a war of high explosive and gas bombs dropped into cities from the air, preparations for which would have to be secured during peace time so that if war did ever come, the country would be ready.[105] This kind of organisation would require a fundamental restructuring of how society related to air warfare. In the First World War the organisation of ARP in Germany, as well as Britain, had in spite of pre-war efforts ultimately been developed as the war progressed. But the consequences of the rapid development of air warfare after 1918 meant that the German public would have to be significantly more airminded than it had been. This was a view that was strengthened within the German military by the belief that it was the buckling of the will of the home front during the war that had cost Germany victory.[106] Only good peacetime preparation of civil defence would prevent a collapse of morale under bombing. Yet it still took several years for this to develop in Weimar Germany. Despite

---

[103] Lemke, *Luftschutz in Großbritannien und Deutschland 1923 – 1939*, pp.127-129.
[104] Defence Ministry memorandum of von Bonin 18 May 1923, cited in Ibid., pp.834-837.
[105] Ibid.
[106] Fritzsche, 'Machine Dreams: Airmindedness and the Reinvention of Germany', pp.688-689.

early recognition of the need to propagandise ARP amongst the public, this was hindered by a lack of clear organisation, and arguments over how ARP would be organised and funded. Development during this period was therefore experimental rather than systematic; an early trial held by the military in Württemberg in 1928 was limited to testing air raid warning systems, as this was the only aspect of ARP they had control over. Power over the other aspects of ARP lay with the Ministry of the Interior, who resisted military pressure to develop ARP more aggressively, and indeed to develop a public propaganda campaign in case it worried the public. The government's more limited ambitions frustrated private, populist associations, such as the Deutsche Luftschutz e.V., established in 1927 to counter what it felt to be a lack of clear direction and public engagement on ARP that had resulted in it becoming a party political issue. The number of ARP associations mushroomed, and the increasing profile of ARP eventually led in 1930 to serious moves within government to address it on a more ambitious and public level. The first large scale trial took place on 3 October 1930 in Königsberg.[107] However, as a result of the range of bodies and opinion on ARP that formed in the last years of Weimar, it was not until the Nazis came to power that the development of ARP became coherent, dissent on which was smothered. Germany's resurgence as a civilian air power under the restrictions of Versailles would be exploited by the Nazis, and the fear of bomb attack by neighbouring states became a vital part of Nazi foreign policy, and useful for the civil discipline and unity it engendered for their domestic policy. In 1933, a few months after the takeover of power, a short pamphlet written by Dr. Edgar Winter, who was responsible for ARP within the National Socialist Association of Teachers, outlined the Nazis' conception of airmindedness. While dealing with the practical matters of ARP, the pamphlet also details the National Socialist worldview with regard to air power, the crux of which remained the same as that of ten years before – the perceived threat from Germany's air-capable neighbours, and the imposition of the unfair restrictions of the Versailles

---

[107] A detailed overview of the development of ARP in during the Weimar years can be found in Lemke, *Luftschutz in Großbritannien und Deutschland 1923 – 1939*, pp.125-206. See also Hampe, *Der Zivile Luftschutz im Zweiten Weltkrieg*, pp.3-14.

treaty.[108] The map below is taken from Winter's booklet, and vividly illustrates German insecurity on air power and how it was used by the Nazis to mobilise awareness of ARP.

'Within two hours Germany will be covered with bombers.' Taken from Edgar Winter, *Luftschutz tut Not* (Berlin: Verlag für soziale Ethik und Kunstpflege, 1933), p.5.

As previously discussed, airmindedness was not a politically neutral space, and within Britain aviation was often the particular cause of the right. The right-wing press were enthusiastic supporters of aviation, and though a number of aspects of airmindedness existed, flight in this period was seen far less as a tool for advocating greater internationalism than as a technology which celebrated the state, empire and Britain's modernity.[109] This was also true of Germany. Fritszche writes that

> ...the most enthusiastic proponents of airmindedness called for a technocratic state in which the rickety forms of democratic governance would give way to the

---

[108] See Dr. Edgar Winter, *Luftschutz tut Not* (Berlin: Verlag fur soziale Ethik und Kunstpflege, 1933).

[109] For an extensive discussion of airmindedness and politics see Millward, *Women in British Imperial Airspace, 1922-1937*, pp.23-29.

streamlined leadership necessary to overcome the debilitating social frictions and parliamentary squabbles that allegedly undermined national defense and inhibited civic virtue.[110]

Where dissent or confusion existed, it challenged not simply the authority of the state but also the idea of airmindedness and ARP as a civic duty to one's fellow citizens. In Britain, where the inter-war period was marked by an anti-war sentiment that permeated into the official mindset, this led to a prolonged public debate on ARP that was open and conflicting, even within government, in contrast to the Nazis' promotion of airmindedness.[111] The muddled priorities of air warfare were brought to light during the Geneva disarmament conference in 1932, where the British government undermined its pursuit of arms limitation agreements while simultaneously defending its right to the controversial policy of _air control' - that of policing dissent and subversion in its Arab, African and Asian colonies through aerial bombardment.[112] The interests of Empire conflicted with domestic policy, and this dissonance was unhelpful in forming a coherent approach for engaging with ARP in Whitehall.

Within the public sphere in Britain, anti-war sentiment during the 1930s linked ARP with a militarization of the civilian population, and was actively resisted by pacifists.[113] As one woman put it when interviewed by Mass Observation in 1939, _We are pacifists, and we're against Air Raid Precautions because we think they're just part of the war machine.'[114] But the specific requirements of the blackout caused a dilemma for pacifists. As JBS Haldane put it, _If I lose my respirator or go onto the roof during an air raid I only endanger my own life. But if I leave a light shining through an uncovered skylight I endanger the King in Buckingham Palace and the Prime Minister in Downing

---

[110] Fritzsche, 'Machine Dreams: Airmindedness and the Reinvention of Germany', p.689.

[111] See Uri Bialer, *The Shadow of the Bomber: the Fear of Air Attack and British Politics 1932-1939* (London: Royal Historical Society, 1980).

[112] See Priya Satia, 'The Defense of Inhumanity: Air Control and the British Idea of Arabia', *The American Historical Review* (111, 2006).

[113] Richard Overy, 'Apocalyptic fears: Bombing and Popular Anxiety in Inter-War Britain', *S-NODI: pubblici und private nella storia contemporanea, I2* (2008), p.13.

[114] MOA, TC23, Box 1, Folder 1A, Casual interviews on ARP, 9 January 1939.

Street.[115] If war came, would submitting to the blackout amount to a tacit approval of the war? A Peace Pledge Union pamphlet in 1936 distinguished between the wartime conditions and resistance to war preparations:

> During a real air raid, it would not, of course, be right for a pacifist to leave the lights in his house burning; for such action might imperil the safety of his neighbours. But during peace time the case is clearly different. Black-outs and gas drill are preparations for war, and it is the duty of pacifists to protest, not only in words, but also in action, against such preparations.[116]

The collective responsibility for ARP and the blackout was only ever as secure as the collective understanding of its purpose. Ultimately, the unsatisfactory manner in which ARP was communicated by government in the inter-war years, coupled with widespread antipathy and active dissent towards it, left the public confused. In January 1939, in the wake of the Munich crisis, a survey of opinion on ARP by Mass Observation in the town of Bolton found a baffled and often almost cynical reaction to ARP.[117] Other interviews from around the country at this time appeared to mirror the confusion. An ARP warden in London told his interviewer I don't know any more than you do. I had my lectures and since then, well, to tell you the truth, I have forgotten all about them.'[118] Another interviewer, on asking a group of women in the London suburbs what they felt about ARP, reported the following:

> One woman of 65 did not understand the meaning of A.R.P. Another, asked what she thought of A.R.P., replied: I'd rather not say, thanks. It's best to leave it alone. A third answered: I can't be bothered with all that now.' (Turning to greengrocer, also at door): I can't be bothered with A.R.P. now, can I, when I've the dinner to get?'[119]

Nevil Shute's novel, *What Happened to the Corbetts*, exemplifies the failure of political communication of the requirements of ARP on the eve of the war. Published in April 1939, it imagined the consequences of a devastating air attack on Southampton. Unremarkable perhaps as a work of fiction, on publication 1000 copies were distributed

---

[115] J.B.S. Haldane, *ARP* (London: Victor Gollancz, 1938), p.81.
[116] The British Library, WP.8951, Pamphlets of the Peace Pledge Union, assorted, circa 1936.
[117] Ibid.
[118] Ibid., report in Evening Herald', 17 January 1939.
[119] Ibid.

amongst ARP volunteers by the publisher William Heinemann, as both a marketing stunt and to offer ARP members a foretaste of what a bombing war might look like.[120] However, the book mirrored the public's confusion, and in its imagined bombing war neglected the blackout, firebombing, and official shelter policy – all of which had been trialled and discussed publicly by the government with increasing frequency since 1935, and were indeed specified to a limited degree in the Air Raid Precautions Act of 1937. In 1938 the prominent left-wing scientist and public intellectual JBS Haldane published his thoughts on ARP, and criticised the government's reluctance to specify ARP and blackout measures outright. This lack of specificity, he felt, left too much uncertainty for the public to quickly adapt to any blackout restrictions. In his words, '...the more we can learn in advance about out[sic] duties the less confusion there will be should war come.'[121] But the development of ARP in Britain, as will be explained in the next chapter, was developed very much within the confines of Whitehall. While concerned groups of professionals outside government developed their own proposals - architects and scientists in the main - they did not affect much of ARP policy. As Meisel writes, 'with the power to sanction and fund ARP projects, the government was able to meet the challenges to its policies.'[122]

In contrast, Nazi airmindedness was constructed almost as an act of faith. Fritzsche writes that 'Only in Germany did the jeopardy of the air age serve as a welcome opportunity for national renewal.'[123] Prior to the Nazi takeover of power, lines of dissent on ARP were most visible on the left. A memorandum circulated in 1932 within the committee of Reichsverband der Deutschen Industrie (RDI), a lobby group representing the interests of German industry to government, noted the intransigence of socialist and communist employees in cooperating with ARP measures. In Weimar

---

[120] Nevil Shute, *What Happened to the Corbetts* (London: Pan, 1965).
[121] Haldane, *ARP*, p.86.
[122] Joseph Meisel, 'Air Raid Shelter Policy and its Critics Before the Second World War', *Twentieth Century British History*, 5/3 (1994), p.301.
[123] Fritzsche, 'Machine Dreams: Airmindedness and the Reinvention of Germany', p.692.

Germany aviation and airmindedness were drawn along political lines. Before the National Socialist *Gleichschaltung* there existed separate gliding and flight clubs, which were aligned with members' political affiliations. These would disappear after 1933, with the unification of all sporting aviation groups. Competing political ideas of airmindedness threatened to undermine a cohesive response to the aerial threat. The 1932 memorandum suggested that coverage within the German press on Soviet Russia's air force and ARP development would encourage _communist' workers to realize that, in its words, they too were worthy of protection.[124] A later memorandum of April 1933 noted that the *Münchener Post* - referred to as an _an organ of the SPD' - had affirmed the commitment of the SPD to ARP preparations.[125] Prior to 1933 the SPD had, alongside centrist and liberal parties, argued for an ARP system that did not engender a militaristic mobilisation of the population. However, none of the parties could counter the increasingly militaristic mood and language of the press and public in this period.[126] The subsequent crackdown on political dissent after 1933 produced a unification of Germany's myriad aviation societies under one official group, and its ARP societies under another, all under the control of the German Air Ministry. This ensured that all public discussion of ARP would take place within the parameters set by the Nazi government.

The irritation of democratic freedoms that had proved so frustrating to those advocating a firmer line on ARP had now been removed, and Nazi airmindedness would develop with a unitary public discourse that was entirely absent in Britain. In doing this, airmindedness and preparations for ARP could be disseminated throughout society with a pervasiveness that extended beyond the media. Schools were a particular focus, in that they provided a forum in which to educate the youth of the nation and transmit knowledge through them to other generations. In 1935 the mayor of Soest, acting as

---

[124] BA Berlin, RS36/2715, memorandum of the RDI, 31 December 1932.
[125] Ibid., memorandum of 5 April 1933.
[126] Lemke, *Luftschutz in Großbritannien und Deutschland 1923 – 1939*, p.67.

Police Chief for the town, directed the headmaster of the high school to remind

students of the importance of ARP in advance of the town's blackout practice. The

mayor hoped that by teaching the children how to correctly blackout a room, they would

then take that knowledge home and teach their parents how to do the same.[127] The aim

of airmindedness and ARP in Nazi Germany was summarised by Erhard Milch, state

secretary of the Reich Air Ministry, in 1937.

> Air raid precautions have fulfilled their purpose when

> 1. The public do not panic in the face of an air raid, even if it were a surprise raid. Nothing strengthens the will to victory more than preparedness.

> 2. When the morale of the nation is not lessened by continuous bombardment.

> 3. When the economic life of the nation, and in particular the war economy, proceeds undisturbed, so that the frontline does not worry over the home front and can commit its full strength to its military tasks.[128]

If airmindedness in the Third Reich had a uniformity of purpose, its central tenet

remained the fear of bombing. In Britain, the fear of the bomber was as much a motive

force for appeasement as it was for developing ARP. Uri Bialer's work traces the

shifting policies of the British government during the inter-war period with regard to air

defence. Stanley Baldwin's warning that ‚the bomber will always get through‘ in 1932

‚mesmerized‘ the lay and professional public, and crystallized a fear that underlay

British policy throughout the decade.[129] Seen in the light of Baldwin's speech that

evening, the despair over the impact of aviation on the security of the state can be

seen as a motive force for appeasement:

> The amount of time that has been wasted at Geneva in discussing questions such as the reduction of the size of aeroplanes, the prohibition of the

---

[127] Stadtarchiv Soest, P22 1055, letter from mayor of Soest to local headmaster, 14 March 1935.
[128] Erhard Milch, 'Was müssen wir tun?', in Dr. Ing. Erich Hampe (ed.), *Der Zivile luftschutz: ein Sammelwerk alle Fragen des Luftschutzes.* (2nd edn.; Berlin: Otto Stollberg, 1937), p.14.
[129] Bialer, *The Shadow of the Bomber: the Fear of Air Attack and British Politics 1932-1939*, p.155.

bombardment of the civil population, the prohibition of bombing, have really reduced me to despair. What would be the only result of reducing the size of aeroplanes? As soon as we work at this form of warfare, immediately every scientific man in the country will turn to making a high explosive bomb about the size of a walnut and as powerful as a bomb of big dimensions, and our last state may be just as bad as the first.[130]

Militarised aviation was an intractable problem for a state that did not want to commit itself to permanent war readiness. Ultimately it was only external pressures that generated any traction within government for ARP, where development coincided with an escalation in the air threat. Indeed, the threat of bombing was balanced in a way that meant German security came at the expense of British security.

After the First World War, the consideration of lighting restrictions within the higher reaches of government was left to one side. The records show that in 1929, discussions on blacking out were held at the level of the Police War Duties Commission, presumably as part of a review of duties for any prospective war. The first mention of blackouts after this period is dated the 27 June 1935, in an Air Staff note written at the request of the ARP sub-committee.[131] This memorandum was written as a response to a recent blackout experiment in Berlin on 19 March 1935, which was reported in *The Times* a few days later.

Out of thin air emerged the machines whose existence had been so vigorously denied. Months of propaganda by the Air Protection League, which claims nearly 5,000,000 members and twenty per cent of the population of Berlin, had taught them how to behave as in war' and preserve good darkening discipline.' Consequently Tuesday's blackout' was a revelation of discipline and organization. Trains coming into Berlin were darkened over a radius of fifty miles; cars drove dead slow with lights dimmed by cardboard; customers in cafes sat behind sheets of blackened paper, and inspectors and police roamed their beats in search of chinks of light.[132]

These air defence exercises finally generated the impetus for a concerted development of blackout schemes for the United Kingdom. It is worth noting here that although

---

[130] Hansard, Baldwin, HC Deb 10 November 1932 vol 270 c634.
[131] TNA, HO 45/18132, Air Staff memorandum for ARP Sub-Committee, 27 June 1935.
[132] 'Bombers Over Berlin', *The Times*, 21 March 1935, p.15.

blackout trials may have begun during this period, as will be seen in the next chapter they were still very much towards the bottom of the list of priorities, and in general match the lack of work on structural ARP preparations such as bomb shelters and preparations for gas warfare.[133] It was not until the Munich crisis that the political will and attention of the population was sufficient to support an increase in blackout preparations.

Conclusion

This chapter has argued that the main distinction between Britain and Germany in ARP preparation during the inter-war years was the extent to which it was mobilised in the public sphere. The experience of air raids during the first world war had in both countries underlined a preference for night-bombing, and the importance of preparing their populations for bombing during peacetime. This latter aspect required a public mandate that was contingent on the perceived security of the nation. After 1933, the Nazis propagandised the idea of Germany as under threat from foreign air forces, which allowed for a militarization of the peacetime population. Discourses of ARP, and public trials of it, were a fundamental part of the militarization of German society. In Britain, the development of ARP also relied on a public mandate. However, this was less forthcoming as Britain's open political culture meant that dissent and apathy were far more present. This affected the extent to which government engaged with ARP in the public sphere, and therefore the extent to which the public understood ARP. Rather than manufacturing a national emergency, as in Germany, the British government had to wait until the situation on the continent allowed for a public mandate to begin public ARP preparations on a larger scale. The events at Munich in 1938 would provide the impetus.

---

[133] Meisel, 'Air Raid Shelter Policy and its Critics Before the Second World War', pp.305-307.

Chapter Three – The Development of the Blackout

Introduction

In March 1936 the film *Things to Come* premiered in Britain. Adapted from HG Wells'

earlier novel - or rather imagined future history - *The Shape of Things to Come*,

Alexander Korda's production mounted an impressive and still terrifying sequence, in

which the city of 'Everytown' is bombed to ruins. Preceding it, a father tells his son as

he leaves for ARP duties that 'You've gotta do your bit, son. Gotta do your bit!', as the

boy beats a march on his drum. There was a stark contrast between the film's vision of

terror and martial civilian life, against the life outside a cinema in Britain in 1936. British

ARP preparations at the time of the film's release were only reluctantly gathering pace.

As chapter two has shown, the public mandate for developing ARP and blackout

preparations was connected to the public's overall sense of security. While the Nazi

state could manufacture a climate and political system in which ARP could be

developed without great hindrance, the authorities in Britain had to wait until the

public's sense of national security gave it a mandate to pursue more open development

of ARP and blackout measures. However, this chapter argues that the differences

between Britain and Germany, at the level of blackout preparations, were ultimately not

as great as may have been supposed. Little material advantage appears to have been

gained by Germany through its earlier development of the blackout, beyond its use as

a propaganda tool as part of the wider rubric of ARP preparations. This was ultimately

due to the fact that a rolling blackout of indefinite length, as would be expected in a

war, was impossible to plan for in peacetime. Blackout trials were restricted in both

countries by the times at which they occurred, and their overall scale. Not even in

Germany, where a public mandate for the interference of ARP trials in peacetime could

largely be taken for granted, was it possible to run a trial blackout for more than a week. For both countries, limited blackout practice could not adequately prepare their populations for life under a permanent blackout. The trials of this period were more useful for raising awareness of the air threat, and developing the administrative framework that defining and enforcing the blackout would require. Both countries succeeded at this level. The British and German blackouts were observed from the air to be the most secure in Europe. Though British planners had to wait until the Munich crisis for a public mandate to begin large scale blackout trials, this appears to have been enough to secure the rudiments of a good blackout. As in Germany, the phoney war would provide an opportunity for fixing the details of the blackout, and alleviating the pressure on the public as much as possible.

Early blackout preparations

The conditions of the Versailles Treaty made the Germany military particularly conscious of its vulnerability to air attack, and it was perhaps inevitable that it became the first country to begin blackout trials during the inter-war period. Following on from early general ARP trials held in 1930, the first recorded trial dedicated to blackout preparations happened at a gas and electrics works in the town of Königsberg in December 1932.[134] Yet the disruption caused by trial blackouts meant that there were limits placed on their length, their scope, the overall reduction in levels of light, and indeed at what time a blackout might be practised. There was the questions of what sort of blackout people and industry should prepare for. Should they prepare for a permanent blackout irrespective of the threat, or for a blackout brought into force on receipt of an air raid alarm? It is not surprising that these questions, though certainly alive in the public domain, chiefly remained the concern of industry and government during the early inter-war period. The difficulty of enrolling entire communities into practising ARP was too great at this early stage for large scale public trials to be

---

[134] BA Berlin, R36/2715, RDI report, 30 December 1932.

considered seriously. Moreover, the relegation of the public to the second tier of priorities in blackout preparations was a feature that would be retained in both countries until the end of the war. Production would always trump public safety.

Initially then, trial blackouts in Germany were concentrated within industrial establishments. The blackout's effect on wartime industry will be dealt with comprehensively later on in chapter seven of this thesis, but it is worth briefly commenting on some of the issues inter-war preparations raised here. Industry, and in particular heavy industry, relied on large amounts of light to carry out work, and used processes that emitted a great deal of it. Given industry's strategic importance in prosecuting any future war effort, it was recognised early on that preparations would have to be made for adequately blacking out complex sites and processes well in advance of a war. A site such as a steel rolling mill would emit light from skylights in roofs, from the molten steel as it was processed, and from the plant's furnaces and chimneys. It would have increased traffic within its vicinity, transporting materials to and from the site. And it would also be easily identifiable, being largely distinct from domestic sources of light. Other open sites such as dockyards, railway yards, sawmills and large industrial plant all had complex processes that needed baffling. All of these lights, if not obscured, would provide telltale markers for enemy craft from several kilometres away. Even if domestic housing were darkened, the constellations of large, light emitting sites in strategically important areas would be enough for enemy pilots to read the terrain. The complexity of screening these processes required not only a great deal of ingenuity in design, but substantial investment in their construction. Compensation for any disruptive effect that preparatory schemes would have on peacetime production was also a key factor that fed into early work on ARP and blackout. Particular attention was therefore paid to developing blackout schemes for sites of heavy industry in Germany and Britain during the inter-war period.

The first blackout trials in Germany appear to have begun in the early 1930s. The files of the RDI indicate that preparations had already begun by this point, with the lead taken primarily by industry itself. By 1932 the union had already undertaken its tenth ‚Luftschutzlehrgang', a series of seminars held in various parts of the country to disseminate and discuss matters concerning ARP in industry. In 1931, the union published a short leaflet on ARP which, amongst other issues, detailed early blackout policy in the following extract:

D – Defence against visibility

...

2. By night

a) Blackout

58. Legislation for the execution of the blackout will, in the event of an emergency, be issued by the authorities.

59. In general, the distinction will made between:

Reduced lighting

60. All unessential lighting for business and traffic are to be extinguished. The remaining lights are to be screened from above and at the sides.

61. Windows, skylights, glass roofs etc. are to be screened with curtains, or else painted. Lighting necessary for daytime work must remain.

Complete blackout

62. The lighting system will most likely be switched off from a central location, in which case a system of emergency lighting sufficient to enable the continuation of business must be prepared.[135]

The guidelines are not very specific, and no mention is made of any particular lighting standards. However, what is evident is that at this stage a partial blackout was envisaged - that is, one allowing for different levels of lighting. Such a scheme would

---

[135] BA Berlin, R36/2715, ‚Industrieller Luftschutz, 1. Merkblatt‚ 1 Dec 1931, p.15.

have involved zoning areas and industries for risk, and allowing them various stages of lighting according to the severity of the air threat. For the union, early planning clearly recognised that the ability of industry to function adequately under blackout restrictions was paramount. Yet while it is clear that preparations were in their infancy, early mistakes are already apparent in the imprecise language of the pamphlet. The guidelines for reduced lighting conditions advise painting or screening skylights and glass roofs. This is easier to write than it is to carry out. These sections of a factory were generally among the most difficult to reach. Opening and drawing curtains that were secure enough to block out light would have been an arduous and time consuming task. Painting windows, as advised, would black them out entirely, but at the expense of any daytime light falling through them to enable work. The easiest solution would have been to leave on electric lights, but this would have the effect of both increasing the temperature of the working space, and the energy costs of the factory. Spread across the country as a whole, the increase in energy demand would be huge. If the intent for developing ARP and blackout was there, the reasoned and practical application of this intent was yet to be seen.[136] As chapter seven will show, in many cases the rather basic but expensive problems of blacking out industry, common to both Britain and Germany, were still in evidence by the end of the war.

Experiments in Germany continued, and the need for striking a balance between blacking out and maintaining production was underlined through small scale blackouts trialled throughout the country, the results of which were disseminated amongst members of the union. In 1932, the results of a trial held in a gas and electric works in Königsberg, proceeding under the restrictions detailed above, noted that while a short blackout had been easily handled by staff, a longer trial had shown the need for

---

[136] For further detail on ARP in industry during this period see Hampe, *Der Zivile Luftschutz im Zweiten Weltkrieg*, pp.72-76.

increased emergency lighting to help workers cope with the darkness.[137] The pursuit of a blackout that would allow a reasonable level of freedom would be recurrent in both countries in the run up to the war, and indeed at times during it, though efforts at finding a scheme that would allow different levels of lighting according to risk would ultimately founder.

Perhaps the greatest distinction between the two countries in this period, beyond the practical trials held in Germany, was the forum in which these matters were discussed. It appears that blackout policy was very much an industrial concern in Germany, whereas in Britain the blackout was primarily discussed in connection with early drafts of the Police War Instructions. The previous chapter made clear the distinction between German and British airmindedness during the inter-war period, and this is reflected in early planning for the blackout. ARP was made more visible in Germany, with the positive attitudes to aviation it prescribed coupled to a particular awareness of the country's vulnerability to an attack by enemy bombers. This made the necessity of ARP more apparent not only to the public, but to industry as well.[138] In Britain discussion of ARP was far less open, and a public mandate for trials that would have enabled early practical development of ARP, which was contingent on the relative security of the country from neighbouring air forces, did not yet exist. There was little enthusiasm in British industry for taking a lead on ARP, since the added costs of developing schemes, along with the weak leadership from government, were a profound nuisance. Development of the blackout during the inter-war years would continue this pattern, where the German public's understanding and assent was taken as far more of an article of faith than in Britain.[139] It was not until later that shifts in the public's attitude to

---

[137] BA Berlin, R36/2715, RDI report, 30 December 1932.

[138] This openness could also seen as a potential weakness, compromising the nation's security. A letter to the union in 1933 notes that public discussion of the specifics of ARP – such as they were at this time – should be limited, so that details of ARP schemes did not reach foreign media. See BA Berlin, R36/2716, RDI letter to members, 8 August 1933.

[139] For a detailed examination of this see Lemke, *Luftschutz in Großbritannien und Deutschland 1923 – 1939*.

ARP in Britain, prompted in no small measure by increasing concern within political circles over German rearmament, allowed the government to pursue a more practical blackout policy, as a Home Office briefing from 1935 makes clear:

> The Air Staff felt... that the complete darkening of a town was impracticable by reason of interference with and stoppage of vital activities. It is, however, possible that, particularly with the ungrudged assistance of the general public and of industry, the control of lighting might not be exercised to a greater degree than has hitherto been considered politic or practicable, on the grounds of interference with essential activities.[140]

The shift in the public's attitude was a necessary condition for the British government to begin practice blackouts. In Germany, the limiting of public debate on ARP after 1933 meant that such a shift in public attitudes was not required, as government could construct and disseminate ARP discourse through the media and through the state. Before 1935, parts of German industry and some towns had held small blackout practices, while in Britain there had been none. It was not until 1935 that concerted efforts at developing the German public's awareness of blackout procedure really began.

The first large scale trials

1935 was a watershed year in the development of ARP in Britain and Germany. It was the year in which Germany unveiled the Luftwaffe, and began extensive blackout trials around the country. As a consequence, the re-emergence of Germany as a military air power provided a motive force for the development of ARP in Britain. The first blackout in Berlin took place on 19 March 1935, and ran from 10pm until midnight. The first hour tested a reduced lighting scheme, and the second hour was a complete blackout. Smaller trials had already been held around the country, but Berlin, as the capital city and prime target for any air raid, was a showcase. Indeed, throughout 1935 and 1936, Berlin hosted visitors from other countries to demonstrate its ARP system, including

---

[140] TNA, HO45/18132, Air Staff memorandum for ARP Sub-Committee, 27 June 1935.

Norway, Yugoslavia, Hungary, Greece, Japan, China and Spain.[141] How well earlier trials had been followed by the public is difficult to discern from material gathered from the archives. No formal powers to enforce trial blackouts had yet been issued during this period, though in 1934 some police forces were using sections of the law related to fire-fighting to enforce ARP measures.[142] A memorandum disseminated to members of the RDI in 1935 carried a report of the Police Chief of Görlitz criticising individuals who had failed to comply with or had sabotaged ARP preparations, and making clear his intention to use all of his powers to prosecute them and make them known through the local press.[143] There is no indication of the politicised dissent that became common in Britain before the war, though some of the reservations articulated by the left in the years before 1933 must have remained after the Nazi seizure of power. However, in an article that perhaps assumed at least some antipathy to the exercise, the *Deutsche Allgemeine Zeitung* reminded Berlin's residents on the day of the practice that it was in their interest to blackout their rooms as completely and economically as possible, and not simply go to bed earlier than usual.[144] And in an indication of the extent to which the state could now enforce blackout practices, residents were asked to keep their front doors open should police, or other bodies working with them, wish to enter the house to secure the blackout. These other bodies would have been either the SA, the SS, or NSKK – the Nazis' motoring organisation, who would secure the blackout for traffic – and all were later employed in practices around the country.[145]

Berlin's two hour blackout was deemed by the authorities to have been a great success. A report produced for the British Police War Duties commission was similarly impressed, and noted that while the reduced lighting had largely failed to obscure the

---

[141] Landesarchiv Berlin, reports of visits filed in A Pr. Br. Rep. 057 – 164.
[142] BA Berlin, R36/2718, RDI letter to members, 1 August 1934.
[143] BA Berlin, R36/2718, RDI letter to members, 29 January 1935.
[144] 'Die Grosse Verdunkelungsübung', *Deutsche Allgemeine Zeitung*, 19 March 1935, p.3.
[145] Stadtarchiv Soest, P22 1055, blackout plan issued by the mayor of Soest, 16 October 1935.

city, the complete blackout had made it almost invisible from the air.[146] However, the general feeling of satisfaction caused some unease amongst officials. The undersecretary of the German Air Ministry Dr. Kurt Knipfer claimed the Berlin blackout had achieved the complete opposite of what it had set out to do. To his mind, the enthusiasm over its success was unjustified, as a blackout where the lights were switched off and everything allowed to come to a halt was no success at all. For him it was not a case of turning out the lights for a short while, but about living and working under those circumstances. In chastising those who proclaimed the successes of Berlin's blackout, he stated that the two-tiered system of lighting – the reduced and the complete blackout – would more than likely not be used in many areas, but rather a full blackout instead. It was under those circumstances that their success had to be judged.[147] Knipfer's assessment was very perceptive. A one-night blackout practice was certainly rather annoying in itself for the population in both countries. But what the First World War had shown, and what the Second World War was to show again, was that the real test of the blackout for the civilian population was in living with it every day, and for a long and unspecified period of time. Knipfer's observation highlights a key problem that could not be solved before the war - that of the public getting used to a blackout. Coupled with the limited hours in which blackout practices took place, the public's awareness of the blackout would never have been as sharp on 1 September 1939 as it would a year later. Later chapters will explore how the blackout developed once the war eventually began, assessing how much had to be learnt by the government and the public, and what effect the absence of bombing during the first few months of the war had on the public acclimatising to the blackout.

The first trial blackout in the United Kingdom was held by the Admiralty as part of Air Defence of Great Britain exercises (A.D.G.B.) on 31 May 1935 in the Medway area of

---

[146] TNA, HO45/18132, Home Office memorandum for Police War Duties Committee, [undated] January 1936.
[147] BA Berlin, R36/2718, RDI letter to members, 19 July 1935.

Kent on the east coast. The following day *The Times* reported that it was the first of its kind to take place in this country since the War.'[148] The exercise covered an area that included the extensive naval facilities at the dockyards at Chatham, as well as the Royal Naval and Royal Marine Barracks. Further tests that year also occurred in prominent naval sites on the mainland – Sheerness on 27 June, Portsmouth on 14 August and Plymouth on 2 October, as well as Gibraltar on 3 December.[149] These blackouts, like the other exercises around the country in the years that followed, took place in the dead of night – 11.30pm at Chatham and Sheerness, 1 am at Portsmouth and 2am at Plymouth. As a report on the exercises held in 1935 made clear: The object... was not to train the civil population in the restriction of lighting but mainly to see whether the town was visible from the air under conditions of more or less complete darkness.'[150] The reluctance to pursue an exercise during the early evening can be ascribed to the practicalities of getting an efficient blackout, when the authorities had no legal powers to coerce citizens and businesses to comply. Running an exercise during the middle of the night when most people were in bed and had no need for lighting made the testing and observation of the blackout that much easier for the authorities. It also limited the potential for accidents and the resulting liability that would fall on the authorities. Despite these limitations, dissent against the early trials resulted in extensive protest from pacifist and civil liberties groups. Tension existed between preparing a nation for war that most hoped would never come, while still maintaining the distance of the state from the ordinary life of the people. Any unnecessary interference in the freedom to go about one's business would have been an unpopular move for any government to make. The blackout, more than other ARP measures of this period, was a form of social control, and this meant that it was contentious from the start. Political dissent could be found running amongst left-wing groups, the clergy, and pacifist organisations. In a letter to the editor of *The Guardian*, the National Council of

---

[148] 'Air Observation Test: "Black-out" over the Medway Area', *The Times*, 1 June 1935, p.8.
[149] See TNA, Home Office memorandum for Police War Duties Committee, [undated] January 1936. See also 'Telegrams in Brief', *The Times*, 5 December 1935, p.15.
[150] TNA, HO45/18132, Home Office memorandum for Police War Duties Committee, [undated] January 1936.

Civil Liberties – formed in 1934, and now known simply as Liberty – questioned the legality of blackout exercises, and reminded readers that following the blackout restrictions was an entirely voluntary act with no legal compulsion. It also questioned the motives behind the blackout itself.

> On the larger issue as to the efficacy of this form of air-raid protection the council is awaiting the results of inquiries which are being pursued by various organisations before declaring its view as to whether the black-out' principle is a genuine attempt to protect the civil populations under aerial warfare, or whether it is designed as propaganda for the creation of armament expansion.[151]

In 1934 an unofficial national ballot on support for the League of Nations, organised with the help of 500,000 volunteers, asked people whether they would support the abolition of all military and naval aircraft by international agreement. 9.6 million answered yes, a figure which as Overy points out was almost half the number who voted in that year's election.[152] This politicised dissent existed alongside one that simply found the blackout trials too much of a nuisance to be bothered with. *The New Statesman and Nation* ran an article shortly after the Munich crisis illustrating the apathy amongst some members of the public.

> A Mass observer who keeps a small tobacconist and news-agent's shop in a working class district in Birmingham, recorded many conversations like this one:
>
> Customer (young man, single, about 23, worker): Well, Betty, how's the Air Raid Wardens going on?'
>
> Me: All right, and it looks as if they will be needed yet. Have you heard tonight's news?'
>
> Customer: No. I heard there was a special out, but I shall hear it on the wireless. I am not bothering though, if I've got to go I shall know soon enough.'
>
> Me: Well you ought to bother. Call yourself patriotic. If you was in Germany and took no interest you would be put in prison.'
> Customer: I don't think it's any good bothering, it's people who keep worrying who are causing all the trouble.'[153]

---

[151] 'Letters to the Editor - "Rehearsals" for Air Raids - Are the "Blackouts" Legal?', *The Guardian*, 15 June 1935, p.5.
[152] Overy, 'Apocalyptic fears: Bombing and Popular Anxiety in Inter-War Britain', pp.16-17.
[153] Mass Observation, 'Sociology of A.R.P.', *The New Statesman and Nation*, November 5 1938, p.717-719.

The ambivalence that attended ARP and blackout education in Britain was a marked contrast to Germany, where ARP policy became increasingly invasive. Yet despite such intrusion, there appears to have been little organised or political dissent against ARP, which given the nature of the state at this time was to be expected. Yet there does appear to have been a similar kind of negligence and indolence in some blackout practices. The mayor of Soest remarked in advance of the town's 1936 blackout practice that care needed to be taken in enforcing the blackout, particularly amongst the town's businesses and shopkeepers, whose precautions in 1935 had not been satisfactory.[154] But these small instances of intransigence do not add up to any kind of concerted, politicised resistance, for the simple reason that such dissent was not allowed in Germany. The collective responsibility of ARP, and the blackout, was only ever as secure as its collective understanding. In public spaces throughout the country monuments were erected to publicise local branches of the RLB. These installations took the form of large bombs attached to a plinth, looking rather like enormous exclamation marks, with reminders or slogans inscribed underneath. Major cities hosted exhibitions of ARP measures and equipment, with all sections of society encouraged to attend. These exhibitions made explicit the link between Nazi ethics and ARP. Prior to an exhibition in Dortmund in 1935, the area's *Kreisfrauenschaftsleiterin* (local leader of the National Socialist Women's League) issued a memorandum exhorting women to visit. Repeating the by now familiar argument of Germany's vulnerability to aerial attack, it stated that:

> No German woman, no German mother that loves their children, their country and their fellow citizens, can afford to miss this opportunity to attend an absorbing exhibition on the aerial threat and air raid precautions.[155]

This contrasts sharply with the voluntarist ethic that the authorities in Britain had so far relied on. From 1935 onwards there was an increasing realisation amongst the public that a confrontation with Hitler's Germany was becoming more likely, and the public's

---

[154] Ibid., D 1397, letter from mayor of Soest to local civil defence bodies, 10 March 1936.
[155] Stadtarchiv Dortmund, 113-12, ¸Aufruf! Deutsche Frauen, Deutsche Mütter!¸ circa June 1935.

appetite for disarmament had started to fade.[156] Publications on ARP, such as

Haldane's *ARP* and *How to be Safe from Air-Raids*, as well as a 1938 National Peace

Council pamphlet on ARP, sold in significant numbers (54,000, 52,000 and 108,400

respectively.) This marked a steady shift of focus in Britain from action against the

cause of the problem to its effects instead.[157] Nevertheless, during the events at

Munich in 1938, councils across the country struggled to mobilise their ARP plans and

to recruit sufficient numbers of volunteers. On 24 September, Bristol city council

estimated a shortfall of almost 8000 volunteers to carry out its ARP plan adequately.[158]

The response by government was to professionalise the service, improve training and,

though it remained a voluntary service, to institute a quasi-military style system of

ranks, uniforms and discipline.[159] This formed a strange paradox; while ARP was

promoted as a voluntary, civic duty, recruitment and retention of volunteers could only

be improved by militarising it. This was perhaps an acceptance of the fact that ARP

made little sense unless set within the framework of an imminent, existential threat. In

Germany, propaganda highlighting the danger from neighbouring air forces had been

used for a long time to instil an awareness of ARP's importance. By the outbreak of war

in 1939, the German RLB counted 15 million members; in Britain, ARP counted 1.6

million members.[160] But these figures, when compared, do not necessarily indicate

preparedness for war, nor even the effectiveness of either organisation. Rather, the

disparity in membership is more indicative of the far larger political role that ARP and

the air threat had played in Germany, and of the desirability to join official bodies and

so demonstrate loyalty to the party and state, though this in itself was no guarantee of

public assent. Goebbels, writing in the journal of the RLB in 1939, spoke of a common

response to officials by those who refused to toe the official line.

---

[156] See Overy, 'Apocalyptic fears: Bombing and Popular Anxiety in Inter-War Britain', pp.25-30.
[157] Ibid., p.22.
[158] BRO, M/BCC/ARP/1, Minutes of the Air Raid Precautions Committee, 24 September 1938.
[159] O'Brien, *Civil Defence*, pp.201-218.
[160] Lemke, *Luftschutz in Großbritannien und Deutschland 1923 – 1939*, p.407.

The Führer doesn't want a war, so there won't be one. So why should I bother with air raid precautions?'[161]

Such attitudes would change only when the Allied bombardment began.

Mitigating the blackout

The effect of Germany's resurgence as an airpower was to quicken the pace of ARP and blackout preparations in the United Kingdom, which was warmly received by the Air Ministry.[162] Discussions on blackout preparations were initially centred on drafts of the Police War Instructions (PWI), point 12 of which dealt specifically with the responsibilities of the police in managing it. The focus gradually drifted away from the PWI as the Home Office began to develop its ARP preparations in earnest, and subsequent revisions of the instructions referred instead to the policy of the Home Office's own ARP department. At the outset, it was clear that there was a will to ameliorate the effects of the blackout as much as possible by dividing the country into three zones, according to the level of threat those areas were thought liable to. The map designating these zones is reproduced below.

[161] Joseph Goebbels, 'Luftschutz-Daemmerung', *Die Sirene, I2* (1939).
[162] TNA, HO45/18132, Air Staff memorandum for ARP Sub-Committee, 27 June 1935.

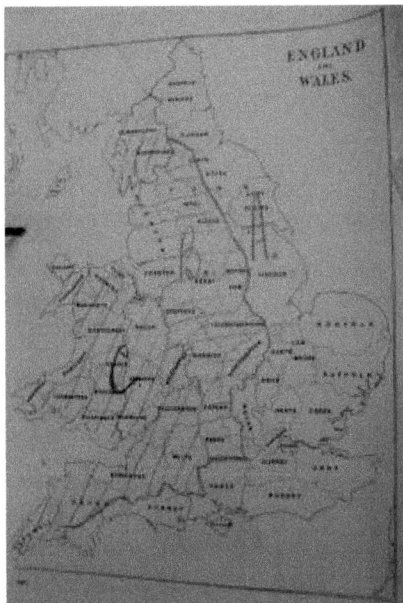

'Zones for Lighting Restrictions.' The division of Britain into zones of threat from an early draft of the Police War Instructions, October 1935.[163]

Broadly stated, this meant that areas in zone A on the east coast most easily reached by raiders from the continent would be permanently blacked out, with no exceptions made save for adequate obscuration of aids to movement of traffic and important industrial work. The central belt of the country, Zone B, would at the discretion of local authorities have some street lighting retained to help movement, and some further exemptions for work vital to the war effort. In both cases however, the ability to obscure or switch off any light on receipt of a warning was a precondition. Zone C, covering much of west England and all of Wales, would be allowed some further exemptions under the direction of regional Police Commissioners. This scheme was not envisioned without some universal restrictions. All residential and commercial properties were to be screened without exemption, and all illuminated advertisements were to be removed permanently. The relaxations in Zones B and C related to street lighting and industrial premises only. Matters to do with lighting on trains, shipping or aircraft were to be decided upon by operators and the government, with the police having no authority on

[163] TNA HO45/18132, 'Zones for Lighting Restrictions', Hodsoll to Andrews, 11 October 1935.

such matters. Likewise, enforcement of restrictions on government property was to be handled by the government.

This scheme continued to evolve in the years leading up to war, with the preferred option within the Home Office and Air Ministry being as dark a blackout as possible. At some point between 1936 and 1937 the number of zones was reduced to two. While no discussions about why this happened apparently remain in the archives, it is likely that the increased range of modern bombers, coupled with lighting experiments undertaken by the Air Ministry, were beginning to have an impact on blackout policy. A joint memorandum drafted by the Air Ministry and Home Office in November 1937 to the Home Defence Committee of the Committee for Imperial Defence reiterated the preference for as complete a blackout as possible, and is one of the few documents in the archive that addresses any potential criticism of the system. It lists two options to be considered for lighting in wartime: unrestricted lighting in spite of air attack; or a modified form of permanent blackout much as the one detailed above, that would allow some lighting for the purposes of industry and traffic movement, and that could be extinguished after receipt of a warning. It is interesting how the memorandum pre-empts many of the complaints about the blackout, addressed in the section on unrestricted lighting.

> ...it may be argued that modern aids to air navigation tend to make aircraft less dependent on the recognition of landmarks, and that even the greatest practicable degree of darkening might still fail to prevent large towns and other important targets from being identified from the air. It may further be argued that reduction of industrial output, and the inconvenience to the civil population resulting from severe lighting restrictions, prolonged over some considerable period, might cause more material damage and loss of morale than any enemy bombing which might thereby be averted.[164]

The rejoinder to these arguments in the document is that other European nations were instituting blackouts and that, under conditions of war, the populace would insist on the

---

[164] TNA, HO45/18133, Air Ministry/Home Office memorandum to Home Defence Committee of the Committee for Imperial Defence, 1 November 1937.

dowsing of lights to obtain greater security from night raids' in the darkness. The

memorandum states that Experience in the last war provides strong reinforcement for

this view.' Thus, the recommendation made to the Home Defence Committee was for

the severest practicable lighting restrictions possible... coupled with a system of decoy

lighting to protect essential industries which cannot be concealed and to confuse the

enemy navigation.'[165]

The eventual recourse to a uniform system of lighting-restrictions on 1 September 1939

appears to have resulted from the cost of centralising lighting systems within local

authorities. From the beginning of blackout planning, the Ministries were concerned

that the ability for immediate extinction of street lighting on receipt of an air raid was

made available. However, lighting systems as they stood at 1935 were varied, and

according to the records few cities had centralised control over their lights, most being

clock or hand controlled. As a result, the ability to switch off external public lighting on

receipt of an air raid warning was severely compromised. Organising an immediate

extinction of lighting across several different forms of lighting control would therefore

have been far harder to organise, and less secure than simply instituting a blackout. On

1 December 1937, a report on available lighting systems to the Committee of Imperial

Defence stated that [t]here are a number of control systems for both gas and electricity

on the market, but we are advised that none is at present fully reliable.' The

memorandum goes on to state of these systems:

> As this war-time system would have to be in readiness in time of peace, would
> have little peace-time value (apart from the possible utility, in some cases, of
> centralised control) and would involve appreciable expenditure, it is a matter for
> consideration whether the conditions of darkness contemplated for Zone A
> should not apply also in the case of Zone B.[166]

Evidently, this view held sway within government. The costs of implementing systems

that could switch off lights from a single point were simply far too great. The only way

---

[165] Ibid.
[166] Ibid.

that such costs could be legitimated would be in the face of a national emergency, and a serious and concrete threat. In less than a year Britain would have one, but by then it was too late to contemplate installing a single switch system. If this reticence is understandable, it is perhaps also the case that its potential cost was dwarfed by the loss of production the blackout would later cause.

The distribution of risk in Germany did not count on any similar system of zoning. While the blackout in the First World War had been confined to the western areas of the country, and then only a narrow strip, Germans had grown used to hearing of the threat now posed to the nation on all sides. Planning for the next war had to take into account that there was now no area safe from modern bombers. However, experience during the war showed that the eastern reaches of the Reich were less troubled by air raids than the industrial and economic heartlands to the west, and some measure of relaxation was allowed in these areas. Hampe writes that where the blackout was maintained in these areas it was largely for the purpose of saving energy, and it was only in the last year of the war that the need for blackouts as permanent as those in the rest of the country became necessary.[167] How formalised this relaxation was is difficult to find from the archives, though discretion would presumably have rested with Police Chiefs in consultation with industry, the party and organizations such as the RLB. Adaptation of the blackout according to the threat does at least appear to have been planned for in the early stages though. A trial blackout held across the entirety of the Ruhr on 23 October 1935 consisted of a reduced blackout for traffic and external lighting from the onset of evening to 9pm, a full blackout from then until 11pm, and a reduced blackout again until midnight. Domestic and business premises were to be blacked out thoroughly during this time, though shops were allowed to adhere to a reduced scheme during the relevant hours.[168] Similar to the schemes being developed

---

[167] Hampe, *Der Zivile Luftschutz im Zweiten Weltkrieg*, pp.556-558.
[168] Stadtarchiv Soest, P22 1055, blackout plan issued by the mayor of Soest, 16 October 1935.

in Britain, what this shows is a willingness to mitigate the effects of the blackout as much as possible. Tying the blackout to the actual threat of a raid would have been ideal, and attempted concessions to this marked inter-war development. In the event however they proved rather optimistic. The level of administration involved was prohibitive save for those areas that could genuinely be seen as low risk. This, coupled to a lack of specificity in the schemes until shortly before the war began meant that despite the years of trials, no one can be said to have been truly familiar with the realities of the blackout regulations until they were called into force on 1 September 1939.[169]

To a certain extent, even when the blackout was being trialled across whole swathes Germany, the myriad problems it would cause were not being acknowledged. Confronting the fact that the blackout would probably have to be almost total was an unappetizing prospect for both the British and German governments, given the effect on movement, production and morale of the people it would inevitably have. Generalized adjustments to the restrictions could not be planned for until either side could gauge the flow of the war and the level of threat posed by enemy aircraft. That both countries should have found themselves in this position is perhaps peculiar, given the importance attached to ARP in Germany. That this was in fact the case is perhaps indicative of the importance of the discursive function of ARP in militarising the population. This did not mean that local officials or the population were very familiar with the specific requirements of ARP. Seen in this light, the absence of a firm grip on ARP in Britain does not ultimately seem to have been much of an advantage for the Germans.

---

[169] Hampe, *Der Zivile Luftschutz im Zweiten Weltkrieg*, p.547.

Decoy lighting

The blackout was designed to minimise the possibility of enemy aircraft recognising their targets, and to make visual navigation of enemy terrain more difficult. Because of this, it afforded an opportunity for deception as part of both nations' air defence systems. Both sides exploited the blackout, rigging chains of lights and decoy installations near cities and strategic targets to trick enemy aircraft into dropping their payloads on empty ground. Their success was used by the British Air Ministry in particular as evidence of the necessity of the blackout; decoys effectively legitimated blackout policy by the extent to which enemy aircraft bombed areas with high concentrations of lights.

Decoy lighting had already been speculated on by the British during the First World War. In 1916, the British Rear Admiral Commanding at Immingham suggested to the Admiralty that since enemy Zeppelins, often confused as to their whereabouts on making landfall at night, tended to steer towards whatever group of lights was nearest, a system of decoy lighting might be used to draw them away from actual towns and cities.[170] While this idea was never developed by the Admiralty, examples exist from the Western Front where decoy lights and dummy airfields had a practical effect.

> ...the men of 54 Night Bombing and Fighting Wing began to lay false flarepaths to deflect night attacks from their landing grounds. Sited around two miles from their ˌparent' stations, lit with paraffin flares and accompanied by small clusters of softly-illuminated dummy buildings, their decoys attracted many bombs, though supervision reportedly proved ˌdangerous and nerve-wracking' for their six-man crews.[171]

In Germany, decoy lighting sites had also been considered during the First World War, but were not constructed until the mid 1930s as part of war game exercises with

---

[170] Colin Dobinson, *Fields of Deception: Britain's Bombing Decoys of World War Two* (London: Methuen, 2000), p.2.
[171] Ibid., p.3.

French forces in 1934-35.[172] Colin Dobinson's comprehensive study of decoy systems in Britain during the war shows that work on decoy lighting sites began in the summer of 1938, having been neglected for many years, and Home Office files show that preparations for decoy lighting were discussed at least as early as 1937. A Home Office and Air Ministry memorandum for the Home Defence Committee from 1937 established the main reasons for decoy lighting:

> The representation in rural districts by means of decoy lighting of important industrial plants and other centres of activity which cannot be darkened completely, would tend to spread' the weight of the enemy bombing attack, and so reduce its intensity on important targets.[173]

A separate memorandum, prepared by the ARP department of the Home Office for a meeting of the Sub-committee on Air Defence Research on 5 March 1937, made a plea for consideration of decoy lighting by committee members as a useful form of defence where light from industrial premises could not be entirely obscured.[174] Correspondence sent after the meeting noted that the idea had also been put forward by Sir Henry Tizard and Winston Churchill, and while notes from this meeting do not apparently exist, it does appear that the evidently less conservative ideas of Tizard and Churchill went beyond what the Home Office and Air Ministry were proposing. A letter sent on 25 March 1937 to Air Vice Marshal Peirse at the Air Ministry by the director of ARP at the Home Office, Wing Commander Hodsoll, said:

> I must say I am not altogether happy about the decoy lighting proposals. It is all very nice for Winston Churchill to talk about having rows of fairy lamps all over the south of England, but it might be even more difficult to do that than to have an effective black-out.[175]

The somewhat vexed language betrays what the Home Office and Air Ministry might have felt was a lack of seriousness in the government's approach to the question of the blackout – in line with ARP preparations more generally until the Munich crisis. Indeed,

---

[172] Edward Westermann, 'Hitting the Mark but Missing the Target: Luftwaffe Deception Operations, 1939-1945', *War in History*, 10/2 (2003), p.208.
[173] TNA, HO45/18133, Joint Home Office and Air Ministry memorandum to the Home Defence Committee, 1 November 1937.
[174] Ibid., Hodsoll to Peirse, 25 March 1937.
[175] Ibid.

Peirse goes on to criticize Henry Tizard, head of the Aeronautical Research Committee, for the 'light-hearted' way he spoke about decoy lighting. In further correspondence, Hodsoll writes on 15 April 1937, 'I have heard unofficially that Sir Henry Tizard is going about saying that there will be no black-out, and that his idea of giving people as much light as they like is going to hold the field.'[176] Ultimately this proved not to be the case. Yet this exemplifies the difficulties for the British in finding a clear blackout policy in the inter-war period, for even at this stage blackouts were not a given for the director of ARP. Eventually, development of decoy lighting was handed to the Air Ministry, though it did not receive great attention until the war began. Dobinson writes of the first experiment organised by the Home Office, which rather confusingly appears to have been done without the knowledge of the Air Ministry.

> These first trials were designed to conceal the faint pinpricks of light showing from a town by smothering it in an array of artificial lights spreading for many miles around. The 'baffle lighting' technique saw its first tests around the Humber on the night of 20/21 May 1939, when no fewer than 4000 hurricane lamps were laid out on a grid (at half-mile intervals) on either side of the estuary... A Whitley bomber was sent out from Dishforth to observe the result, which the crew and representatives from the ARP department found strangely convincing.[177]

Despite this apparent success the system was never developed, owing to what one must assume to have been the enormous logistical problems such a system would involve, particularly in a long war. In the event, decoy lighting was discussed but never adequately developed until the war began. In contrast, German decoy sites were more established in the build-up to war, with Hamburg alone having eleven sites by the end of 1935.[178] These sites multiplied throughout Germany in the inter-war period. Their early success in the war can be measured by the instruction of the Luftwaffe's General Hugo Sperrle in June 1940, commanding Air Fleet 3 at the time, to construct more decoy installations within his command without heed to material and expenses.[179] Their construction, like those in Britain, involved using large tracts of countryside to simulate

---

[176] Ibid., Hodsoll to Peirse, 15 April 1937.
[177] Dobinson, *Fields of Deception: Britain's Bombing Decoys of World War Two*, p.14.
[178] Westermann, 'Hitting the Mark but Missing the Target: Luftwaffe Deception Operations, 1939-1945', p.208.
[179] Ibid.

industrial and town lighting, and the methods used were ingenious. Galleys were rigged to simulate the spark from a tram's overhead power lines. And in a technique that perhaps says much about uniform adherence to the blackout in Germany, sites mimicking towns would be designed to portray a poor blackout, parodying it with intermittent lighting. Flak batteries and searchlight units were placed around these sites, furthering the illusion in the hope that they would lure enemy bombers. British systems developed along similar lines. Control over the development of decoy systems was handed Colonel John Turner, then director of Work and Buildings at the Air Ministry, at the outbreak of war in September 1939. Owing to conditions of secrecy that were strict even within government circles, the decoys section of the Air Ministry became known simply as _Colonel Turner's Department'.[180] Here too the skills of building illusions were imported from the British film industry to construct Britain's decoy defences. Crowdy writes of Turner's auditions:

> After viewing the early attempts of cinema prop makers to simulate cheap and convincing dummy aircraft, Turner was most impressed with work of Sound City Films at Shepperton Studios. Sound City was owned by the Scottish businessman Norman Loudon. With a slump in movie work, Loudon had planned to build a theme park called Sound City Zoo and Wonderland, which was scheduled to open in 1940. Unfortunately the war put paid to this project and the studios were crying out for work. The contracts from Turner proved something of a life line.[181]

Early work on day time decoys switched to night time systems as the Luftwaffe altered its tactics in 1940. The network of QL (lighting) and QF (fire) sites mushroomed around the aerodromes and towns of Britain. They were a noted success. A Home Office review and defence of the blackout from the summer of 1941 cited numerous instances where _thedisplay of lights frequently catches the enemy's attention and attracts bombs in places which would otherwise not have been subject to attack.'[182] In 1942, Arthur Harris noted the continued importance of visual identification for bomber crews.

---

[180] Terry Crowdy, *Deceiving Hitler: Double Cross and Deception in World War II* (Oxford: Osprey, 2008), pp.58-61.
[181] Ibid., p.59.
[182] TNA, HO 186/428, _Black-Out – Notes for the Minister', 6 August 1941.

The multiplication of enemy decoy-fire sites in the 1942 greatly added to the problems of target location – as the Luftwaffe had found over here. GEE' [one of the RAF's early radio navigation systems] was not sufficiently accurate to indicate whether a promising-looking fire was one started by our own aircraft at the aiming point (or, mistakenly, in the wrong place), or was an enemy decoy some miles distant from the target. Only in clear weather conditions and with the assistance of moonlight could we have reasonable hopes of success. Even in the best possible conditions, however, industrial haze generally prevented visual recognition of Ruhr targets.[183]

In this passage, Harris vindicates not only the use of decoys, but the blackout itself. Yet the extension of the zone of danger from urban areas into the countryside would not be without its cost or protest. This will be looked at in greater detail in chapter four of this thesis. In contrast with much of the material presented in this study, decoy sites were one of the few aspects of the blackout that required structural preparations, and were held secret from the public as much as was practicable. Indeed, people in Britain were forbidden to refer to them in public.[184] Decoys were to a great extent free of the more common problem of inter-war development, that of how much involvement the public could expect to have in blackout trials, and how best to mobilise awareness and understanding of it in peacetime. This was exacerbated by the extent to which the state was liable for any accidents that occurred during trials, by compromising public safety. This problem is outlined in the following section.

Liability and blackout exercises

In Britain, the question of liability for any accidents occurring during blackout exercises was fudged until the outbreak of war. A letter sent by the Admiralty to the Home Office on 15 November 1935 outlined the problem.

On a recent occasion of Air Defence Exercises at Portsmouth, the Town Clerk of the Borough of Gosport, while agreeing to extinguish the lights on Gosport landing stage and Gosport wharf, stated that his Council must hold the Admiralty responsible for any damage which might be caused as a result of the action. My Lords are advised that the fact that lights have been extinguished at

---

[183] Arthur T. Harris, *Despatch on War Operations, 23rd February, 1942, to 8th May, 1945* (London: Frank Cass, 1995), p.10.
[184] TNA, HO 186/428, Black-Out – Notes for the Minister', 6 August 1941.

the request of the Naval authorities would afford no defence to a claim for damages and that so extinguishing the lights might, if a fatal accident resulted, find himself faced with a charge of manslaughter.[185]

The response to this letter was long in coming, and was eventually sent on 23 June 1936, agreeing with the position as set out by the Admiralty and noting that the Secretary of State was investigating how the exercises might be conducted under existing law. These discussions were ultimately fruitless, since the position, as stated in a response to the Admiralty on 18 April 1938, remained the same.

> I am directed by the Secretary of State to say... that it is not at present his intention to introduce such legislation [to delineate responsible authorities], but to rely upon the conduct of exercises in a manner which minimises the possibility of claims being made against the Government or local authorities.[186]

It is not clear from the files whether any legislation was introduced before the outbreak of war, but given the prevarication over three years on this issue it seems unlikely. What is clear is that the lack of legal accountability and tools for coercion hindered any large scale exercises that could take place during hours when most people were awake. Conducting blackout exercises so as to ‚minimise' the chance of accidents, and to avoid authorities becoming liable for damages or injury as a result of them, inevitably meant restricting the scale and times at which exercises could take place. Without evidence of a national emergency, there was no mandate to inconvenience the public and trade. Indeed large scale exercises, such as those reported by *The Times* in Berlin in 1935, were not used by the authorities because of the odd legal situation the exercises placed everybody in. A note from 1936 advising the Home Office on this issue outlines the nature of the problem.

> As regards motor cars, I will assume that it is contemplated that the police, in accordance with arrangements agreed between the local authority and the A.R.P.D. would request all motorists on entering the ‚blackout' area to put out their lights and side lamps. A motorist who complies with such a request commits a criminal offence (i.e. failure to carry at night he lights requested by law); and the constable who made the request might, in theory, be charged with procuring or aiding and abetting the offence. In addition to his criminal liability, the motorist incurs abnormal risk of causing damage to other people and to

---

[185] TNA, HO45/18132, Admiralty to Home Office, 15 November 1935.
[186] TNA HO45/18133, Home Office to Admiralty, 18 April 1938.

property by driving his car without lights. The fact that the motorist was doing this at the request of the police would not afford him any defence in civil proceedings for damages or criminal proceedings for careless or dangerous driving or driving without proper lights.[187]

So, in the absence of any legal requirement for a motorist to turn off their lights in a blackout zone, the local authorities had to ask drivers to break the law. In the event, many exercises simply asked drivers in advance of an exercise to refrain from driving, which was easy enough given the hours they took place in. If they were stopped on entering a blackout exercise, they were asked to park up and take shelter until the exercise was finished. This was in effect a test of the administrative practicalities of the blackout, rather than a test of how civil society might cope with it.

By extension, the same the same legal reasoning that could make a motorist in a blackout a criminal might do the same for local authorities charged with providing adequate lighting. Some confusion existed over whether this was in fact the case. The legal note referred to above, written in 1936, stated that since local authorities were legally responsible for lighting the streets under its supervision, they would be offered no protection from legal proceedings should anything go wrong during an exercise. Any defence by a local authority on the grounds that the lights had been turned off on instruction from a government department would not hold up in law, since there was no legislation ceding legal authority over lighting to the government. The idea of the government indemnifying local authorities in such cases was floated within the Home Office, but seems to have come to nothing. However, a guidance note issued to local authorities in the summer of 1939, in advance of an extensive blackout trial held nationwide with the cooperation of the RAF, contradicts this advice, stating that there is not generally any obligation in law on local authorities outside London to maintain street lighting where it has been installed.'[188] Confusion on this issue will not have

---

[187] TNA HO45/18132, letter to Scott, 19 March 1936.
[188] TNA, HO 186/19, ARP Department circular, 27 June 1939.

helped the preparation of blackout exercises, and it is worth asking whether the trial blackouts were more useful for those organising them than the population at large. Indeed, the government's confusion over the development of ARP and blackouts was by 1938 already being satirised by the cartoonist David Low. Geoffrey Lloyd, the Under-Secretary of State for the Home Department, asks his colleagues to imagine themselves buried under rubble, before immediately calling time for lunch. This prompts Thomas Inskip, the Minister of Coordination for Defence, to announce ͟Oh Lor! I've forgotten the sandwiches.'

'Trial Blackout': George Low cartoon from *The Guardian*, 27 January 1938, p.12.

Since the method of trial blackouts was for them to be held late at night and in the early hours of the morning, it is debateable whether, when the lighting restrictions were imposed on 1 September 1939, the public were ready for its effect on their lives. Guidance on lighting restrictions, in the first months of the war, was something that was very much learnt on the job. As much as the trials had benefited the development of technical methods of compensating for the blackout, the first few months of the war were the test for how it affected the lives of the population. An indication of how much was learnt in these few months can be illustrated in the increase in size from the first set of lighting instructions issued under the emergency orders, to the second; 8 pages of instructions for those issued on 1 September 1939, as compared to the 28 pages for those issued on 19 January 1940. The additional 20 pages of detail is a good indicator of how encompassing the blackout was, and how much of it was not reckoned with before the war.

German blackout tests, while they began much earlier, were still faced with the problem of their relatively limited scale. Despite propaganda efforts to make Germans aware of ARP after 1933 and the threat from foreign airpowers, the Nazi government dragged its heels in actually formalising ARP in law. It wasn't until 1935 that the first *Luftschutzgesetz* (Air Raid Law) was introduced on 25 June, and it was another two years until the by-laws governing the detail of the regulations were signed by Göring, on 4 May 1937. There appears to have been no great discussion on liabilities for blackout exercises, though insurance from the state for ARP practices was covered under the regulations. What is notable from the four years of trial blackouts is the gap between the rhetoric of ARP and its adherence on the ground. Press reports of the large scale Berlin trial from 1935 may have been enthusiastic, but as already mentioned, were by no means indicative of the public's ability to cope with a rolling blackout. It is in fact difficult to separate press assessments of trial blackouts from their use as propaganda, and they cannot be taken as reliable indicator of the blackout's thoroughness or quality. Some more sober assessments from the German press give hints of less enthusiastic reception. A report of a trial blackout from the Ruhr city of Essen in October 1935 writes of countless lapses' visible from a water tower.[189] An apparently more successful trial in Dortmund in 1935 still suffered from problems with industrial blackouts that despite substantial investment are still not satisfactory', and with many people staying home to avoid the trial.[190] This was not normal life under a blackout, and whatever successes may have been claimed, a real test could not be seen until the extensive trials of 1937. The city of Hamburg, along with much of

[189] 'Eine Probeverdunkelung', *Rheinisch-Westfälische Zeitung*, 20 October 1935, p.4.
[190] 'Die Verdunkelung in Dortmund', *Rheinisch-Westfälische Zeitung*, 1935, p.2.

northern Germany, was blacked out for seven nights between 20-26 September. The first reports claimed a huge success – discipline on all sides' cried one headline from the Party affiliated *Hamburger Tageblatt*, though it was only practice for a more limited reduced' blackout.[191] The following night's complete blackout was less successful, and the *Tageblatt's* report asked for no slacking in the blackout!'[192] Berlin, which had been holding a rolling blackout during the same period, had its practice lifted when Mussolini arrived in the city. Göring's reasons for doing this belie the problems of peacetime blackout exercises, and the politics of good adherence to them.

> The reason for the lifting of the restriction was with regard to the commercial and economic life of the capital and above all the immaculate attitude of the entire population of Berlin, who have made the blackout practice in Berlin a complete success.[193]

One can only imagine how the people of Hamburg, who were made to continue with their blackout for the next few days, felt on reading this. Some parallels with the British experience must be drawn. While the German authorities had more extensive plans for trialling blackouts than the British, they still rather underestimated the task. The week-long trials of 1937 were the last of their kind until the war began, and even these were confined to specific regions of Germany. Their scale pales in comparison with the wartime rolling blackout, and it is probably unfair to imagine any amount of practice could make the public familiar with the true task of living with an indefinite blackout before a war. But the gap between rhetoric and what actually happened on the ground is, in this, rather large.

Conclusion

This chapter has examined how the blackout was developed in Germany and Britain prior to the war. Despite earlier development, and larger scale exercises, little

---

[191] 'Im tiefsten Dunkel war Hamburg die ganze Nacht', *Hamburger Tageblatt*, 21 September 1937.
[192] 'Hamburg war Gestern noch dunkler', *Hamburger Tageblatt*, 22 September 1937.
[193] 'Berlin braucht nicht mehr verdunkeln', *Hamburger Tageblatt*, 23 September 1937, p.2.

advantage was gained by Germany over Britain during this beyond the militarisation of the population through the wider propaganda of ARP, and the discipline it encouraged. That this was so lies in the intractable nature of trialling blackouts over an extended period during peacetime, given its detrimental effect on civilian and economic life. While both country's blackouts were organised at the administrative level successfully, it was therefore difficult for either country to adequately prepare the public for the difficulties of living under an indefinite, rolling blackout. The delayed start to the bombing war was invaluable in allowing the public to become used to blackout discipline, and to iron out the flaws and unforeseen problems that restricted trials had failed to identify. Hence while interwar trials were no doubt important, they were of more practical use for administrators and air forces, rather than the civilian population.

Chapter Four – Adherence and Enforcement

Introduction

The blackout's nightly routine and its focus on the rights of the community over the individual was an important element in the construction of a unified home front in both countries. Adherence to the blackout by civilians, by business, and indeed by the state, was a visible measure of wartime discipline. The universality of the blackout meant that fairness, as applied to the policing of the blackout, the punishments handed out for infractions, and the shouldering of the blackout's burdens, became one of its central features. Because of this, the blackout played an ambiguous role in reifying the wartime community by emphasising collective security, and also undermining it through the tensions it brought out between the people and the state, and between people themselves. This is made clear in the following chapter, in which space – public space and private behaviour within it – is a recurring issue in the blackout, as well as the monitoring of blackout discipline by the state and by the people themselves.

The beginning of the blackout

As the two previous chapters have established, preparations for the blackout, despite some attempts at trialling it throughout both countries, brought more of an administrative benefit than any great familiarity with it for the public. How the population would react to and live with a rolling blackout was something that pre-war planning could only try to imagine. As the previous chapter showed, the conditions of war were far more conducive to actually planning the blackout in Britain than the restricted practices of the inter-war years. The ambiguity of the first months afforded the public and administrators in national and local government a period in which to acclimatise and plan, without the fallout from a catastrophic incendiary or gas attack to impede their efforts. Yet though the blackout began with the declaration of war, the willingness of the public to go along with the blackout was not assumed to be an article of faith in Britain. Where in Germany blackout discipline had acquired a normative power of allegiance to the state under the umbrella of ARP in general, scepticism and antipathy surrounding ARP remained far higher in Britain. The war did not begin with any one event that would melt the feelings of cynicism, or intransigence, towards ARP. Rather, the greatest justification for it would always be falling bombs. Because of this, and despite the efforts of politicians and those involved with organising ARP, it did not acquire a strong normative power in Britain. It was this difference that distinguished the two nations as the war began.

The assumption that Britain and Germany were run under fundamentally different systems during the Second World War can mask their often intriguing similarities. Germans were by this point familiar with the rhetoric of the Nazi *Volksgemeinschaft*, even if the reality was more complicated. There were now parallels in how total war modified the needs of British society that bear comparison with Nazi ideas of individual responsibility. Though a state of war existed, it had yet to manifest itself in any appreciable way for British citizens, barring the interruptions of ARP and the blackout. In the very early days of the war in Britain, newspapers regularly reported on blackout transgressions amongst the population. The *Bristol Evening Post* ran a story on 7 September 1939, relating the response of an ironmonger in Bournemouth to a policeman who had ordered him to stop showing a light. Off back to Germany where you belong' he told him, I have got some work to do, so clear off.'[194] His response, bridling against the obligations of the blackout in a country that saw itself as more free than Hitler's Germany, exemplifies the change the war brought to ideas of individual responsibility. That same day the paper ran an article by Duff Cooper, the former

---

[194] 'More People Fined Over Lights', *Bristol Evening Post*, 7 September 1939, p.7.

Secretary of State for War and future Minister of Information, who told readers that a good first rule for behaviour in wartime is obedience to orders and abstention from criticism, whether it be of the Prime Minister or local air warden.'[195] This language, unthinkable in peacetime, underlines how ARP and the blackout would redefine the idea of the individual's role within the community. The idea of Britain fighting a People's War' was quickly appropriated by the government, and is still present in popular memory several decades on. The blackout formed an important and little acknowledged part of this construction of a cohesive, unified nation.

Consent in securing and policing the blackout

The years from 1933 onwards saw the German police force organised around a principle of protecting the German public from malign outside influences. Broadly, these were defined as anything that was not enshrined in the tenets of National Socialism.[196] The criminal and legal system became one of the more important systems for tying together the threads of race-consciousness that characterised public discourse in Nazi Germany. It provided a system of thought and punishment for boxing dissent, whether criminal, political, sexual or biological, into neat categories of transgression. The legal system at the beginning of the war quickly adapted to punish blackout offences that exploited it.[197] Yet failing to secure the blackout properly was not necessarily a criminal act. How the blackout was exploited for personal gain is described in chapter five of this thesis. In contrast with those types of offences, the majority of blackout transgressions were not the result of active or wilful sabotage, or of people seeking advantage. Their main causes were laziness, thoughtlessness and carelessness. These in themselves were resistance of a sort, in that they demonstrate the limits of Nazi ideology, and state power in general, in regulating people's behaviour.

---

[195] Duff Cooper, 'Sound Rules for Behaviour in Wartime', Ibid. p.6.
[196] Robert Gellately, *Backing Hitler: Consent and Coercion in Nazi Germany* (Oxford: Oxford University Press, 2002), pp.40-50.
[197] See Nikolaus Wachsmann, *Hitler's Prisons: Legal Terror in Nazi Germany* (London: Yale University Press, 2004), pp.192-208.

Though one would hesitate to say they were rarely more than passive examples, not blacking out nevertheless flew in the face of the heightened rhetoric that the Nazi state had attached to ARP in the preceding years. Göring issued a statement at the beginning of the war that exemplifies the kind of language that was attached to ARP.

> You warriors in self-defence, know that in your duty you protect not only the lives and health of your wife and your children, but also the fate of millions of fellow citizens... Our enemies will retreat from our unbreakable will to resist. Long live the Fuhrer! Long live Germany![198]

Given the status of ARP in forging the national consciousness and the siege mentality of the Nazi war state, the question of consent is of great importance for the blackout measures. The extent to which Germans willingly followed the Party line has been increasing in prominence in scholarship on Nazi Germany. Indeed, the tone of scholarship has shifted markedly since the war's end. In the immediate post war years, the general consensus amongst historians was that Nazi Germany was a classic totalitarian state, with public freedoms severely restricted. The subsequent shift in focus from top-down histories towards bottom-up, social histories, has chipped away at the foundations of this idea. Nazi Germany has therefore been increasingly understood as a dictatorship by consensus, with the Party's influence and the state's apparatus of terror revaluated and reduced in importance. Its power therefore emanates from the willingness of ordinary Germans to cooperate with the state, with citizens placing tremendous faith in the tenets of National Socialism, however they might understand them.

In assessing these developments in the historiography of Nazi Germany, Richard Evans argues that the consent of the German people in being governed by the Nazis has been overstated, and argues for a more sophisticated understanding of consent that goes beyond what Neil Gregor has criticised as the rediscovery of the vocabulary

---

[198] Hermann Goring, 'Luftschutz sichert die Heimat', *Berlin Lokal-Anzeiger*, 5 September 1939, p.3.

of -political religion" as a means with which to analyze —or, rather, to analogize—the Nazi dictatorship.[199] This study's contribution to the debate on coercion and consent in Nazi Germany can be seen in this chapter by outlining how an as yet little researched area of the German home front contributed to the heterogeneous character of cooperation and dissent in this period. That blackout offences were committed at all gave local officials and party functionaries a great deal of concern; neither criminals nor good citizens, how these offenders were dealt with, and how the blackout was made secure throughout the war, provides an interesting place from which to consider the character of Nazi policing and justice.

Because of the universal character of the blackout, these considerations also play a part in how it was policed and adhered to in Britain. The work done by the Nazis in the years before the war in fostering a coherent national identity in Germany has no comparison in Britain. Yet the implications of exposing a light and endangering the rest of the community carried the same weight. As Rose writes, despite attempts to foster popular ideas of togetherness across the classes in Britain, the war still found cases of defiance, resistance and indifference.[200] Though the political climate and structure of Britain was very different to Germany's, similar language and justifications were used in both countries. During the war years, the official narratives of the conflict together with the tighter restrictions on the media tried to construct Britain as a unified nation, with a common goal. This in turn influenced much of the post-war representations of the social effects of the war in Britain, which again focussed on the unity and community cohesion the war was alleged to have fostered. Harold Smith singled out Richard Titmuss' *Problems of Social Policy* as especially guilty of overestimating the extent to which the war generated a community of likeminded citizens. By concentrating too

---

[199] See Richard J Evans, 'Coercion and Consent in Nazi Germany', *Proceedings of the British Academy,* 151 (2007). & Neil Gregor, 'Politics, Culture, Political Culture: Recent Work on the Third Reich and Its Aftermath', *The Journal of Modern History,* 78/September (2006), p.644. See also Jill Stephenson, 'Generations, Emotion and Critical Enquiry: A British View of Changing Approaches to the Study of Nazi Germany', *German History,* 26/2 (2008).
[200] Rose, *Which People's War? National Identity and Citizenship in Britain, 1939-1945,* p.8.

much on this Dunkirk spirit', Titmuss and others who followed a similar line paid insufficient attention to behaviour inconsistent with that idea'.[201] Smith's work, with its trenchant criticism of Titmuss' influence on post-war consensus, argued for an examination of Britain's home front that engaged with the disparities and myths that Angus Calder had begun to demolish in his key work *The People's War: Britain, 1939-45*, published in 1969, and *The Myth of the Blitz* in 1991. The examination of inequalities - of food and clothes rationing, the class divide where urban populations sheltered during air raids - were all aspects of the war that required reassessment. With the blackout, the idea of equality in prosecution, and fairness in how it was administered means that it too requires a deeper appreciation of its role in both fostering and undermining ideas of the national community.

Angus Calder noted in *The People's War* that by the war's end almost one in fifty Britons had been convicted of some sort of lighting offence – about 925000.[202] It was almost certainly more, considering those who had been let off by wardens and those whose infractions had not been noticed. Given the comparative saturation of ARP's importance in Germany when compared with Britain it might be assumed that the quality of the blackout, and adherence to it, was far better and indeed stricter than in Britain. But a report compiled by the Air Ministry in the first months of the war shows that this does not appear to be the case. In fact, the experience of British pilots flying to Germany was that, certainly in the early stages of the war, the blackout was not as comprehensive in Germany as it was in Britain. In a report that gauged the effectiveness of the blackout from the opinions of pilots and other members of aircraft crews, it described the transition in flight over different countries with relation to the blackout.

[201] Harold L. Smith, *Britain in the Second World War: a Social History* (Manchester: Manchester University Press, 1996), p.2.
[202] Calder, *The People's War: Britain, 1939-1945*, p.337.

A pilot leaves England which is ‚blacked out' and his first impression is one of thankfulness for neutral countries. In reasonable weather conditions he sees Holland, a blaze of light, and later perhaps Denmark with a blacked out area between them. At first the blackout in Germany was not complete. Towns like Hamburg and Bremen could be identified by the fact that there were large lighted areas in the positions where the pilot expected to find these towns.[203]

Curiously, an intelligence report from September 1940 noted that the standard of blackout for private houses in Germany had been applied far more rigorously in exercises prior to the war than during it, even after a full year of war.[204] This is perhaps strange, and there is nothing to corroborate this observation elsewhere in files either in Germany or Britain. It might be the case that the zeal with which officials pursued blackout offences over the short periods that ARP exercises took place could be far greater than in wartime. The RAF's survey of the blackout eventually notes a tightening of the blackout across Germany during these first few months; blackout discipline did, it would seem, find its hold amongst the German population. Yet despite this, there remained infractions that helped British bomber crews find their target, or else confused them. The report noted that ‚sometimes our aircraft find lights in use when they approach but they are extinguished immediately it is known[sic] that bombers are in the vicinity'. And in a reference to observations of both Germany and Britain, the report noted that ‚occasionally the position of towns is disclosed by numerous separated lights', which the report presumes to be ‚individual instances of non-compliance with the regulations'.[205] This report surely illustrated to policy makers in the Home Office the importance of the blackout. Though political and public reaction in Britain began to question both the severity and the necessity of the blackout, aerial observations of the German blackout, and the use of blackout infractions for navigation, would have reiterated the importance of maintaining it. Indeed, all later discussions on this matter by the government would defer to the opinion of the Air Ministry. No adjustments were made to the blackout for purely political reasons, and the RAF was

[203] TNA, HO186/1395, report from Bomber Command, [undated] February 1940. Guy Gibson also noted the poor blackouts in neutral countries, as well as France. See Guy Gibson, *Enemy Coast Ahead* (Manchester: Goodall, 1998), p.76; p.84.
[204] TNA, HO186/2042, intelligence briefing, 3 September 1940.
[205] Ibid.

always invoked as an independent arbiter of the blackout's continued existence. A ministerial briefing before the winter of 1941 was unequivocal.

> It should be made clear at the outset that there can be no question, at this stage, of modifying the basic principles of blackout policy. This policy and its applications are under constant review in consultation with the Air Staff, and due account is taken of any fresh development as it occurs; but the Air Staff assert that the maintenance of a strict black-out is as useful and necessary now as at any stage of the war.[206]

Though this may have seemed reasonable in Whitehall, the blackout nevertheless had some vociferous detractors in Britain. The associations and double meanings of the blackout were never pleasant. Lant offers this index of its miseries.

> The noun blackout' referred to the fabric of or paint used to cut out light, and to the government regulation of blacking-out. It also designated, in older use, the condition of being without information or news, and the temporary, complete failure of memory or loss of consciousness. In the context of flying, it referred to transient blindness resulting from centrifugal force incurred when a sudden turn was made. As a verb, it meant to obscure or obliterate, particularly lights escaping from windows.[207]

While it may have been seen a necessity by the Air Ministry, the technicalities of justification could seem remote and alienating in a war fought between nations which, though seemingly at a peak of civilization, had imposed barbarous conditions not only on the front but at home too. From the very start of the war, Churchill was concerned with the impact of the blackout on the morale of the nation. Apparently taking soundings from members of the naval staff when First Lord of the Admiralty, Churchill argued in War Cabinet meetings for a relaxation of the blackout that was in keeping with the scale of the threat, and cautioning against over-reaction. He felt sure that the Germans wouldn't launch indiscriminate attacks on civilians yet. The danger was that the advantages in increased security... might well be outweighed by greater disadvantages in other fields of our war effort.' [208] At the beginning of the war correspondence between the naval staff outlined not only the extent to which the

---

[206] TNA, HO 186/428, Black-Out – Notes for the Minister', 6 August 1941
[207] Antonia Lant, Blackout: Reinventing Women for Wartime British Cinema (Princeton: Princeton University Press, 1991), p.124.
[208] TNA, CAB/73/15, minutes of War Cabinet meeting 30 November 1939.

effectiveness of the blackout was being debated amongst senior staff, but also its range over the Empire. The blackout in Gibraltar had caused a seven month delay to the widening of a dock; Malta too was blacked out, as was Colombo in Ceylon.[209] And at the appearance of a lone raider in the Mozambique channel, the whole of the East coast of Africa was blacked out – though we may wonder at how well this was followed, bearing in mind distances and the level of infrastructure for lighting. The scale of measures in these early months seemed entirely out of keeping with the threat. The Deputy Chief of the Naval Staff argued that

> the effect on morale of all this blacking out must be very bad indeed, and I should not be surprised if we are the laughing stock of the world over it. How anybody with any sense of proportion can black out East Africa because raiders appeared in the Mozambique Channel I find it difficult to conceive. I suppose the chances of an aircraft from this raider trying to bomb anywhere in East Africa are certainly not more than one in a million.[210]

Making clear that he agreed with these criticisms and passing them onto the War Cabinet, Churchill nevertheless tolerated the blackout during the war, in spite of his own misgivings. However, he argued for relaxations wherever possible. At the third meeting of the interdepartmental lighting committee in November 1939, he argued for a relaxation of the regulations that, in view of what was to come over the following years, betrays the uncertainty of the war's first months.

> I venture to suggest to my colleagues that when the present moon begins to wane the black-out system should be modified to a sensible degree. We know it is not the present policy of the German Government to indulge in indiscriminate bombing in England or France, and it is certainly not in their interest to bomb any but a military objective. The bombing of military objectives can best be achieved, and probably only achieved, by daylight or in moonlight. Should they change this policy, or should a raid be signalled, we could extinguish our lights again.[211]

Quite what 'modified to a sensible degree' means is rather vague here. Certainly, despite pre-war preparations, the consensus that something had to be done to alleviate the very worst effects of the blackout was well established before Christmas, and by

---

[209] TNA, CAB/67/2/58, Churchill memorandum to War Cabinet, 20 November 1939.
[210] Ibid.
[211] NAS, CAB 73/16, Churchill memorandum to Ministerial Committee on Lighting Restrictions, 30 November 1939.

January 1940 a new Lighting (Restrictions) Order set out on paper the various modifications now allowed under a new lighting regime.[212] Responsibility for lighting in districts was devolved to local authorities. Yet despite the apparent enthusiasm amongst the public for the what was known as the _starlight' system, some councils chose to forego installing it. Despite this reticence, the speed of movement on alleviating the blackout as much as possible was both a practical consideration and a political one. Practical in the sense that the restrictions had taken a severe toll not only on the cultural life of the nation – as previously described – but also on the flow of people, traffic, goods, and the ability of industries gearing up for war to maintain output. This will be explored in chapter seven, but for this section it is important in understanding the political impact of the blackout.

Justification for the blackout's inconvenience and danger relied on a threat that was yet to appear. Had the war begun with a surprise attack by German aircraft, as long feared, the blackout's necessity would have been apparent and uncontested. In the absence of this, the response by government in Britain to alleviating the strain of the blackout was evidence of the link between it and the perception not only of the war, but its handling by the government. Though a few people found it exciting, it was for most a burden, and with its frustrations and contraction of public space, minister's consideration of its impact on morale was not unwarranted. The following conversation, caught at the beginning of the war, betrays the class antagonism and anger with Chamberlain that the blackout brought out of one girl:

> Me: _How do you like these new blue lamps?'
>
> Single girl, civil servant, 19: _Lovely, when you want to read. I'd like to have Chamberlain for myself, for a day. I'd sit him in a darkened tube, give him an all-day ticket, and leave him there under the eyes of two watchful navvies with pick-axes on their shoulders, so that he couldn't escape.'
>
> Me: _But, still, perhaps they know best.'

---

[212] O'Brien, *Civil Defence*, pp.322-323.

Girl: Know best? What can they know about what it's like to travel with the proletariat on crowded tubes and trains, in semi- or complete darkness? Good heavens, they could switch them off, if there was a warning, if that's what you're worrying about.'

Married woman, clerk, 37: But that might cause panic.'

Girl: Well then, they switch to fainter lamps in case of a raid. That should be satisfactory.'[213]

Churchill's views on the blackout may in part have been influenced through his occasionally fractious friendship with the newspaper magnate Lord Beaverbrook, whose stable of papers maintained a steadfast line against the blackout. Beaverbrook's positions in government during the war brought him into direct confrontation with the blackout's effect as a brake on the wartime economy, through his roles as minister of aircraft production (2 August 1940 – 1 May 1941), minister of supply (29 June 1941-4 February 1942) and a short-lived term as minister of war production (4-19 February 1942). But at a Regional Commissioner's Conference in August 1943, the weight of the opinion of the Air Ministry was made clear.

> The Minister said that a Cabinet Committee under his chairmanship had been considering the industrial aspects of the blackout. Its findings had led to some relaxations, without prejudice against the main position. The Beaverbrook press had been conducting a campaign against the blackout, using the arguments (a) that to dispense with it altogether would give no real advantage to the enemy, and (b) that, in any case, arrangements could be made to mask or extinguish lights on the approach of enemy aircraft. As to (a), the Air Staff had said that the R.A.F. would be very grateful if the enemy would lift their blackout.[214]

No amount of cabinet influence could overcome the insistence of the Air Ministry in the blackout's worth. Antipathy to the blackout had perhaps more to do with politics than with its practical application, or its effectiveness as a defensive measure. The only appeal that could ever be made for its abolition was on the grounds of prosecuting the war effort – as will be seen in the following chapter. The Beaverbrook press pursued its agenda against the blackout with a vehemence that was puzzling, and with no small amount of disingenuousness. Anderson became an early target of the Standard's editorials – according to the paper, it was he who had decided on the present system of

---

[213] MOA, Folder 1/D, Blackout in Trains, 24 October 1939.
[214] NAS, HH50/132, Minutes of the Regional Commissioners' Conference, 19 August 1943.

lighting, and had done so on the back of _one night when Sir John trudged through the streets.'[215] This was nonsense. The Home Office was convinced that Beaverbrook was pursuing a grievance against Anderson.

> ...this inspiration comes from the proprietor. Both Editors [of the Express and Standard] were present at the Minister's recent press conference and know the facts – that the black-out is imposed by the Air Ministry and that the deciding tests are made from the air and not from the ground.[216]

The steadfast attitude against the blackout may to a certain extent have been commercial – none of the other national papers took a hard line stance against it. And perhaps because of this, there may have been a need for a voice to articulate a grievance against the blackout, that found it too craven a reaction to the circumstances of the war, and too reminiscent of a level of state control more familiar to its enemy.

The political impact of the blackout was such that the state might have been expected to have lead by example when the war began, by blacking out its property efficiently. Given the inconvenience of the blackout, and the penalties for breaching it, it was obvious that the restrictions would have to be applied to civilian and state alike. But perhaps one of the most interesting aspects of the early days of the war was the difficultly the state found in blacking out its own property adequately, and the potential for undermining the integrity of the blackout this caused. While officials from both countries exhorted their fellow citizens to follow correct procedure, they found themselves undermined by poorly secured blackouts in state buildings and facilities, to the irritation of citizens. Despite the rhetoric of community and unity, the maintenance of the blackout was very much an imposition by the state on the population, and few welcomed it in the ambiguous days of the Phoney War. Whether from Government offices, police buildings or military installations, a shaft of light emitted by employees of the state was damaging, not only for the community ethic of ARP, but also in the

---

[215] 'One Man Against London', *The Evening Standard*, 12 December 1939, p.6.
[216] TNA, HO 186/1012, Crutchley to Mabane, 12 December 1939.

respect of each government's handling of the war. Any breach by the state in blackout precautions was an immediate, visible failure of the state in managing the war. While the management of any large building might reasonably have been expected to have had a few teething problems in the first days of the war, continued incidences of Government offices showing lights proved to be a recurring problem.

On 3 September 1939, a few days after the lighting restrictions had come into force, a civil servant took a stroll around Whitehall to see how well the area had blacked out. Not very well, as he found out. In a note to the Lord Privy Seal, he reported the War Office as being particularly bad, with 'about a dozen windows revealing strips of light from 2-4 inches down the sides of the blinds.' Night watchmen were found wandering around with oil lanterns exposed, and the telephone exchange nearby was also poorly secured.[217] All of these problems were of course easily fixable. Yet a later survey found continuing problems around Whitehall. Mass Observation took a general survey of the blackout in Whitehall in early November 1939. Despite the intervening months, it still found lax adherence amongst many of the buildings, which the following extract from their survey illustrates.

> Imperfectly blacked out (generally merely a slit of light showing at the edge of the blind. This would not be visible either from above or any distance from ground level).
>
> Admiralty   17
>
> —Arch   17
>
> Home Office   35
>
> War Office   4
>
> Buildings in Storey's Gate (Office of Works etc)   29
>
> Charles St.   45
>
> Windows that were poorly blinded and showed light through. (Doubtful if these would be visible from a distance on ground level)

---

[217] TNA, HO 186/720, Chapman to Lord Privy Seal, 3 September 1939.

Admiralty Arch 5

Foreign Office 6

No windows show direct beams of light, and none had no blinds (OBs has seen them here with no blind at all – in Dominions Office).[218]

The press was not slow in taking this up. While criticising the variable rates at which blackout offenders were fined, *The Daily Mirror* told its readers that if they MUST offend', then Whitehall was the cheapest place for them to show a light.[219] This was not a problem peculiar to the early days of the blackout. Over a year later, a letter from the Metropolitan Police to the Home Office in March 1941 again complained of government offices not adequately blacking out. Buildings occupied by the Treasury, having caused local police touble on several occasions', and the Air Ministry were cited as particular examples. The Met laid the blame at the Office of Works, and the generally poor quality of blackout material available.[220] These infractions by the state also extended to militarised areas. In the village of Burford in Oxfordshire a correspondent for Mass Observation wrote that

> by the end of October the military had moved in, and were illuminating the landscape vividly through their rectory skylight and other sources, although they had already been in occupation of un-blacked out places for as much as a week. This pleasantly infuriated many of the villagers, nursing their quiet grievances of the blackout, which is quieter in Burford than in most places, because there are two enormous aerodromes in the immediate vicinity.[221]

Perhaps rather unfairly, the writer Vera Brittain blamed the poor discipline and moral laxity' of British troops for the destruction of the large country estate she lived near and at which they were stationed, their lighted cigarettes at night providing a beacon for a feat of precision bombing' by the Luftwaffe.[222]

---

[218] MOA, Folder 1/D, Government Offices in Blackout', 9 November 1939.
[219] 'Black Outlook', *The Mirror*, 7 November 1939, p.1.
[220] TNA, HO 186/720, Scotland Yard to Home Office, 14 March 1941.
[221] MOA, Folder 1/D, Account from Burford village, 19 October 1939.
[222] Paul Fussell, *Wartime: Understanding and Behaviour in the Second World War* (Oxford: Oxford University Press, 1990), p.17.

The corollary to all state infractions was who would take responsibility for them. Fault could easily be established for the ordinary householder showing a light through a poorly arranged curtain. In buildings where many people lived or were employed this became a trickier problem, and where the authority of the crown was invoked even more so. A lack of uniformity in who took responsibility for poor lighting in government offices, and how they could be sent to court, forced the Home Office into formulating a policy in the early months of 1940. The most common situation, familiar to office and tenement buildings in the private sector too, was that a member of staff would often be held responsible and charged by the police for infringing the blackout, where in many cases they were not in fact directly at fault. If at the end of the working day an office worker failed to draw a blind, a cleaner working at night might find themselves inadvertently breaching the blackout simply by turning on the light when coming in to clean an office. This was common to cleaners in Germany and Britain. Over a year from the start of the war, the journal of the RLB ran an article in 1941 that found it was still a problem. A cleaner complained:

> Look, when we arrive to clean it's already completely dark. So for us to get to the window in order to put the blackout blinds in place, sometimes we have to climb on tables. Ask yourself, could you do that in the dark?... The people from the Reichsluftschutzbund should make sure that people arrange the blackout themselves, before they leave the office.[223]

When such infractions were prosecuted, the common method of dealing with them was through appointing somebody within that building who would take responsibility for the infraction and pay the fine, whether at fault or not. This applied in instances where the person to actually blame for the infraction could not be identified. It was always assumed that where blame could be established, those at fault would be held responsible. Bristol City Council issued notices to all of its depots reminding their employees of this, after reimbursing an employee at a depot who had been fined

---

[223] 'Wir gehen auf Verdunklungs-kontrolle; Das „Nachtleben der RLB-Amtstraeger', *Die Sirene,* 3 (1941), p.50.

£1.10d for a breach of lighting regulations, despite not being responsible.[224] This was

the pattern for similar offences around the country, and included government property.

However, one of the peculiarities of blackout offences on government occupied

buildings in Britain was that they were technically immune from prosecution. A legal

note from the Treasury solicitor to the Treasury secretary made it clear that the Crown

had immunity from prosecution under the Defence Orders, including matters of lighting,

though in their opinion it did not extend to cover negligent officials. Recognising the

political impact exercising this immunity would have, the memorandum stated that:

> If, as a matter of policy, it is desired not to take full advantage of this immunity, I
> do not think that there is any objection to each department appointing some
> senior official on whom the summons can be served who will, if so advised,
> defend the proceedings and whose fine (if any) will be reimbursed by the
> department.[225]

This advice appears to have been heeded by the government. As previously noted,

there was already a keen popular interest in how those in authority adhered to the

blackout. Had the state exercised its immunity, it would have caused huge damage to

the integrity of the blackout, and of the government too.

The importance of the state in maintaining a correct blackout extended to Germany as

well. It is easy to imagine Hitler at the *Kehlsteinhaus* at Berchtesgarden, perched high

in the Bavarian Alps, looking down at the valley floor and scrutinising the blackout in

the surrounding towns and villages, each chink needling his sense of authority. In

memoranda regarding blackout awareness campaigns throughout the war in Germany

the centrality of the Party in organising and maintaining it is always fore-grounded.

Hitler maintained a keen interest in the blackout, and throughout the war was provoked

to intercede personally in matters of poor lighting, the technicalities of the blackout, and

blackout judgements. No publicised notices of blackout infractions by government

departments appear in the press – though this is not to say they didn't occur. Indeed in

---

[224] BRO, M/BCC/ARP/2, Minutes of the Engineering Sub-committee, 16 November 1939.
[225] TNA, HO186/720, Treasury solicitor note copied to Home Office, 2 January 1940.

1940, on passing a poorly blacked out army barracks, Hitler complained and ordered for it to be corrected.[226] But the relationship between ARP and the successful prosecution of the war had been politicised to such an extent that any infraction by the state would have been profoundly embarrassing not just for the offending department, but for the Party as well. By 1940 it had long been repeated throughout Germany's public sphere that the home front should conduct itself in a manner befitting the sacrifices their soldiers were making on the fighting front; a failure in any property owned by the state or party to correctly blackout would have been extremely damaging. In the autumn of 1941, as the nights grew longer, the Party instigated a propaganda campaign to underline correct blackout discipline amongst the population. It was feared that people were likely to have become complacent in maintaining the blackout, having become too accustomed to organising it later in the evening. Party members, having been made central to the maintenance and policing of the blackout, were reminded of their duty to support the campaign and be aware of and ready to be questioned about any aspect of ARP.[227] The importance attached by the Nazi state to blackout discipline, coupled to the harder line taken on criminal offences in general, meant that blackout punishments for repeat offenders were more severe. Lax blackout discipline became such an issue that in August 1940 Hitler's office issued a decree stating that persistent blackout offenders would have their electricity suspended for a minimum of eight days. But though this punished individual irresponsibility, this note also made provision for entire communities, so that if a town were to be persistently poorly blacked out, their electricity would be shut off for a minimum of seven days.[228]

Lax discipline, in a country where ARP had been so fundamentally drawn into the fabric of the society and constructed as a patriotic duty, was an affront to the unity of the

---

[226] BA-MA, RL/2/II/97, Reinecke to Oberkommando des Heeres, Kriegsmarine, Reichsminister der Luftfahrt und Oberbefehlshaber der Luftwaffe, 3 October 1940.
[227] BA Berlin, NS18/1311, RLB circular, 28 October 1941.
[228] BA-MA, RL/2/II/97, letter from Borman to all Gauleiters, 17 August 1940.

nation and the authority of the party itself, and the increased severity of the

punishments reflected this. In the south of Germany, an increasingly poor standard of

blackout discipline forced local authorities into addressing the problem. The note

issued by Hitler's office in 1940 set in chain an overhaul of blackout monitoring in the

areas surrounding Munich. Officials had noted an increasingly relaxed attitude to the

blackout. This was attributed to the relatively few incursions into German airspace in

the south so far – the link between the state of the war and willingness to follow the

blackout was not peculiar to Britain. Indeed, it was noted that communities in the

countryside were especially lax.[229] The lack of discipline was by no means uniform;

rather, differing standards of blackout were blamed on differing standards of

punishment. A comprehensive SD report written in December 1940 stated that the

same offence would in the one area be dealt with by issuing a warning, whereas in

another it would be prosecuted by a local commissioner. And in the latter case, where

monetary penalties were sought, there was a great deal of difference in the amounts

being levied. As previously noted, this was a complaint heard in Britain too. Differences

were also found in how complaints and prosecutions against blackout offenders were

processed; where some local courts had fined offenders 100RM, others had been

jailed, and some had yet to receive any court prosecution whatsoever. This lack of

uniformity, it was felt, had brought about lax discipline.[230] Despite the report identifying

these issues and making recommendations to fix them, poor blackout discipline

continued into the following year. An SD report in March 1941 noted that where some

courts were charging first time offenders the sum of 5RM, 10RM or 15RM, others

started at 100RM or more.[231] Though the wide variation in fines was generally

attributed to judgements taking account of the specifics of each case, there was

nevertheless a feeling that sentencing might seem capricious and unfair. In responding

---

[229] BAYHSTA Minn, 71874, SD report circulated to Higher SS and Police leaders in military districts VII and XIII, 5 December 1940.
[230] Ibid.
[231] Ibid., SD memorandum to Higher SS and Police leaders in military districts VII and XIII, 10 March 1941.

to the SD's criticism, the office of the Regierungspräsident outlined the variety of ways in which local authorities were handling blackout offences.

> Some rely primarily on warnings, others with warnings and punishment handled by the police, others with warnings and punishments handled through public prosecutors, and only some choose to prosecute according to the letter of the law.[232]

There does not appear to have been a unified system for fining blackout offenders. But the Bavarian Ministry of the Interior did recognise the wildly different manner of fining and prosecuting blackout offences, and so by the end of 1941 had developed a set of standard practices for local authorities to follow. These fines were graded according to severity and how often an offence occurred. First time offences garnered a warning, or else a 1RM fine when corrected by the police, but only in instances of minor infringements. After this fines increased in scale. Where the blackout was poor fines of 5RM to 25RM could be considered; where an offence was repeated 10RM – 50RM; and in severe cases fines of 50RM to 150RM could be considered. After this, arrest was also a possibility, as was the removal of electricity from the premises for eight days.[233] There is some indication of a later revision of the fines as the war progressed, owing to the pressure to amend them in light of increasingly damaging attacks by Allied bombers. Again though, it is doubtful if this was done at a national level. Just how much of an issue blackout offences became later can be seen in one letter, forwarded in 1942 to the Bavarian Ministry of the Interior by the Gauleiter's office, which asked that enormous fines of 500RM and 1000RM be made possible for blackout offences.[234] Some people were clearly still not doing as they were told. The gradual petering out of archive sources that discuss these sorts of blackout problems may indicate an eventual level of satisfaction in how it was administered, though this is not to say that offences did not continue throughout the war.

---

[232] Ibid., Witt to Bavarian Ministry of the Interior, 21 March 1941.
[233] Ibid., Bavarian Ministry of the Interior to District Presidents, 26 May 1941.
[234] Ibid., Chancellery of the Gauleiter of Munich to Bavarian Ministry of the Interior, 5 October 1942.

Similar concerns about disparities in fines and sentencing were raised in Britain. At the opening of the York assizes in 1940, a judge criticised magistrates for failing to take full advantage of their powers. In his words:

> There are some places well within my knowledge where you do not get an effective and complete black-out. It is for that reason that magistrates have been given a weapon to punish those who do not obey. But there are those who use it so gently and sparingly that if I were minded to be naughty and show a light I could do so every day of the week and not be much poorer. The punishments are inadequate and must be administered even more strictly and heavily than ever before.[235]

The policing of the blackout, and in particular the fines issued to poor and wealthy blackout offenders, could serve to undermine community cohesion in Britain. In November 1939, the parish council of West Dean in Gloucestershire was already fed up of the blackout. Holding a meeting to air their grievances, it was claimed that the police were playing a cat and mouse game with the public. Speakers described the district as _living in a state of terror'.[236] And in late 1940, Bow Street magistrates were in particular noted for large fines that in the view of the Home Office, were apt to cause grievance and undermine the national interest.[237] There was a balance to be struck between the need to punish blackout offences and make an example of the crime, against the social background of the offender. Magistrates' rulings in this matter were not uniform across the country. The ability to pay one's fine was as much a political question as it was a matter of justice. As one respondent to a Mass Observation survey put it, _3 pounds isn't enough to make Lord Nuffield stop and think, but it's enough to make my mother go without breakfast for a fortnight.'[238] Sentencing could therefore serve to undermine social cohesion, though it is notable that in the same Mass Observation report, a survey found an overall acceptance of the severity of sentencing, with 30% claiming they were in fact not severe enough.[239]

---

[235] 'Judge Warns 'Keep Dark'', *Manchester Evening News*, 25 June 1940, p.5.
[236] 'Blackout 'Terror' by Police', *The Daily Mirror*, 1 November 1939, p.11.
[237] TNA, HO45/18628, Harris to Dummett 5 October 1940; McKenna to Dummett 21 October 1940; Harris to Maxwell 30 October 1940.
[238] MOA, 304.2-3 People's attitude to the blackout, 27 July 1940.
[239] Ibid.

Countryside and adherence

Viewed at night from above, cities and towns are distinguished by the dark spaces between them. What the blackout was designed to achieve was the obscuration of towns and cities by hiding them in the darkness found in the countryside, and this created a tension between these different parts of the landscape. The extension of decoy lighting systems into the countryside, and the erroneous release of bombs from aircraft confused by the blackout, meant that it was an ambiguous system for people living in the countryside. While it was designed to keep cities and towns safer, it was at the expense of increasing the risk to people living outside of them. As detailed in the previous chapter, decoy sites employed various tricks to fool pilots, fashioning the illusion of either a poorly lit town, a blazing target, or a dummy facility. When flown towards by enemy bombers, these sites would become flak traps, or simply absorb the majority of ordnance. Yet these sites also had the potential for attracting stray bombs onto outlying villages and towns. The citizens of Lauffen, a village near one of the decoys for the city of Stuttgart, lost forty houses in an air raid, and they complained to officials in the city that they had protected urban facilities and denizens at the reckless expense of villagers.[240] However, the success of these sites in Germany meant that, when protests came from local officials, they were ignored.[241] No similar protests appear in the record in Britain, possibly owing to the lower intensity of bombing. O'Brien does however note that though Morrison shelters were distributed to householders who lived near airfields, this was not extended to people living near decoy airfields, nor to people near searchlight batteries or anti-aircraft guns.[242]

---

[240] Jill Stephenson, *Hitler's Home Front* (London: Hambledon Continuum, 2006), p.157.
[241] Westermann, 'Hitting the Mark but Missing the Target: Luftwaffe Deception Operations, 1939-1945', p.10.
[242] O'Brien, *Civil Defence*, p.539.

The tension between urban areas and the countryside was important to how the blackout operated.[243] Those that lived in the countryside sometimes coped with the blackout differently from people in urban areas. At the start of the war at least, this resulted in a different level of adherence. Perhaps the most immediate effect of the blackout on life in the countryside was in work. In particular, fire was no longer allowed in open spaces, and in Germany transgressions were threatened with severe penalties.[244] Hop pickers in Kent bemoaned the restrictions, with their days in the fields no longer ending with a gathering around a campfire but with the onset of night.[245] Travelling past the oast houses in the darkening countryside on her way to London, Jan Struther wrote in her *Mrs Miniver* column in *The Times*:

> and all the way up in the train that wretched lovely line from *Antony and Cleopatra* kept running in my head:-
>
> Finish, good lady; the bright day is done,
> And we are for the dark.[246]

What is perhaps most apparent was the difference in how people in the countryside coped with the dark. When it began, newspapers ran commentaries on how country dwellers found all the fuss over the blackout a little bemusing. The dark was for them far more a part of their lives than those in the towns. The ribbons of electric and gas streetlights that had extended the life of towns into the night were far less common. When the blackout arrived it was, to a certain extent, far less trouble for people in the country to get used to it. A writer for the *Münchner Neueste Nachrichten* wrote of showing a friend of his from the countryside around his city before the war. Dazzled by the myriad red, greens and yellows of the city at midnight, his friend looked up at the

---

[243] For a wider examination of the relationship between town and country in Nazi Germany see Stephenson, *Hitler's Home Front*, pp.1-22.
[244] Stadtarchiv Dortmund, Signatur 424-1, wartime scrapbook of city archivist Luise von Winterfeld.
[245] 'Changes in the Hop Gardens', *The Times*, 11 September 1939, p.5.
[246] 'Peace-in-War: a Letter from Mrs Miniver', *The Times*, 6 October 1939, p.11.

sky and cried _The moon! You've killed the moon!'[247] Now the tables had turned, and it was the town and city that became strange and unfamiliar.

Adherence to the blackout was taken somewhat as an article of faith amongst urban populations; it was they, after all, who were expected to take the brunt of any bombing. The platonic ideal of the *Volksgemeinschaft* would have mitigated any difference in threat, with everyone pulling together for the sake of the community. However, this was not borne out by the reality. In 1940 a memorandum sent to local officials in the areas surrounding Munich identified a particular drop in blackout discipline in the countryside, which was attributed to a relatively quiet summer and the longer hours of daylight.[248] Other correspondents complained that, rather than stick to the prescribed hours of the blackout, people living in the countryside tended to blackout when *they* believed darkness had fallen.[249] The solutions to this were both higher penalties, and a greater focus on educating the public. Recognising the need to broaden the administration of the blackout amongst a sometimes reticent rural population, the Gauleiter of Munich and the surrounding area had made the Hoheitstrager - the functionaries of the party - responsible for the maintenance of the blackout.[250] As a county director put in a memorandum to local chapter directors, doing so was urgent since it was _clear that police bodies, as well as ARP wardens and other such functionaries, cannot possibly maintain the required measures without the help of the Party.'[251] Doing this implied that it was not just the organisational breadth of the party, but also its authority, that was fundamental in raising the standard of the blackout amongst the population. By moving

---

[247] Carl Haensel, 'Die abgedunklete Stadt', *Münchner Neueste Nahrichten* 16 September 1939, p.4.
[248] BAYHSTA Minn, 71874, Higher SS and Police Leader to Bavarian local authorities, 26 August 1940.
[249] Ibid., letter, 27 September 1940.
[250] These being the bearers of sovereignty of the party, each responsible for their own sphere of influence. These were, with their sphere and in order of decreasing authority: The Fuehrer – The Reich; The District Directors (Gauleiter) – The District; The County Directors (Kreisleiter) – The County; The Local Chapter Directors (Ortsgruppenleiter) – The Local Chapter; The Cell Directors (Zellenleiter) – The Cell; The Block Directors (Blockleiter) – The Block.
[251] BAYHSTA Minn, 71874, Chief Inspector of Police to District Presidents, 3 September 1940.

it from being mainly the focus of administrative bodies to the Party as well, it underlined the political importance of the blackout within Germany.

In Britain, the fact that the countryside differed politically and socially from the towns was perhaps something of a truism. However, the differences in social and community bonds between urban and rural areas had an effect on how the blackout operated. These differences had already occupied the minds of Labour party members in the inter-war years, more used to dealing with urban society. The blackout had already made life difficult for local organizers in every party, impacting on their ability to hold meetings and maintain membership through doorstep collections in the evening.[252]

For them, the rural constituencies were foreign lands, inaccessible backwaters that no fellah could reach except he were a Stanley or Livingstone.'[253] Working to establish an electorate in the countryside required a different approach to that for the towns. What Clare Griffiths makes apparent in her study of Labour's relationship with the countryside were the idiosyncrasies of organisation and informal networks that gave it a different character to urban areas.[254] These aspects found an expression through the blackout too, and are apparent in the Mass Observation report from the Oxfordshire village of Burford at the start of the war, which gives a vivid picture of the differences between town and country life, and the weight that the local community placed on offences. In the observer's opinion, because relationships amongst members of the community tended to be closer than those of urban communities, this gave the act of illicitly showing a light a subtle difference. In their words, one of the main reasons why

---

[252] Thorpe, *Parties at War: Political Organization in Second World War Britain*, p.154.
[253] *Labour Organiser,*1941, cited in Clare V. J. Griffiths, *Labour and the Countryside: the Politics of Rural Britain 1918-1939* (Oxford: Oxford University Press, 2007), p.53.
[254] Ibid., pp.67-73.

the blackout is so effective in villages appears to be that immediately anybody shows a light someone else comes and sneaks on them to the ARP warden.'[255] She writes:

> The effect of the local warden coming and ticking one off for not blacking out in a village is rather one of feeling that a village delegate is coming to censure you and that you, the outsider, have behaved rather shamefully. In London, on the other hand, the feeling rather tends to be that when a warden knocks on your door he is a damn nuisance and you suppose you've got to see to it about the curtains.[256]

In towns and cities, this act could be far more impersonal, and while there is perhaps something of a caricature about the report's account of village pettiness, the tighter relationships within a small community must surely have given the act of snitching to the warden a different kind of weight. The report notes there was a 'latent resentment' against the influx of evacuees in Burford, who villagers, especially the elderly, were 'only too happy to report.'[257] Recent arrivals setting up home in the countryside were also liable to fall foul of censure. A correspondent for *The Times* noted during a survey of their village's blackout, that 'the newer quarter, where the curtains had always been of the lightest as became recent converts to the country, let the village down badly.'[258] But despite the arrival of evacuees, the observer found a community spirit under the blackout that they felt was unique to villages. In their words, 'In large towns, which have no such feeling of local entity, there is no such spirit. There is not even a street loyalty.'[259] Those features of country life that were so unappetizing for the urban population - the limited entertainments, and the pace of life in general - were in the early days of the blackout conditions that now affected them. In Germany, commentators found this to work in the country dweller's favour.

> Much of what living in the city makes difficult is solved by itself in the country... The farmer prefers to stay at home in the evenings. And if he leaves the house, he can find his way home in the pitch black.[260]

---

[255] MOA, Folder 1/D, Account of Blackout in Burford, 19 October 1939.
[256] Ibid.
[257] Ibid.
[258] 'The Perfect Black-out', *The Times*, 25 September 1939, p.11.
[259] Ibid.
[260] William Hegeler, 'Dorf im Krieg', *Berliner Lokal-Anzeiger*, 8 November 1939, p.5.

And indeed when the blackout came to an end in Britain, the distinction between the city and town was again made apparent, as a poem from an issue of *Punch* in 1944 illustrates:

> Black-out had blessings, friend, as well as banes;
> We lost our ways at times, but there were gains
> In ugliness unlit, in beauties shown
> That, but for black-outs, we had never known.
>
> Town-dwelling folk, I mean – the countryside
> Saw no great difference and had less to hide;
> But some who knew so long the darkened city
> May say, when lights go on again, A pity![261]

It is perhaps the case that though the blackout was certainly an imposition, the link between the dark and rural life made the transition to the wartime blackout far less troublesome than for those in the towns. As will become apparent towards the end of this thesis, though it created entirely novel problems, the blackout also served to amplify existing differences in both British and German society. The differentials in how urban and rural populations coped with the blackout were important in how these different parts of society related to the war, and could sometimes run against the rhetoric of the unified wartime nation. The difference in experience also underlines the fact that the blackout was a problem of modernity; it was the urban population and infrastructure that were most affected by bombing and by the blackout restrictions. Problems suffered by rural populations in the blackout were largely a result of urban life and infrastructure extending into rural spaces, either through mobile populations or else the cover given to towns and cities by the countryside. The tensions that the blackout caused specific to the denser urban populations are explored in the next section.

Common areas of disagreement

In the towns, the density of the population and the greater need for light made public space a key pressure point in the blackout's operation. Lights shown at roadsides and

---

[261] '"When the Lights go on..."', *Britain*, 3/5 (March 1944).

by vehicles, by industry and other transport, and in particular railways, formed a large part of complaints made about the blackout by citizens in both countries. These matters of transport, industry and business are dealt with in a later chapter, and therefore this section restricts itself to analysing the impact of the blackout on public spaces. Most importantly, the architecture of buildings and the design of public spaces was one of the main points of contention during the war. As simple as it may seem for buildings to be blacked out, there were great variations in the style of buildings that had to be secured, with correspondingly different requirements. In one of Mass Observation's reports on blackout adherence from the start of the war, a survey which examined different housing areas according to class found a higher rate of blackout infringement in middle class areas than in working class ones.[262] These results, while undoubtedly an honest observation, can only be indicative up to a certain point. Though the report's author does not mention this, consideration should firstly be given to the larger size and number of windows in larger middle-class houses, and secondly the amount of light that each family could afford to have on. Simply by having a larger house and greater income, middle class houses generally had more sources of light, whether electric or gas. The potential for it to leak from the bigger and more numerous windows of middle class houses was therefore correspondingly greater. Unfortunately, a similar survey for Germany does not exist, though this fundamentally practical problem may have been repeated there too, in line with other structural problems in blacking out common to both countries.

Blackout offences in Germany frequently occurred within shared spaces, and most typically the landing or stairwell of a shared block of housing. Pre-war, the housing architecture of Britain indicated a preference for the rows of terraced or semi-detached single family units still common in many parts of Britain, and a general predominance of

---

[262] MOA, Folder 1/D, 'Light Count in West London', 6 September 1939.

houses over flats, even in cities.[263] In Germany housing had developed rather differently, with new housing in the inter-war years generally adding to existing stock, rather than replacing it through slum clearance as in Britain. The preference was for single family units in Britain, with a higher and increasing rate of owner-occupancy. [264] This is in contrast with Germany's continued preference for rented housing and higher proportion of apartment housing in urban areas.[265] This latter feature correlates with the comparatively higher incidences in Germany of complaints about these areas, and official concern regarding them. Early news reports in Berlin reminded people that responsibility for securing the blackout in apartment blocks was placed on both the landlord and the tenant.[266] This could, however, lead to complications, as one particular case from Berlin vividly illustrates. ·

In January 1941 the landlady of a small apartment block wrote, via her solicitor, to the Police authorities to dispute a blackout fine that had been levied against her elderly mother. Though the landlady, Frau Haupt, had paid the fine on behalf of her mother already – a sum of 15RM, with 50RM costs – she contended that in the event her mother was not at fault. Rather, it was her accusers, who lived in the same block of apartments. At issue was the fourth floor of the stairwell which, according to her accusers the Hahns, who lived in the building, had not been blacked out appropriately. Since Frau Haupt's mother was the building's manager, it was she who the Hahn's had blamed. But as Frau Haupt's mother was elderly, it was the building's porter, Frau Hammer, who was nominally charged with arranging the blackout each night. According to the solicitor's letter, there was a general agreement amongst all the residents of the building to secure the blackout on their respective floor of the stairwell.

---

[263] Anne Power, *Hovels to High Rise: State Housing in Europe Since 1850* (London: Routledge, 1993), pp.183-185.
[264] Ibid., pp.179-185.
[265] Ibid., pp.105-107. See also Silverman's discussion of Weimar Germany's struggle to build enough apartments for the urban workforce in Dan P. Silverman, 'The Housing Crisis in Weimar Germany', *Central European History*, 3/1/2 (1970), pp.130-133.
[266] 'Jetzt täglich verdunkelung!', Berlin Lokal-Anzeiger, 2 September 1939, p.3.

All residents that is, except the Hahns, who lived on the fourth floor. Because of this, the residents of the building undertook to secure the fourth floor's blackout as a favour to Frau Hammer. When this couldn't be done, Frau Hammer either did it herself or else sent her son to secure it. The result of this byzantine arrangement was that on the night of 18 October when the offence took place, no-one could be sure who was in fact responsible for the infringement. However, a counter accusation, with evidence based on access to keys for unlocking the 4th floor window and the testimony of a neighbouring train driver, indicated that it had in fact been the accusers who had left the window open, having been witnessed doing so previously by the train driver when resting outside on his balcony. This defence was not, however, accepted by the police. After months of subsequent wrangling, all sides agreed that since the offence had occurred what was now a long time ago, there was no possibility of the Hahns being sentenced for it. Yet despite this apparent acceptance of their being at fault, the police rejected Frau Haupt's appeal on the grounds that since she was aware of the Hahns opting out of the agreement to secure the blackout on the 4th floor, ultimate responsibility for securing the blackout rested with her.[267]

This case, with its complications that lend it the narrative of a farce, perfectly illustrates not only the difficulties and banalities of securing a regular blackout, but also the agreements that had to be reached not only between the state and the citizen, but amongst citizens themselves. The design of buildings and public space in towns and cities was one of the main sources for problems in adhering to the blackout regulations. This was the case not only for those in charge of large public buildings, but also for the people working in them, and for private houses too. The all-encompassing quality of the blackout required a physical adaptation of space, as well as an adaptation of behaviour within it. Maintaining both required a remarkably intrusive system of

---

[267] Landesarchiv Berlin, A Rep. 358-02-3863, sequence of letters, 3 January 1941 – 7 July 1941.

monitoring by the state, and the next section will examine the role of the person who had the state's authority for maintaining the blackout in these areas - the *Blockwart*, or ARP warden.

Blockwart and Warden

The warden, whose equivalent was the *Blockwart* in Germany, was the personification of the state's maintenance of the blackout and its authority over the citizen in matters of ARP. In Britain, public memory has cast the ARP warden as a nuisance to the lives of ordinary citizens, and they were no more liked in Germany. However, as Schmiechen-Ackermann writes, their prominence in narratives of the home front in Germany has been remarkably understated. As well as this, the division of responsibilities between the Party and the RLB in ARP is rather ambiguous.[268] Nominally, the *Blockwart* was the representative of the RLB in the block. They were helped by the *Luftschutzwart*, who secured the ARP measures within buildings. The *Blockleiter* was the party representative in the block. Yet while the administrative functions of officials were generally neatly ascribed to various bodies, the melange of officials tasked with maintaining order within a block meant that the average German citizen used the term *Blockwart* to describe the myriad different authorities monitoring them.[269] The distinction was further confused as the war went on by the increasing interest of the Party in ARP, and the gradual absorption of the RLB into the Party itself in 1944.[270] Indeed, this confusion is apparent in subsequent writing on the Third Reich, where the terms are used interchangeably. As a result of this, amongst the *Blockwart*'s other functions in managing the ARP of each block, their role in policing the blackout and their relationship to the *Blockleiter* made the maintenance of the blackout explicitly political. Though the maintenance and policing of the blackout in Britain was

---

[268] Detlef Schmiechen-Ackermann, 'Der "Blockwart"', *Vierteljahrshefte für Zeitgeschichte*, 48/4 (2000), pp.575-578.
[269] Ibid., pp.582-583.
[270] BA Berlin, R43 II/665, edict from Hitler's Office, 25 August 1944.

undoubtedly a political issue, its organisation was free of any one party's influence. Complaining and grousing was allowed, provided one carried it out anyway. But in Germany where the mobilisation ARP had been fundamentally bound to the survival of the state itself there was little space between the *Blockwart* and the Party at the beginning of the war, and none whatsoever by 1944. In an article published in 1939 in *Die Sirene*, the journal of the RLB, one writer, himself a *Blockwart*, wrote that they should consider themselves the ARP-father of the block.'[271] The paternalism enthusiastically promoted by the writer imagined the German public under ARP as a family, happily lead by the *Blockwart*, as seen in the image from the article reproduced below.

The idealised German ARP 'family'. Taken from 'Einer Von 700,000: Der Unbekannte Luftschutzmann Hat Das Wort', *Die Sirene*, 5 (1939), p.124.

Such fantasies could only be dreamt of in peacetime. The role of ARP in maintaining discipline within the block has perhaps been overlooked in studies of the German home front. By extension, more consideration should perhaps be given to the blackout's importance in maintaining a visible sense of discipline amongst the German population, as well as its role as a mechanism for mobilising ARP awareness amongst Germans.

The caricature of the *Blockwart*'s British equivalent the ARP warden had a basis in fact, and was largely a result of the awkward months of the Phoney War. As Juliet Gardiner writes, they were accused of being parasites and slackers... of standing around doing

---

[271] 'Einer von 700,000: Der unbekannte Luftschutzmann hat das Wort', *Die Sirene*, /5 (1939).

nothing and being paid handsomely to do so.'[272] Protests against wardens tended to centre on perceptions of fairness and a warden's temperament. One woman in Bolton told the following story to a Mass Observation correspondent.

> Mr. Lamb used to come round and make trouble... He's a domineering kind of man. He didn't come in a nice way. There's a big Irishman who lives up Church Street and Mr. Lamb used to go up there and shout over his back, 'Put those lights out,' and the Irishman would shout back, 'I'll put your lights out.' Then Mr. Lamb would go away.[273]

Sometimes arguments over a warden's behaviour could lead to violence. One man in Manchester was fined £5 for assault and £2 for a breach of lights, and in his evidence alleged that the warden had used obscene language at which the defendant had flung him against the garden wall after telling him to look at another house where a naked light was showing.'[274] And as in similar instances of government adherence to the blackout, correct discipline amongst wardens was equally important in how the relationship of power was perceived. A fish and chip shop keeper in Bolton illustrated this in an interview with a Mass Observation correspondent.

> A man came in here with a torch. I said 'You're another with a torch.' He said, 'I need it,' and showed the badge on his coat, 'I'm an air-raid warden.' I said 'Oh, are you.' Then a girl came in and said, 'Shall I close the door?' I said, 'It doesn't matter, he's an air-raid warden and they can't say anything while he's in here.' He didn't say a word.[275]

Despite the sometimes strained relationship between the warden and the community they were policing, the powers of the warden were not as extensive as the animus towards them might imply. It may be the case that part of the trouble of being a warden was having to be a nuisance while having few powers other than to knock on doors and tell people to fix their curtains. Certainly, when seen against the authority of other positions of authority in the public sphere, their powers were rather few. Section 24 of the Lighting Restrictions only allowed members of the police and military to enter premises and forcibly put out the lights, or adjust the blackout. Some wardens

---

[272] Gardiner, *Wartime: Britain 1939-1945*, p.68.
[273] MOA, Folder 1/D, Blackout comments, 3 November 1939.
[274] 'Knock Out Blow from ARP Man', *Manchester Evening News*, 1939, p.7.
[275] MOA, Folder 1/D, Blackout comments, 3 November 1939.

complained that they had even less power than the Home Guard to enforce the restrictions. Wardens who were charged with maintaining public shelters eventually had to be given legal powers under the Defence Regulations to enforce order.[276] Discussions amongst Civil Defence authorities to give wardens similar powers to the police for maintaining the blackout proved fruitless, possibly due to the political impact this extension of powers would have amongst the population, as well the conflict with the Police this would have inevitably brought. However some Chief Constables circumvented the regulations by arranging to enrol wardens as Special Constables, and by doing so automatically giving them the power to enter premises.[277] Yet this was not standard practice, and the warden's reputation as a fusspot seems a rather unfortunate consequence of their relative lack of power. Given their importance in maintaining the system of ARP when the bombers finally did arrive, some small measure of sympathy is perhaps due. The Wardens' Service was the first line of civil defence, and their responsibilities extended far beyond the day to day operation of the blackout. They would be the first at the scene of any bombing, and beyond their initial responsibilities for reporting the location of bombs and guiding people to safety, they also had to cope with first aid, putting out incendiaries, and using their local knowledge to locate missing persons in damaged buildings.[278]

The contrast between the wardens' with Germany is interesting, given the difference in freedoms, and relative power of the wardens. That both were sometimes unpopular is understandable. They formed one of the key points at which the state was at its most intrusive. That the title of the ARP warden in Germany was conflated with all types of local authority is perhaps symptomatic of this. In both cases then, the importance of the blackout to the state could lead to tensions between its representatives and the general

---

[276] O'Brien, *Civil Defence*, p.566.
[277] NAS, HH50/9, Minutes of the Scottish Regional Training Officer's Conference, 25-26 January 1943.
[278] O'Brien, *Civil Defence*, pp.565-570.

population. The intended discursive and structural function of the blackout was to strengthen the integrity of the wartime state. However, maintaining the blackout also complicated the relationship between the citizen and the state.

The end of the blackout

There is perhaps an assumption that the end of the blackout would bring with it enormous relief. In lifting the blackout, one would finally be free of the obligation to conceal any light, and with it the attendant fuss and disruption of securing the blackout every night. The end of the war in Germany has left few clues as to how civilians dealt with their eventual freedom to show a light again. The collapse of the German state had followed years of its increasingly fragile infrastructure being regularly assaulted with ever greater force by Allied aircraft, leaving German civilians with far more to cope with than their British counterparts.[279] Interruptions in the electricity supply were frequent, and any relief by the blackout's absence was tempered by the continued difficulties in living. Olaf Groehler described the blackout in years following the invention of radio guidance systems as a ‗hysterical mania' for the Nazi state, a view instanced in the following example.[280] On 13 April 1945, shortly before the Red Army began to overrun the city's defences, local officials in Berlin received a memorandum from the Police President calling for yet tighter control of the blackout. Amidst the devastation of hundreds of bombing raids from previous years and the city's failing infrastructure, the memorandum's content gives an indication of just how perverse the restrictions had now become.

> Every householder must, in their own interest, secure their blackout... should any break in the supply of electricity be followed by an air raid, during which the householder leaves the premises, it is best that any lights are turned off and pulled from sockets... As well as this, upon returning it is advised that blackout materials are checked <u>before switching on any lights</u> in case any were damaged during a raid... Even when the All Clear has been given, bright light

[279] Stephenson, *Hitler's Home Front*, pp.313-343.
[280] Groehler, *Bombenkrieg gegen Deutschland*, p.240.

should not be allowed to fall on the street, since it is possible that enemy aircraft may still be over the city district.[281]

By this stage, the restrictions must surely have become useless, serving only to bolster what faltering sense of collective will to resist and fight the Nazi leadership tried to instil amongst German citizens.[282] Across the rest of Germany, the blackout was lifted with the announcement of Germany's surrender. People living in the small village of Lienen, having witnessed fierce fighting in the area as the Allies advanced through north-west Germany, were finally able to take down the blackout on 8 May 1945.[283] Domestic life in this period was made strange by the chaos of the Nazi state's collapse, and the period of transition that followed meant that when the blackout was eventually lifted there was little to cheer about. In a series of letters written to her children in case she did not survive the war, Else Tietze, writing from her flat in Berlin, told her children of how difficult these days of transition were. In April 1945, shortly before the Battle of Berlin began, she apologised for not writing sooner, as the cellar in her tenement building was too dark and they were sparing their candles. Electricity supply at this time was erratic, and what light they had was far from consistent. Life at night is always made possible by light, and when this failed in the inside of homes as well out on the streets, the result was periods of confinement in darkness. On the 6 May 1945, a day before the general surrender of German forces, she wrote:

> I stayed in bed until 9.15 this morning, even though I'd gone to bed at 9.30 last night. It's just so cold in the flat, colder than we ve ever known it. I'm sitting in a woolly jumper, coat and blanket; since you can't do anything at night without a light, you simply go and sit in bed. [284]

Later, as the situation gradually stabilised, she struggled to adapt to the imposition of Berlin's new time zone – in areas controlled by the Russians daylight now began an hour earlier. Yet despite the peace that the city now had, amidst its ruins, Else reflected

---

[281] Berlin Landesarchiv, F Rep. 240/B0058, Public notice from President of Police, 13 April 1945.
[282] Beck, *Under the Bombs: the German Home Front 1942-1945*, pp.188-189.
[283] Friedrich E. Hunsche, *Lienen am Teutoburger Wald: 1000 Jahre Gemarkung Lienen* (Lienen: Gemeinde Lienen, 1965).
[284] Tagebucharchiv Emmendingen, Signatur 1303, letters of Else Tietze , 28 April 1945 onwards.

that though people were free to show lights through their windows, she longed to see the moon through the darkness of the blackout again. The series of letters closes with a postscript from her son who, released from a POW camp after the war, returned home to find a light shining from the living room. How strange,' he wrote in the final sentence, no blackout...'[285]

While both countries had begun the war under generally comparable circumstances, by the war's end they were entirely different. The ending of the blackout provided some small relief for a demoralised population in Germany. In Britain, the public had felt over the course of 1944 an increasing sense of eventual victory. Reactions to the lifting of the blackout are by comparison far easier to gauge. As the war drew perceptibly to a close, the end of the blackout came in two stages. The first, known as the dim-out, came on 17 September 1944. With the threat from Germany's Luftwaffe effectively neutralized, and recognising the limits of the blackout in defending London against V1 and V2 strikes, the government allowed for a higher standard of lighting. Preparation for the dim-out had been cautious. A report of the Committee on Black-Out restrictions in July 1944 made clear that public opinion of it was tied to the overall course of the war, since despite the public not liking the blackout they were convinced that it is an essential means of defence should attack be made by piloted aircraft.'[286] The political fallout from any premature lifting of the restrictions was a key consideration. A raid from piloted aircraft seeking to counter the propaganda effect of the lifting of the blackout had the potential to cause great damage. Were that to happen, the public would in the opinion of the Air Ministry blame the government for the attack. With this and with the visibility of the eastern coast to enemy aircraft flying from Holland kept in mind, the dim-out was eventually instituted across selected parts of the country.

---

[285] Ibid., [postscript not dated.]
[286] TNA, CAB 66/53/17, Report of the Committee on Blackout Restrictions, 28 July 1944.

Sections of the coast defined as special coastal areas' were not allowed to show more light, and neither was London. Surrounding counties in the East had to apply to the Ministry for Home Security for consideration. The rest of the country was allowed to implement the new restrictions.[287] However, despite the caution, some misunderstood the new relaxations, and in confusion caused more light to be shown than was allowed. In Caterham, a woman living by herself opened up her curtains, switched on every light, and stood outside to admire her brightly lit house. Her neighbours hurried out to tell her of her mistake.[288] But the immediate response to the dim-out was not one of unbridled enthusiasm, but was instead far more cautious. Years of living under blackout conditions where light in the dark implied insecurity for the community meant that, though commercial enterprises were keen to exploit the new freedoms, the population at large were hesitant, as a Mass Observation report 17 September 1944 illustrates.

> Practically everyone with whom [the investigator] has spoken continues to enforce the blackout regulations, perhaps not so carefully as in the earlier days of the war, but they haven't taken advantage of the revised regulations. The general feeling is, that the war isn't over yet. When it is, they'll pull down the blackout curtains, and make a bonfire of them.[289]

Others commented that the new freedoms gave them the sort of feeling that I had as a child when I picked an apple that wasn't yet ripe and had thrown it away'.[290] These reactions were, perhaps, entirely natural. During the course of the war the blackout had changed from an imposition with no apparent purpose during the Phoney War, to a necessity that was grudgingly accepted. And as previously stated, it was the bombs rather than the threat of war that provided the greatest reason for the blackout. For some, the protection that it had offered extended to more than enemy bombers. Protection from the outside world in general had mingled with the protection from the Luftwaffe, and the resumption of lighting left them conflicted. One young woman, living

---

[287] London Met Archives, LCC/CL/CD/1/291, memorandum to Local Authorities from Ministry for Home Security, 9 September 1944.
[288] 'It Wasn't Even Twilight', *The Caterham Times*, 22 September 1944.
[289] MOA, Box TC23/12/H – A note on the relaxation of the blackout, 17 September 1944.
[290] Ibid. Lifting of the blackout, 27 September 1944.

with her mother in the Welsh countryside, wrote the following of the gradual resumption

of an almost full blackout in her house after the dim-out:

> September 17th 1944
>
> The beginning of the dim out.' I put some different curtains on the bedroom windows but left the rest.
>
> September 18th 1944
>
> I've just been outside and the light from the living-room through the green curtains seems a blaze of light! I almost felt scared when I saw it, but it does light up the road.
>
> September 25th 1944
>
> It's no good. We're too used to a black out. Having no curtains at all on the scullery and bathroom windows made us feel too guilty, naked and unprotected, so I've had to put some back. Mum, knowing there was a light showing outside while I was at choir practice last night was frightened of being alone.[291]

Though there were, of course, many reasons for this lack of enthusiasm, the duty to the

community that had been a focal point of the blackout's operation over the years of the

war remained one of the reasons for this reticence. But just as people had become

used to the blackout at the war's beginning, so they became used to living with light

again. An article from *The Times* in 1945 stressed that now the war was over, and after

months of people leaving the curtains and letting the light shine out on principle, it was

time to draw the curtains; now that the black-out is once more voluntary we can with a

clear conscience and an unwounded vanity allow cosiness to resume its empire.'[292]

The speaker of the House of Commons who illuminated Parliament's Victoria Tower on

24 April 1945 did so with the words I now switch on our Lantern light.'[293]

Conclusion

By the end of the war the blackout had become part of the fabric of life in both

countries. This chapter has argued that the blackout played a constitutive role in the

---

[291] IWM, Box 82/37/1 – Diaries of Miss EG Davies, 17-25 September 1939.
[292] 'Drawing the Curtains', *The Times*, 22 September 1945, p.5.
[293] Lant, *Blackout: Reinventing Women for Wartime British Cinema*, p.133.

active construction of a unified home front. This fore-grounding by the blackout of community and citizenship has been little remarked upon in the literature of the home front, and this chapter makes the case for its consideration in discussions of how and to what extent the wartime communities of Britain and Germany were unified. Though the universal aspect of the blackout brought with it inevitable tensions in how the restrictions were applied across society, these tensions were the result of adherence being measured against an ideal of behaviour that was appropriate to the threat of bombing, and the protection that the blackout was supposed to afford the wartime community. The blackout was also a system that involved the policing of the behaviour of the population by the state, and the population themselves.

Chapter Five – Crime and Sex

Introduction

This chapter focuses on crimes and behaviours that deliberately exploited the blackout.[294] Whereas failing to secure the blackout was more often than not the result of individual tardiness, exploitation of it for personal gain was seen as a gross breach of acceptable wartime behaviour, which the sentences for such crimes reflected. In Germany it led to death sentences; in Britain to some of the heaviest sentencing of the war. This was a recognition of the fact that darkening the streets to make people safe from enemy aircraft had the paradoxical effect of making people feel less safe from each other. Yet incidences of crime attributable to the blackout during the war also need to be set against the *perception* of crime during the war. Drawing on post-war studies examining the relationship between crime and light, and the perception of personal safety relative to darkness, this chapter argues that in Britain especially, where crime figures rose during the war, levels of crime have to be contextualised within a political and social climate that had sharpened against wrong-doing. An increase in recorded crime can just as well reflect higher rates of detection and reporting of crime as it can of more incidences of it actually occurring.[295] This is also

---

[294] Surprisingly little has been written about crime on Britain's home front during the war. Studies of the home front all acknowledge it, and in most cases address it in some form, but subject specific studies are limited to two books; Edward Smithies' 1982 study *Crime in Wartime* and Donald Thomas' 2003 work *An Underworld at War*. In Germany the situation is much the same, with most studies looking beyond aspects of home front criminality to encompass wider ideas on Nazi justice. See Edward Smithies, *Crime in Wartime* (London: George Allen & Unwin, 1982); Donald Thomas, *An Underworld at War* (London: John Murray, 2004).

[295] The history of crime and statistics is its own field of study, and despite statisticians assembling more sophisticated audits of criminality, there is still much debate on how to interpret crime data. Extrapolating trends in crime from historical datasets must necessarily come with the caveats that many crimes may have gone unrecorded, that collection of data may not have been uniform across towns and cities, that figures may have been massaged for political purposes, and that detection and conviction rates may simply indicate more attention paid to those crimes than had previously been the case. Added to this, there are of course difficulties in accessing statistics on criminality – particularly so in the case of Nazi Germany. The problem is doubled when comparing statistics across two countries, and in particular two

true of sexual activity during the war. Though the blackout provided a framework for unifying the wartime home front, as argued in previous chapters, the blackout's high profile association with transgressive behaviour could also destabilise it. However, this relationship was ambiguous; the blackout was by no means the only factor involved in wartime criminality.

The relationship between crime and light

The most notorious post-war blackout occurred in New York in 1977. As a result of a cascading power failure, caused by lightning strikes to several power cables that fed the city, New Yorkers found themselves entirely without electricity on the hot summer's night of 13-14 July. The events of that night, marked by mass looting, vandalism and arson in certain districts, left the city with a repair bill of $300 million. Following criticism from black leaders over a failure to recognise the scale of urban poverty, President Carter made a surprise visit in October that year. As he walked through the post-blackout ruins in the South Bronx, observers noted that they were more akin to the bombed cities of wartime Europe than an American metropolis.[296] Such devastation, from one night of darkness, had far deeper roots than the blackout itself. Contemporary fears of chance blackouts such as the one in New York rest on a fear of crime and disorder. If these fears do not seem unreasonable, they must be set against the paradox of both an increasing standard of lighting in Western cities over the last century, alongside a parallel rise in historical rates of crime and perception of crime and security in late-modern society.[297] The relevance for the wartime blackout is that more light does not necessarily lead to less crime. Therefore any analysis of the blackout

---

countries with such markedly different views on liberty, the rights of criminals and the rule of law. See Paul Lawrence Barry Godfrey, Chris A. Williams, *History and Crime* (London: Sage, 2008).
[296] Joshua B. Freeman, *Working-class New York: Life and Labor since World War II* (New York: New Press, 2000), p.276. See also Jill Jonnes, *South Bronx Rising: the Rise, Fall, and Resurrection of an American City* (New York: Fordham University Press, 2002), p.311.
[297] David Garland, *The Culture of Control: Crime and Social Order in Contemporary Society* (Oxford: Oxford University Press, 2001), pp.139-140.

requires both an understanding of the prevalent trends in crime at the time, and the effect the darkness had in exacerbating or dampening them.

In 1973, a group of schools in America instituted what was called a _dark campus' policy, because they were tired of repairing vandalism to their property. This was in effect a localised blackout. The rationale was simple; that where little light existed, vandalism would be that much more difficult to carry out. The results of the experiment appeared to show a dramatic decrease in the rate of vandalism, with a concomitant decrease in the cost, labour and energy consumption associated with building repairs. The study does not appear to have been seriously followed up by local authorities, and it has not since been scientifically reappraised. It has nevertheless led to a continued, though not apparently systematic, use of dark campus lighting in America. Within Britain there has been an ongoing debate on the effectiveness of light and surveillance in deterring crime. Two review papers published by the Home Office, the first in 1991 and the second in 2002, assessed the body of research looking at the impact of lighting on crime in public spaces. The 1991 study noted that _improvements to street lighting can help to reduce the public's fear of crime, but that they make less of a difference to the prevailing level of crime than many people would expect.' The second review from 2002 was more emphatic, saying that _improved street lighting can be effective in reducing crime in some circumstances' and that _improved street lighting could often be implemented as a feasible, inexpensive and effective method of reducing crime.'[298] This latter report has not been without its detractors, and campaigns to reduce the glow from towns and cities have seized on the 1991 report as evidence that crime is not deterred by street lighting, despite popular opinion favouring the lighting of public

[298] Brandon C. Welsh David P. Farringdon, 'Effects of Improved Street Lighting on Crime: a Systematic Review', *Home Office Research Studies* (London: Home Office Research, Development and Statistics Directorate, 2002); Rosemany Newton Malcolm Ramsay, 'The Effect of Better Street Lighting on Crime and Fear: a Review', in Gloria Laycock (ed.), *Home Office Crime Prevention Unit* (London: Home Office, 1991). For an extensive if rather rambling overview of the effect of lighting on crime see Duco Schreuder Kohei Narisada, *Light Pollution Handbook* (Dordrecht: Springer, 2004), pp.563-603.

spaces.[299] What is important is the presence of fear itself, and how this affects the perception of space and one's sense of safety within it. Over the past few decades, research has established the fear-of-crime paradox - that those who most fear crime are those least likely to be a victim of it.[300] Within this there is a distinct gender bias; women tend to feel more vulnerable than men, and often associate the threat of crime with sexual assault. While this thesis is not the place to weigh the merits of these arguments with any degree of authority, it should make the reader aware that the effect of lighting on crime remains an ongoing debate, and that the perception of crime is not always linked to its actual presence. The implications of this will be drawn out over the course of this chapter.

Later studies of the New York blackout found that latent issues within the communities most affected by the rioting had contributed to the dissatisfaction and anomic behaviour expressed during that night, and were exacerbated by the freedom the blacked out city invited.[301] The relationship between extant social dissatisfaction and community relations must therefore be taken into account when looking at the impact of the wartime blackout. Previous chapters have sought to explain how the blackout was trialled before the war, and how both nations attempted to form a sort of community ethic of ARP. But though this was one of the consequences of the blackout, and ARP more generally, the blackout also undermined the war community by allowing for

---

[299] See Brandon C. Welsh David P. Farringdon, 'Measuring the Effects of Improved Street Lighting on Crime: a Reply to Dr Marchant', *The British Journal of Criminology*, 44/3 (2004); P.R. Marchant, 'A Demonstration that the Claim that Brighter Lighting Reduces Crime is Unfounded', *The British Journal of Criminology*, 44/3 (2004). See also the website of the *Campaign for Dark Skies*, established by the British Astronomical Association [http://www.britastro.org/dark-skies/index.html].

[300] Stefaan Pleysier Diederik Cops, "Doing Gender' in Fear of Crime: The Impact of Gender Identity on Reported Levels of Fear of Crime in Adolescents and Young Adults', *British Journal of Criminology*, 51 (2011), p.58-59. On the relationship between the fear of crime and poverty see Christina Pantazis, "Fear of Crime', Vulnerability and Poverty', *British Journal of Criminology*, 40 (2000).

[301] Seymour R. Kaplan Louis Genevie, Harris Peck, Elmer L. Struening, June E. Kallos, Gregory L. Muhlin, Arthur Richardson, 'Predictors of Looting in Selected Neighbourhoods of New York City during the Blackout of 1977', *Sociology and Social Research*, 71/3 (1987).

140

dissenting and illegitimate behaviour. The most feared of these was assault, which the following section examines.

Assault

In April 1944, Lynne Burgess was attacked by a group of American GIs (presumed to be deserters) while on her way home from the office during the blackout. They threw her to the ground and kicked her, almost breaking her finger while attempting to steal her wedding ring. The attack caused the miscarriage of her and her husband Anthony Burgess' unborn child.[302] This tragedy would later form one of the inspirations for Burgess' novel of anomic juveniles, *A Clockwork Orange*.[303] Burgess' extrapolation of this event into his fiction was founded on one of the greatest concerns of the wartime blackout - the possibility of being assaulted. For women in particular, the potential for inappropriate advances, stalking, and sexual violence was far greater under the cover of darkness. Before the war began, police chiefs in Britain had already anticipated an increase in these types of crimes.[304] Within the first few days of the war, Glasgow police were already advising for female ARP wardens to be escorted home in the dark, after increasing incidences of molestation.[305] The experience of one girl, 15 at the time, is exemplary.

> I was nearly home when I heard footsteps behind me. It sounded like a man who would walk much faster than me so I moved to one side. He didn't pass but came along-side of me and started talking. I expect he knew that I was a girl because of the torch showing my legs... Soon after this I had to turn into a little road which runs along the back of some shops. He must have thought I was encouraging him and taking him somewhere quiet because he put his arm round my waist. I was a little bit scared but I knew that I was nearly home so I just kept walking. We turned into our street which is very short, only about eight

---

[302] Andrew Biswell, *The Real Life of Anthony Burgess* (London: Picador, 2007), pp.107-109. In other versions of this story told by Burgess he alleged that his wife was raped, though given his alleged propensity for altering his past on a whim it was never certain if this was, in fact, the case.

[303] Anthony Burgess, *A Clockwork Orange* (London: Penguin, 1962), p.xiv (introduction to the 1996 Penguin edition).

[304] Glasgow Record Office, SR22/40/1, Chief Constable's annual report 1939.

[305] Glasgow Record Office, SR22/43/56, Chief Constable to all Superintendents, 4 September 1939.

houses on each side. We live about in the middle so I casually walked down the path on our side and then I moved away from him, popped into the gate and shut it saying goodnight. I couldn't see his face but I could sense he was very surprised. I daren't tell Mum or she'll stop me going to the club.[306]

As the public grew used to the blackout, reports of assault became more common. The response of many, certainly in the early days of the war, was to remain at home and avoid the streets. But for those who worked nights or late shifts this was not always an option. Similar problems were experienced in Germany, and by December 1939 the SD was noticing a high level of dissatisfaction over how these assaults were being handled by the authorities. In particular, the variation in how they were dealt with by the police caused consternation amongst the population. The molestation of women in the darkness was a major problem, and the report cites _groping of the breast' as being especially prevalent.[307] Physical contact was not the only way in which women were troubled by the blackout. Following and stalking were easier to do under the cover of darkness. A woman living in London wrote the following in her diary for Mass Observation.

> Just before my stopping place the bus stopped at a pub and several people got on including a youngish looking man who dithered about and eventually sat immediately behind me and tried to attract my attention. When I got off the bus he followed and walked on my heels (a terrifying experience in the black-out.) When I could stand it no longer, I turned and flashed my torch full in his face and then ran for home. Felt very shaken. Had bath and turned in.[308]

Such cases could also develop into physical assault, and attempted rape.

> The little girl who works next to me, aged 14 years, was attacked by a man last night going home from work about 7 p.m. She was nearly home, and walking slowly behind a man in order to not get in front of him, when he suddenly turned and put his hand over her mouth and threw her down. She screamed and fought; luckily she was so near home her people heard her and ran out, and the man made off. Her face is sore this morning and it was a big shock. She lives in a newly developed estate which is rather lonely, so she isn't going out night now when she gets home, and has asked permission to leave at 5 p.m. and work Saturday mornings to make her hours up.[309]

[306] IWM 89/4/1, letter no.24, undated, circa 1941.
[307] BA Berlin, R58/146, SD mood report, 13 December 1939.
[308] MOA, Folder 1/D, _Blackouts', 12 September 1939.
[309] MOA, Box TC54/1/B, Extract from *Mass Observation's Weekly Intelligence Service* (US publication), 17 February 1940.

Despite the awareness of the danger to women, responses in both countries were not always typical. In 1940, the SD reported of an NSV volunteer in Berlin who had been assaulted during the blackout, and had refused to identify her assailant on the grounds that she did not want to upset his family. But the continued presence of the attacker had disquieted other women in the neighbourhood, and it was at the behest of her Ortsgruppenleiter that she eventually brought charges. In the report's words, this was done to reassure the community.'[310]

However, the repercussions of such incidents were not always traumatic, and sometimes surprising. One girl, reflecting on being approached and held as she walked home, wrote in a letter to a pen-pal that when I thought about it later in bed I remembered that I had enjoyed the feeling of someone holding me', remarking that We aren't the kind of family who go in for hugging at all, perhaps I miss it or perhaps I'm growing up.'[311] However, caution was the more common response to the threat of assault. In Germany, the reports of the exiled Social Democratic Party noted that, by January 1940, women in particular were far less willing to journey out onto the streets after sunset, not simply due to the sharp rise in accidents, but also because of the increase in robberies and burglaries.[312] Such was the concern that one shopkeeper advertised his walking sticks as good protection in the blackout'. The small print underneath stating they helped to tap around in the darkness and prevent falls was presumed by the SPD's reporter to ward off accusations by the police of alarmism.[313]

This new caution modified men and women's behaviour in public spaces during the blackout. At major train stations in London, where people idled in the gloom while

---

[310] BA Berlin, R58/146, SD mood report, 13 December 1939.
[311] IWM 89/4/1, letter no.24, undated, circa 1941.
[312] *Deutschland-Berichte der Sozialdemokratischen Partei Deutschlands (Sopade) 1934-1940* (7; Frankfurt-am-Main: Verlag Petra Nettelbeck, 1980), p.26.
[313] Ibid.

awaiting connections, evenings were characterised by a distinct separation between men and women, and an increase in tension that a female Mass Observation reporter described as 'not even equalled by the ordinary rush hour.'[314] As the train stations gradually emptied, women could be found clustering in cloakrooms, 'partly because they couldn't see outside, partly because they felt nervous standing around.'[315] The separation of the sexes seems automatic, in apparent deference to the potential threat that women now faced in public spaces after dark.

> The main places in which the travellers were grouped were firstly any well-lighted place in which there were chairs or benches... As for the remainder of the travellers they either collected together in small groups – the men smoking – the women collecting against a pillar or wall in the company of others of their sex. During a period of about ten or fifteen minutes I joined one of these 'groups' and found that in that time that it was constantly being added to by other strays – not without a certain amount of reason for I found when standing alone I was approached several times with a hopeful 'good-evening'.[316]

This again shows the impact the blackout had on public spaces, and how it modified behaviour - in this case, along gender lines. However, interaction depended on the degree of security people expected from particular public spaces. The community of travellers on a train was different to the community waiting at the station, since the train was a fairly stable, closed space. Here, people could generally be more certain of the behaviour of their fellow passengers. On the other hand, the station was far more open; a generally poorly lit, liminal space, in which people waited to continue their journey. Because of this, security was that much more unpredictable.

The blackout intensified awareness of personal safety, and the acuteness of any traumatic incident on the streets. But despite the apparently decreased security afforded by the blackout, the increase in crime, and of violent crime, was generally not treated as a cause for concern. This was the case in both countries. The general consensus amongst Police Chiefs in Britain shows a satisfaction with the level of crime

---

[314] MOA, Box TC70/4/C, 'Stations in the blackout', 19 and 22 October 1939 (est.)
[315] Ibid.
[316] Ibid.

throughout the war. There appears to have a been an expectation that the war would bring about a large escalation in all offences, and in fact the figures published by the Home Office do show an increase in almost all indictable offences over the course of the war. Robbery rose from 342 cases in 1940 to 1033 by 1945. Violent crime similarly rose from 7392 in 1940 to 14322 in 1945.[317] These figures, which are solely of offences reported to the police, may in fact seem lower than expected, and it is almost certainly the case that these offences were underreported. However, historical data on crime, and indeed current crime data, provides an incomplete record of crime levels when used on their own. It is in fact more useful to consider levels of reported crime as contingent on wider social processes and changes in the criminal justice system. Godfrey et al. write that

> [W]hen reported instances of property crime rose massively in the mid-twentieth century, an interactionist perspective (giving weight to the interaction between state institutions and social forces) would be to state that this might be due to more criminals stealing goods, but we know that changes in public willingness to report crime, and police willingness to register it, were so large that we cannot draw any firm statements about increases in criminality.[318]

This may explain the relative sanguinity of British Police Chiefs, despite the marked rise in recorded offences over the course of the war. Yet this rise followed a generally increasing level of recorded offences throughout the 1930s, and perhaps more to the point, indicate increased police vigilance of the police in detecting and prosecuting sexual offences over the course of the war. As can be seen in Table 5.1 below, the level of rapes and indecent assaults on women in Britain seem to have risen quite dramatically over the course of the war. These national figures contrast with those released for the cities of Manchester and Bristol, which report no significant rise. This may indicate two things. Firstly, a corresponding increase of those types of offences in other parts of the country, as well as a higher level of detection and reporting in those areas; and secondly, underreporting in other areas. Indeed, it seems altogether unlikely that no rapes occurred in an area as large as Bristol during 1940.

---

[317] 'British Recorded Crime Statistics, 1898 - 2001/02', (Home Office).
[318] Barry Godfrey, *History and Crime*, p.36.

Table 5.1 - Sexual offences against women in Britain, 1935-1945[319]

	Rape	Indecent assault on a female	Unlawful sexual intercourse with a girl under 13	Unlawful sexual intercourse with a girl under 16
1935	104	1964	71	417
1936	99	2200	67	420
1937	108	2382	92	501
1938	99	2593	80	477
1940	125	2381	65	433
1941	169	2589	76	542
1942	200	2745	117	651
1943	257	3302	108	700
1944	416	3639	109	767
1945	377	3904	114	820

The city of Manchester published one of the more detailed city surveys, from which the following data on indecent assault and rape was gathered; comparable data for the city of Bristol only exists for the first three years of the war.

Table 5.2 - Sexual offences against women in Manchester, 1939-1944[320]

	Indecent Assault	Rape
1939	40	4
1940	36	1
1941	44	1
1942	46	1
1943	39	4
1944	49	6

---

[319] 'British Recorded Crime Statistics, 1898 - 2001/02', (Home Office). Note that figures for 1939 are not available from this dataset.
[320] Manchester City Council archives, Chief Constable's annual reports 1939-1945.

Table 5.3 – Sexual offences against women in Bristol, 1939-1941[321]

	Indecent Assault	Rape
1939	34	2
1940	30	None recorded
1941	25	3

Comparing the British and German statistics for assault can only lead to very general conclusions, both for the rates at which offences occurred and the extent to which they were prosecuted by the state. The difference in population size must also be kept in mind – roughly 70 million in Germany compared to 47 million in Britain. Indeed, given the rather patchy nature of sources, any trends corroborated between them must remain very tentative. Tables 5.4 and 5.5 give some indication of how much sexual offences declined by in Germany.

Table 5.4 – Sexual offences in Germany, 1937-1943[322]

	Rape	Sexual Offence against person under 14
1937	613	6969
1939	642	6285
1940	445	4345
1941	431	4054
1942	380	3640
1943	112	1240

---

[321] BRO, Chief Constable's annual reports 1939-1941.
[322] Bruno Blau, 'Die Kriminalität in Deutschland während des zweiten Weltkrieges', *Zeitschrift für die gesamte Strafrechtswissenschaft,* 64/1 (1952).

Table 5.5 – Sexual offences committed by juvenile Germans and foreigners, 1942-1943[323]

	Sexual Offences	Rape	Unnatural Sexual Offence (female)	Sexual Offence with person under 14 (female)
1942	2042	172	665 (1)	868 (20)
1943	752	45	243	346 (8)

The blackout lies hidden within both the British and German sets of figures. As previously stated, the paradox of the blackout was that it compromised the safety of the individual for the protection of the community, and sexual offences which exploited the blackout were amongst the most serious crimes. It is impossible to assess the extent to which degree the rise in the British figures was a result of an actual increase in offences. What is certain is that the political and moral climate of the war, to which the blackout and its obligations contributed, lent itself to a greater focus on reporting and prosecuting such crimes. This undoubtedly contributed to the increase in numbers being reported. The reasons for the general decrease in sexual offences in Germany are again complex, and given the issues outlined regarding the methodological problems of crime datasets and the paucity of existing research, the conclusions must remain speculative. Underreporting may have contributed to the decrease, as well as a prioritising of police resources towards other types of offences. The decrease may also have been indicative of the increasing severity of sentencing for all types of offences, including sexual ones, as well as the reduced number of men on the home front.[324] These are, however, speculative. What is certain is that while the number of recorded sexual offences in Germany appears to have declined during the war, the severity of

---

[323] Ibid.
[324] Evans argues for this latter point, but contends that the marked drop in sexual offences when compared with the rise in other crimes can mainly be attributed to the German police being so concerned to enforce wartime restrictions that they were starting to neglect other areas of the criminal law.' This might indeed have contributed to the drop, but it cannot be said to be the main cause. See Evans, *The Third Reich at War*, p.213.

punishments for them increased. Though fewer sexual offences were recorded in 1941 than in previous years, two offenders were executed for a violent sexual offence against a woman, and three were executed for rape. This increasing severity extended to juvenile justice too; in 1943, a juvenile was sentenced to death for rape and murder.[325] However, execution for rape was not limited to Germany. When American troops arrived in 1942 they also brought with them their system of military justice, and though Britain had abolished the death sentence for rape in 1861, the American military sentenced several soldiers to death, the majority for sexual offences or for incidences relating to sexual encounters. 18 American soldiers were executed in Britain, of which six were convicted of rape, and four of rape and murder. The racism endemic to the American military during this period meant that minorities were over-represented in death sentences. Of the six rape convictions, five were against African American soldiers and one against a Mexican American, with the rape and murder convictions being against two white Americans, one African American, and one Mexican American.[326] The severity in sentencing of sexual offences was fostered within a wartime climate where the profile of sexual relations, and what was acceptable in wartime, had a higher profile in both countries. Indeed the fear of violence, and the fear of sexual violence, has a corollary in how sex as a whole was treated in both countries during the war. Wilton writes that the war served to crystallize long standing discourses on gender, sexual preference, and sexual activity: Homosexuality (in men) joined childless women, prostitutes, abortion and STDs as a danger to nation or race."[327] The blackout was an enabler for these vices'. Fear over the sexual health of the nation mingled with the fear of the dark, and the paradox that while the honest citizen might fear or resent the blackout, there were elements in society for whom it was an opportunity to exercise traits deemed immoral, and even damaging to the nation. This

---

[325] Blau, 'Die Kriminalität in Deutschland während des zweiten Weltkrieges', pp.75-76.
[326] J. Michael Thomson J. Robert Lilly, 'Executing US soldiers in England, World War II: Command Influence and Sexual Racism', British Journal of Criminology, 37/2 (1997), pp.268-269.
[327] Tamsin Wilton, EnGendering AIDS: Deconstructing Sex, Text and Epidemic (London: Sage, 1997), p.64.

occurred in both countries and, as will be explained, both drew on discourses of nationality, citizenship and morality. However, the density in how they were articulated and accepted differed according to each country's relative freedoms.

At the beginning of the war in Britain there was, as Rose writes, widespread public apprehension about the declining morals of girls and young women in British cities and towns.[328] The war brought with it not only a freedom in women's ability to define themselves economically, through taking on a greater role in previously male dominated areas of work, but also in how they could act sexually. The blackout provided opportunities for women and men to pursue casual romances, though it was women and girls who were deemed to be the greatest potential problem. The public's perception of the ordinary woman and the prostitute began to change. According to one London gangster, Good-time girls became brazen tarts' and ordinary wives became good time girls.'[329] Such behaviour was at variance with the more noble perceived role of mother' that women were usually ascribed. In Germany, the ideal of the German mother, as envisioned by the inherently masculine worldview of the Nazi party, was, according to Jill Stephenson:

> the married woman who bore several children and worked contentedly at maintaining a clean and orderly home, shopping thriftily and making limited demands as a consumer, educating her children to be both conscious of their racial identity and eager to engage in a life of service to the Aryan' community.[330]

Motherhood had by the start of the war an established link with the ability of nations to compete in the arena of world politics, and their military strength. British colonialism had been bolstered by a Victorian medical discourse that associated the success of expansion abroad with, as Wilton writes, the reproduction of a fit and healthy

---

[328] Sonya O. Rose, 'Sex, Citizenship, and the Nation in World War II Britain', *The American Historical Review,* 102/4 (1998), p.1147.
[329] Billy Hill, quoted in Thomas, *An Underworld at War,* p.272.
[330] Jill Stephenson, *Women in Nazi Germany* (Essex: Pearson Education, 2001), p.18.

fighting/labour force.'[331] The rise in sexual activity for its own sake was counter to this idea of _healthy' sex. Elizabeth Heineman offers a description of these first few months of the war in Germany that is worth quoting at length.

> When the war began, government authorities anticipated a rise in sexually transmitted disease (STD) and illegitimate pregnancy. The picture they found was uneven: in some regions and cities rates rose; in others they did not...local health departments were to raid bars and dance halls and test female employees and patrons for STDs. Employees of the health department soon required military protection in at least one major city as raids degenerated into brawls between male customers, including SS and Gestapo men, and health officials... Of particular concern to local police were young women who hung around soldiers' quarters. In the winter of 1942, Hamburg health authorities estimated that two-thirds of young women with STDs had been infected by soldiers.[332]

Through sexual adventure, women were now perceived to be a threat to the health of the country's military, and therefore the capacity of the nation to fight a war. The blackout forms part of the backcloth to the sharpening moral climates of both countries. As a site of opportunities for liaisons, whether illicit or not, the morality of women in the wartime blackout became a great concern. While Britain and Germany are perhaps not comparable in the scale of rhetoric and action, they were certainly both heading in the same direction. For example, in 1940, concern over reports of hooliganism and other _undesirable occurrences' in Raphael Park in London was such that they were eventually brought up in council meetings. Subsequent reports in the *Romford Recorder* and *The Evening Standard* led to a Mass Observation reporter asking around in the neighbourhood what people knew. Those that were willing to talk explicitly linked trouble to women's behaviour.

NM: _Do you go to the park much?'

F20C: _Yee [sic], quite a bit? [sic]'

NM: _Know anything about -goings on" reported in *The Recorder*?'

F: _Well, I've never seen anything, myself, but I suppose you can guess. I think one or two girls got into trouble, over there – the soldiers, you know.'

---

[331] Wilton, *EnGendering AIDS: Deconstructing Sex, Text and Epidemic*, p.62.
[332] Elizabeth D. Heineman, *What Difference does a Husband Make?: Women and Marital Status in Nazi and Postwar Germany* (Berkeley: Univeristy of California Press, 2003), pp.53-54.

She declined to give details.

NM: Do you know anything about Raphael Park?'

M25B: No, only as a place where young women go if they want a night with a soldier.'[333]

Rose writes that:

> Newspapers in geographically dispersed rural and urban districts increased widespread anxiety by printing lurid headlines, feature articles, a proliferation of letters to the editor, and editorials that dissected the causes and consequences of teenage girls running wild' or going out for a good time.' Routine reports often went into excruciating detail describing their indiscretions,' fuelling the panic by exciting both outrage and prurient attention.[334]

Levels of sexual activity and official concern over it can also be inferred by the dramatic increase in prosecution for procuring illegal abortion and concealment of birth.

Table 5.6 – Birth control offences in Britain, 1935-1945[335]

	Procuring illegal abortion	Concealment of birth
1935	116	71
1936	141	58
1937	197	71
1938	172	69
1940	110	62
1941	171	82
1942	344	80
1943	461	98
1944	649	121
1945	464	123

Before the war, German policies on sex and birth control were already heavily politicized according to National Socialist race ideals, and between 1933 and 1945 they developed into a sophisticated system of genetic selection. Acquiring an abortion was made more difficult for German women. This occurred at the same time that the legal

---

[333] MOA, Box TC54/1/B, report on hooliganism in Romford, 25 June 1940.
[334] Rose, 'Sex, Citizenship, and the Nation in World War II Britain', p.1150.
[335] 'British Recorded Crime Statistics, 1898 - 2001/02'.

system was developed to allow for legalized abortion for solely eugenic purposes, which was targeted at foreign women.[336]

Table 5.7 – Convictions for illegal abortion in Germany, 1937-1943[337]

1937	5737
1939	4943
1940	1962
1941	2715
1942	3126
1943	1372

The sharpening of the law on abortion after 1943 shows a heightening of the state's concern over sexual activity, with the punishments for abortion again diverting along racial lines.[338] Concern over this aspect of sexual activity was mirrored in prosecutions against German women soliciting with POWs, a problem which became a 'mass crime' despite efforts by the Party.[339]

Table 5.8 – Prosecutions for liaisons with POWs in Germany, 1939-1943[340]

1939	3
1940	924
1941	2650
1942	6451
1943	3972

This level of concern at controlling and limiting the sexual appetites of the public, especially women, to maintain the nation's birth-rate and eugenic standards, sometimes masked the extent to which control was also sought over sex for its own sake. Indeed, historians of sexuality in Germany have noted that the attentions paid by

---

[336] Gisela Bock, 'Antinatalism, Maternity and Paternity in National Socialist Racism', in David F. Crew (ed.), *Nazism and German society, 1933-1945* (London: Routledge, 1994). See also Cornelie Usborne, *Cultures of Abortion in Weimar Germany* (Berghahn, 2007), pp.216-223.
[337] Blau, 'Die Kriminalität in Deutschland während des zweiten Weltkrieges', p.51.
[338] Gabriele Czarnowski, 'Hereditary and Racial Welfare (Erb- und Rassenpflege): The Politics of Sexuality and Reproduction in Nazi Germany', *Social Politics,* 4/1 (1997), p.130.
[339] Hubert Speckner, *In der Gewalt des Feindes: Kriegsgefangenenlager in der "Ostmark" 1939 bis 1945* (Vienna: Oldenbourg, 2003), p.157.
[340] Blau, 'Die Kriminalität in Deutschland während des zweiten Weltkrieges', p.55.

the police and officials in Nazi Germany spiralled beyond the concern of procreation to include any sexual activity, and an eroticization of normal social interaction.[341]

After the Nazis came to power, prostitution in Germany had gradually become instrumentalised according to the needs of the Nazi war state. It had been assumed by anti-prostitution activists that the state would now seek to eradicate it, and to a certain extent this was true. State control over the sexual appetites of the country was tethered to the Nazis' notion of the _asocial' woman. This label, as Timm writes, referred to prostitution, promiscuity, interracial sex, and even becoming too easily sexually aroused or creating a -strongly erotic impression."[342] Set against the de-eroticised ideal of the German mother, protecting the home and hearth, these asocial women – of which the prostitute and the VD carrier were the most vilified – were liabilities to the Nazi state. But this is not to say that prostitution was entirely removed, or that it did not have a use in the Nazi worldview. Safeguarding the health of the population from the eugenic damage of VD had to be balanced with the apparent need for men – and perhaps more importantly German soldiery – to satisfy their sexual appetites. By 1936, the military were calling the construction of military brothels _an urgent necessity', and Himmler was so concerned by moves during the 1930s to clamp down on prostitution that he feared a decline in the Army's morale, and an increase in homosexuality amongst its members.[343] Subsequent Nazi policy organised these brothels along _racist hierarchies', with brothels for foreign workers in Germany separated from those for German citizens and soldiers. The intent of Nazi brothels was, above all to _maintain the physical fitness and morale of -Aryan" men.'[344] When the war began in Germany,

---

[341] On this see Elizabeth D. Heinemann, 'Sexuality and Nazism: The Doubly Unspeakable?', in Dagmar Herzog (ed.), Sexuality and German Fascism (Berghahn, 2003), pp.22-66.

[342] Annette F. Timm, 'The Ambivalent Outsider: Prostitution, Promiscuity and VD Control in Nazi Berlin', in Robert Gellately and Nathan Stoltzfus (ed.), Social outsiders in Nazi Germany (New Jersey: Princeton University Press, 2001), pp.192-211, p.194.

[343] Ibid., p.195.

[344] Julia Roos, 'Backlash Against Prostitute's Rights: Origins and Dynamics of Nazi Prostitution Policies', in Dagmar Herzog (ed.), Sexuality and German Fascism (New York: Berghahn Books, 2005), pp.67-94, p.93.

prostitution was removed from the streets and organised instead through a system of brothels, both private and military. These were designed to minimize the visibility of the sex trade, decrease its threat to the health of the German military, and make the availability of sex a resource for maintaining military morale. A letter from the Bavarian Ministry of the Interior to police officials on 9 September 1939 set out the arrangements for the policing of prostitution during the war; it was to be confined to bordellos and the houses of prostitutes, provided no children lived there. Soliciting was to be allowed in guesthouses with the agreement of the police, but outdoor trafficking was forbidden.[345] The intent was to remove prostitution from the public space into a state-private one, and the general decline in convictions for procuration bears this out.

Table 5.9 – Convictions for procuration in Germany, 1937-1943[346]

1937	1266
1939	913
1940	604
1941	754
1942	708
1943	319

No such control over prostitution existed in Britain. Pre-war discourses of prostitution were disproportionately tied up with ideas of foreignness; of white-slavery, Latin pimps, and nebulous ideas of the eroticism of the continent.[347] As will be discussed in chapter five, this link between sexuality, otherness, the unknown, and the blackout already existed, and was naturally mapped onto cultural representations of the blackout during the war. Existing ideas of prostitution and otherness were readily disseminated through the press into the public domain. Phillip Ziegler writes that:

> Towards the end of 1941 the Evening Standard reported an epidemic of beatings-up during the black-out in the West End; the following year the journalists themselves seem to have become a favourite target as they left their

---

[345] Munchener Staatsarchiv, Polizeidirektion München, Nr.7950, memorandum, 9 September 1939.
[346] Blau, 'Die Kriminalität in Deutschland während des zweiten Weltkrieges', p.50.
[347] See Stefan Slater, 'Pimps, Police and Filles de Joie: Foreign Prostitution in Interwar London', The London Journal, 32/1 (2007).

offices in the middle of the night. _The black-out makes for some petty devilry,' wrote James Hodson. _The papers report the prosecution of two negro soldiers working in conjunction with a decoy prostitute. The unsuspecting fellow is taken along a lonely street and thereupon -bashed" by the soldiers.'[348]

For those prostitutes who could only, or perhaps preferred to, conduct their business outside, the effect of a more open market led to a need to stand out on the darkened streets. Prostitutes working on the streets of Manchester adapted in novel ways. Margaret Hill, a diarist in Manchester, noted the following.

> We walked home across the town in the blackout, under dripping bridges and railway tunnels – a sort of nightmare at midnight. In High St. ... we met the High St. _fairies' (i.e. local prostitutes) in their white mackintoshes to show up in the blackout.[349]

The anonymity of the blackout was also exploited by homosexuals. Gay life in the blackout was made a little easier. In his memoir *The Naked Civil Servant* Quentin Crisp wrote of how the blackout changed the conditions for gay life during the war:

> By heterosexuals the life after death is imagined as a world of light, where there is no parting. If there is a heaven for homosexuals, which doesn't seem very likely, it will be very poorly lit and full of people they can feel pretty confident they will never have to meet again. It is only partly because they are so ashamed of themselves and wish to remain unrecognized that this environment seems so desirable. The chief reason is that it makes possible contacts of astounding physical intimacy without the intervention of personality.[350]

With the greater freedom afforded by the blackout came a higher level of recorded incidences of homosexual activity. Homosexuality was classed as an indictable offence in Britain, under the Offences Against the Person Act 1861, and the national records show a general increase in detection over the course of the war.

---

[348] Phillip Ziegler, *London at War 1939-1945* (London: Pimlico, 2002), p.229.
[349] Manchester City Archives, Box M720, papers of Margaret Hill.
[350] Quentin Crisp, *The Naked Civil Servant* (London: Penguin, 1968), p.151.

Table 5.10 – Homosexual offences in Britain, 1935-1945[351]

	Buggery	Indecent assault on a male	Gross indecency between males
1935	78	535	227
1936	125	690	352
1937	102	703	316
1938	134	822	320
1940	97	808	251
1941	177	757	390
1942	208	998	582
1943	245	1208	623
1944	277	1186	449
1945	223	1318	459

As with those on prostitution, the rise in offences is slightly misleading. On seeing that the authorities were interested in certain kinds of offenders, young officers wanting promotion found it far easier and a good deal safer to pursue homosexuals and prostitutes than burglars.[352] It may have been easier for homosexuals to associate during the blackout, but they were also the subject of greater attention by the police. Homosexuality was similarly classed as a criminal offence in Germany, though was altogether far more vigorously punished. Pre-war measures had already led to a huge increase in the amount of prosecutions for homosexuality. The discourses of a _healthy' sexuality, one that served the state's need to breed its idealised Aryan population, were as prevalent for homosexuals as they were for women. By 1937, the head of the Reich Office. Dr Josef Meisinger, stated that in his office's view:

> Since... homosexuals are useless for normal sexual intercourse, homosexuality also has an effect on young blood and will eventually lead to a drop in the birth rate. The result is a general weakening of the nation's strength of the kind that

---

[351] 'British Recorded Crime Statistics, 1898 - 2001/02'.
[352] Montgomery, cited in Smithies, *Crime in Wartime*, p.149.

threatens not least a nation's military capacity. In the end... homosexuality is a permanent threat to order in the life in the state.[353]

The clampdown on gay life intensified when the war began, and official statistics during the war indicate that ‗unnatural intercourse' declined from 7614 in 1939 to 2126 in 1943.[354] Since homosexuals were classed as *Volksschädlinge* (racial vermin), the police in Munich monitored homosexual activity as well as they could, and staked out known gathering spots to make arrests and generate intelligence for future operations. Here, the darkness worked in the favour of those being monitored, as a report from 1943 illustrates.

> On Saturday 3rd July 1943 at 11pm, a group of nine men gathered in an unlit public lavatory who, at the switching on of a torch, were alarmed and fled the location. A raid on this location would certainly be successful. From my observations, the best time for a raid would be a Saturday at around 11pm.[355]

By 1944 however, the police were finding it increasingly difficult to monitor the usual sites well enough in order to make any arrests. The loss of younger detectives who were drafted into the war, coupled with the blackout restrictions, meant that detectives' observation of locations was made more difficult; faces and clothing could not be recognised, and as such the time suspects spent in location could not be judged accurately.[356] The blackout gave a measure of protection not only from enemy aircraft, but also from the monitoring of the state; a small measure of security for a group so persecuted by it.

The link between sexual activity and the blackout was evident in both Britain and Germany. The blackout created a tension between the potential freedom for liaisons at night, and anxiety over the sexuality and safety of women during the blackout. As with

---

[353] Jeremy Noakes, *Nazism 1919-1945, Volume 4, The German Home Front in World War II* (Exeter: University of Exeter Press, 1998), p.391.
[354] Ibid., p.136.
[355] Staatsarchiv München, Polizeidirektion München, Nr. 7975, Schutzpolizei report, 6 July 1943.
[356] Ibid., Berchem to Inspectorate of the Security Police and SD, 12 December 1944.

criminal behaviour, overt or excessive sexual activity during the blackout was seen as antithetical to the system of obligations and responsibilities that the blackout, and the wartime home front itself, represented. Quantitative and qualitative data on the levels of sexual activity during the war is scarce, and as with the other crime statistics in this chapter, the tables above may reflect more attention to paid to certain behaviours by the authorities, and people reporting them, than a marked increase in sexual activity. Indeed, Simon Szreter and Kate Fisher's oral history of sexuality in Britain notes that their respondents did not see the war as a period of particular licence.[357] But the link between transgressive behaviour and the blackout was firmly embedded within the home front. As a consequence, the blackout could also work as a destabilising part of the home front communities of Britain and Germany.

Juvenile crime

If the modest rise in overall crime did not worry the Police Chiefs of British cities terribly, the same could not be said of juvenile offences. Indeed, the dramatic rise in crime amongst this group as a result of the blackout alarmed the governments of both countries. The freedom of the blacked out city for wayward or bored youths invited mischief; the German cartoon from 1937 reproduced below, which was published after a series of one night blackout trials in major cities, anticipated this.

---

[357] Kate Fisher Simon Szreter, *Sex Before the Sexual Revolution: Intimate Life in England 1918-1963* (Cambridge: Cambridge University Press, 2010), p.59.

'Why on earth did you smash the streetlight?'
'But constable, we were only playing Blackout.'

Anticipation of juvenile blackout crime. Taken from 'Lustige Verdunklung', *Tageblatt Wochenshau*, 28 September 1937.

By 1940, Göring had already made the link between the blackout and juvenile delinquency explicit. In an address to the Ministerial Council for the Defence of the Reich, he stated that ‗the blackout and general wartime conditions facilitate a lack of discipline and the commission of offences by young people, but do not generally explain them.'[358] This last point referred to the social circumstances of youth offenders, and in some cases their political outlook. The cover of darkness provided criminal opportunities for German youths who either fell through the infrastructure of schools, parents, the Hitler Youth and other Nazi social organisations, or else found themselves growing up antithetical to the aims of the Nazi state. The crime rate amongst this group soared; by 1943 54% of incidences of serious theft were attributed to juveniles, an increase of 120% from the start of the war.[359] In Britain, the statistics released by Police

---

[358] Noakes, *Nazism 1919-1945, Volume 4, The German Home Front in World War II*, pp.440-441.
[359] Blau, 'Die Kriminalität in Deutschland während des zweiten Weltkrieges', p.61.

Chiefs on juvenile crime are similarly unequivocal. In his report for the year 1939

Glasgow's Police Chief referred to juvenile crime specifically.

> There is no doubt that the present complete absence of illumination during the hours of darkness tends to encourage the commission of such crimes as theft by the method commonly known as smash and grab', and by house breaking generally, by persons who, under normal circumstances, would have lacked the necessary courage. There exists, in such circumstances, a very real danger that juveniles in particular will be influenced, by the apparently reduced risk of detection, to venture on a career of crime, and the ultimate return to peace-time conditions might well reveal a consequently abnormal increase in criminal activity. [original emphasis][360]

Next year's report bore out his warning.

> In the case of crimes the major increases are shown in Theft and Housebreaking, the figures for which have risen by 420 and 376 on last year's figures. For the less serious offences the figures for Malicious Mischief and contraventions of the Glasgow Police Acts (Stone Throwing, Hanging on Rear of Vehicles, etc.) have increased by 325 and 297.[361]

The following table lists the punishments issued for juvenile offences in Glasgow, which

show in particular a large rise in fines issued and the use of whippings as punishment.

---

[360] Glasgow Record Office, SR22/40/1, Chief Constable's annual report 1939.
[361] Glasgow Record Office, SR22/40/1, Chief Constable's annual report 1940.

Table 5.11 – Punishment of youth offences in Glasgow, 1939-1940[362]

Disposal	1939	1940
Charge withdrawn or acquitted	117	92
Otherwise discharged	-	3
Charge proved-dismissed	149	175
Put on probation	859	1109
Sent to institution for defectives	1	1
Sent to Prison	1	-
Sent to Remand Home	49	59
Sent to Borstal institution	17	17
Sent to Approved School	181	271
Committed to care of Fit Person	2	-
Whipped	14	111
Fined	93	396
Ordered to find caution	6	2
Admonished	430	573
Totals	1919	2809

Writing on a similar rise in juvenile crime, Manchester's Police Chief was unequivocal in ascribing the rise to wartime conditions on the home front.

> ...the exceptional increase shown in the figures for 1940 can only be ascribed to the abnormal conditions prevailing in consequence of the War. In many cases the fathers of juvenile delinquents are serving in His Majesty's Forces and the mothers are employed on essential Government work; consequently there is an unavoidable lack of parental control.[363]

Contemporary academic analysis also followed this line, attaching most importance to the novel familial and social conditions of the war.[364] The war was felt to have had a coarsening, degenerative effect amongst some sections of the population, especially amongst the working class. This had an effect on the morals of youths. The ease with which some could either commit crime, or witness what was thought of as morally corruptible behaviour – a mother's relationship with a man other than the father is cited as an example – could only serve to contribute to delinquency. This reasoning would

---

[362] Ibid.
[363] Manchester City Council archives, Chief Constable's annual report 1941.
[364] Walter A. Lunden, 'War and Juvenile Delinquency in England and Wales, 1910 to 1943', *American Sociological Review*, 10/3 (1945).

inform post-war attempts to reform youth supervision.[365] In comparison with Germany, where the state's control over youth behaviour was exercised to a considerable degree through legal sanctions or else through state youth groups, there does not appear to have been a serious attempt at regulating youth behaviour from the British government. In Germany, officials worried at the susceptibility of the nation's youth to outside influences. To counter this, an increasing criminalization of youth was mirrored in a renewed focus on determining the shape of children's and adolescents' lives through Nazi youth groups and family organisations.[366] However, gangs of youths continued to roam the blacked out city streets. By 1944, this was a serious concern for the regime. A report by the Reich Ministry of Justice had identified three types of gangs present in Germany: Politically hostile gangs; liberal-individualistic gangs; and criminal anti-social gangs. The report states that one of these groups, the Edelweiss Pirates, meet at night on street corners, in doorways or in parks.' They were politically hostile to the community, and despised authority. Another group, the Swing Youth, admired American music and dressed like English dandies:

> The members dress in clothes which imitate English fashions. Thus, they often wear pleated jackets in tartan designs and carry umbrellas. As a badge they wear a coloured dress shirt button in their lapels. They regard Englishmen as the highest form of human development. A false conception of freedom leads them into opposition to the HJ (Hitler Youth).[367]

Amongst the third type of group were gangs of youths drawn from the criminal classes, and genetically inferior, antisocial family clans.' All of them met at night, and their existence was linked directly to the conditions of the blackout. As Kebbedies writes, the problem in controlling German youth during the war was that free time was inevitable,

---

[365] For a discussion of juvenile delinquency in Scotland during the war see David Smith, 'Official Responses to Juvenile Delinquency in Scotland During the Second World War', *Twentieth Century British History*, 18/1 (2007).
[366] See Jörg Echternkamp, 'The Essential Features of German Society in the Second World War', in Jörg Echternkamp Ralf Blank, Karola Fings, and Jürgen Förster (ed.), *Germany and the Second World War: Volume IX / I: German Wartime Society 1939-1945: Politicization, Disintegration, and the Struggle for Survival* (Oxford: Oxford University Press, 1990), pp.1-101, p.35; Noakes, *Nazism 1919-1945, Volume 4, The German Home Front in World War II*, pp.396-464.
[367] Noakes, *Nazism 1919-1945, Volume 4, The German Home Front in World War II*, p.453.

yet also immoral, particularly in wartime.'[368] In both countries, the link between the blackout and youth crime was explicitly tied to ideas of morality and social cohesion. While this was present in all instances of adult crimes that were either facilitated or occurred during the blackout, these ideas found their clearest expression in the surge in youth crime during the war.

The language of blackout justice

The foundation of Nazi justice was based on securing the integrity of the national community. As a result, criminal law was specifically driven along the Nazis' characteristic political, ideological, and biological lines. As Noakes writes, the law held two specific functions in Germany: firstly, to maintain the morale of the home front by limiting any political or criminal disruption; and secondly, to make sure that the losses of the best ‑human material" at the front were not exacerbated by the survival or even proliferation of the worst elements at home, thereby producing a negative selection in terms of population quality.'[369] The national community, as ‑thehighest interest protected by the law', superseded the rights of the individual, and any ideas of rehabilitation.[370] The Decree against National Pests was issued on 5 September 1939, creating three classes of ambiguously defined offenders – the plunderer, the exploiter of blackouts, and the anti-social saboteur. Sections 2 and 4 of the decree relate specifically to blackout offences:

> 2. Crimes committed during air raids
>
> Anyone who commits a crime or an offence against life, limb or property by exploiting the measures which have been taken to protect against air raids with penal servitude for up to 15 years or with penal servitude for life or in particularly serious cases with death.
>
> 4. Exploitation of the war situation as grounds for increasing the sentence

---

[368] Frank Kebbedies, *Ausser Kontrolle: Jugendkriminalität in der NS-Zeit und der frühen Nachkriegszeit* (Essen: Klartext, 2000), p.141.
[369] Noakes, *Nazism 1919-1945, Volume 4, The German Home Front in World War II*, p.121.
[370] Michael Stolleis, *The Law Under the Swastika: Studies on Legal History in Nazi Germany* (Chicago: University of Chicago Press, 1998), pp.72-73.

Anyone who commits any other offence with the aim of exploiting exceptional wartime circumstances will be punished in excess of the normal with penal servitude for life or with death if this is required by the response of healthy popular feelings to a particularly heinous offence.[371]

Differences in how the law was applied were evident across the country, and pressure from the Party on the judiciary to give harsher sentences mounted during the war. When the war began, Roland Freisler, State Secretary in the Reich Justice Ministry for penal affairs, asked ‗If the community needs to be securely protected against the criminal personality for years on end, why not snuff it out and thereby ensure perfect protection at one blow?‘[372] Such reasoning, asserting the safety of the community as the key factor in harsher sentencing, found increasing expression through the law courts as the war carried on. While there are no statistics that break down death sentences by types of offence, the use of capital punishment across all offences escalated dramatically once the war began, as the following table illustrates.

Table 5.12 – Executions in Germany, 1938-1945[373]

	Executions
1938	85
1939	139
1940	250
1941	1292
1942	4457
1943	5336
1944	4264
1945	297

The following example, found in the archives of the Münchener Staatsarchiv, illustrates how this manifested itself in an individual case, and provides a remarkable view of both the legal reasoning of blackout death sentences and how they were carried out. The file, marked with a cross to indicate execution, relates the crime of Johann Weilnahmmer. Caught and sentenced before the bombing had even begun, it is

---

[371] Noakes, *Nazism 1919-1945, Volume 4, The German Home Front in World War II*, pp.129-130.
[372] Ibid., p.122.
[373] Ibid.

exemplary of German blackout justice at the start of the war and affords a wider view into both the political and cultural justifications for severe blackout justice.

Weilnahmmer was born in Munich on 9 June 1914. His file refers to him as being an ‚illegitimate child‘, whose mother died when he was two years old. He was subsequently raised by foster-parents Isidor and Rosina Meier in the village of Hönning, near Munich. A poor student, he repeated a year at school and, on leaving, worked on his foster-parents‘ farm. At 18 he began working for a brewery for half a year, and from 1935-1937 performed his national service at a flak-battery in Kitzingen. He left the service as a private and attempted to join the police, but did not pass the exam. Instead, he began work as a truck and tractor driver, and shortly before his arrest was working as a driver on a building site. He earned roughly 150RM a month, 50 of which he estimated went on food, and the rest of which he spent on the weekends in Munich in pubs and at dances.

On Saturday, 2 December 1939, he was asked to drive a truck to Munich for repairs. As they could not be undertaken immediately, he used his free time to frequent cafes and ‚carouse‘ with girls, and quickly outspent his earnings. Though he picked up his pay of 40 RM the following Monday, by Thursday he was once again penniless. It was at this point that he decided to steal a handbag that evening under the cover of the blackout, and so continue his ‚pleasure-seeking‘ in Munich. At 6pm he stationed himself on Bayerstrasse, and began to follow a 34 year-old stenographer called Mathilde Haushofer. Approaching her from behind, he grabbed her handbag. In her surprise Haushofer did not defend herself, and as she was not carrying the bag very firmly he quickly escaped, throwing it and Haushofer's photo ID away and keeping the 5.10 RM he found, which he spent that evening. The following day he carried out a similar crime at almost the same time on Maria Fleischmann, a 42 year old unskilled

166

worker, on Pariserstrasse. Surprised, she again did not defend herself, though she did raise the alarm. At this a soldier apprehended Weilnahmmer. The bag and its contents were estimated to have been worth about 5RM.[374] For these two crimes, and their paltry reward, Weilnahmmer was sentenced to death.

The language of the written judgement is revealing. Though Weilnahmmer pleaded that he did not use force and would have given up had he encountered any resistance, this did not mitigate his crime. He was judged to have knowingly used the blackout in order to steal, understanding that it would make it that much easier. His choice of hour, at the moment when most people were leaving work for home, showed an opportunism that, would have terrible consequences if not punished by the state and simply allowed to continue. By choosing working women as his victims, he was also judged to have selected them knowing that they did not belong to ‚wealthy circles.' He committed his crimes not from economic necessity, but because of his reckless spending. In the judgement's words, his ‚lust for dancing set him on the wrong path.' Other personal circumstances, his young age, his apparent ‚weakness of spirit' - a euphemism for his intelligence - and previous good behaviour was judged as insufficient grounds for mitigation, in light of such a serious transgression. As a result, the only sentence left for the court was execution.

After the sentencing, a letter from the Chief Public Prosecutor of Munich was sent to Johann's foster-parents on 3 January 1940. He informed them of the decision of the court, and that the matter of a pardon was with the Minister of Justice, a decision on which had not yet been reached. He offered his foster parents the right to take the body. If no reply was sent, it would be assumed that the body was not to be retrieved. Johann's foster parents never replied. On 14 February a letter sent by the Office of the

---

[374] Munich Staatsarchiv, adapted from the written judgement of the People's Court, 15 December 1939.

Minister of Justice to the Chief Public Prosecutor confirmed that no pardon would be given. Johann's body would be sent to the Anatomical Institute of Munich University, and his head to the city's psychiatric institute. The following extract is from the minutes of Weilnahmer's execution.

> At around 6am the condemned was led from his cell by two prison wardens, accompanied by the Prison Chaplain Kinle. He sat down at a table, on which stood a crucifix and two lighted candles. The public prosecutor, Mr. Schmucker, then read the relevant section of the judgement of the Munich Special Court of 14 December 1939, and the decree of the Reichsminister for Justice of 12 February 1940. After the chaplain had given a short prayer, the condemned was given over to the executioner. The executioner's assistants blindfolded the condemned and walked him to the guillotine, on which he was bound by two leather straps and his neck moved under the blade. Executioner Reichhardt released the blade, which separated the head of the condemned from his body. At this the chaplain said the Lord's prayer. The prison doctor satisfied himself that the condemned was indeed dead. From the blindfolding to the falling of the head fourteen seconds passed, during which time a bell was rung. The entire operation, which proceeded without difficulties, lasted approximately 1 minute and 41 seconds from his leaving the cell.[375]

It is difficult to assess how common such judgements were during the war – as noted previously, the figures for execution are not broken down by types of offence. What is notable in this case is the degree to which the judiciary in Munich had already adjusted to the political climate of sentencing fostered by the Nazi state. In this case, the interpretation of the law followed Nazi imprecations to secure the community against undesirable elements. However, other special courts at this time did not always follow this reasoning – for the similar crime of robbery in the blackout, the Hanseatic Special Court sentenced four men on 8 September 1939 to 8 to 10 years hard labour. Rulings against offenders sometimes took their personal circumstances into account. In May 1941, a story in the *Völkischer Beobachter* of a 19 year old robber who had used the blackout for his crime left Hitler incensed. The offender's punishment of 10 years hard labour was far too lenient, and he demanded his position on such offences be reiterated to the State Secretary for Justice, Schlegelberger.

---

[375] Munich Staatsarchiv, Staatsanwaltschaften (Public Prosecutor), Nr. 9230, minutes of execution, 27 February 1940.

The Führer cannot understand this verdict. It is the opinion of the Führer that if we wish to keep robbery under the cover of darkness to an absolute minimum, then in such cases the death penalty must be used. In any case, as the Führer has said time and again, given the heroic efforts of our soldiers we must strike hard against such robbers.[376]

Interfering in this manner was a habit that Hitler maintained during the war, with a concomitant effect on the severity of sentences handed down by the judiciary.[377] With some measure of grovelling, the Justice Secretary's reasons for the leniency of the sentence were outlined in a lengthy response, and drew Hitler's attention to facts not covered by the newspaper's report. The offence was similar to the case study above - an opportunistic theft of a handbag at night from a war widow. However, the circumstances of the offender's personal situation were mitigating factors. A sickly father, humble circumstances, and previous good character all played a role in the offender escaping the death sentence. However, the exigencies of these cases notwithstanding, the interpretation of the law during the war became increasingly harsh at the encouragement of the Nazi state. The application of ever harsher sentences escalated with the bombing war, with looting under the cover of the blackout becoming a particular focus in the later years of the war.[378] The language of justice also sharpened in Britain, and looters were threatened with similar severity. The Lord Mayor of London asserted that forthcoming legislation would put looters into the category of murderers', liable to suffer death or penal servitude for life'.[379] Though the maximum sentence for looting was indeed execution, no such sentence was ever given during the war. Yet the fact that it was discussed in such terms gives at least an indication of the strength of feeling surrounding exploiters of air raids and the blackout. However, there was a balancing act between severity and leniency. In 1941, Churchill asked Herbert Morrison to review the sentences of six firemen convicted of looting, and

[376] BARCH, R43 II/645a, Lammers to Schlegelberger, 29 May 1941.
[377] Evans, The Third Reich at War, pp.515-519.
[378] Ralf Blank, 'Wartime Daily Life and the Air War on the Home Front', in Jorg Echternkamp Ralf Blank, Karola Fings, Jurgen Forster, Winfried Heinemann, Tobias Jersak, Armin Nolzen, Christoph Rass (ed.), Germany and the Second World War Volume IX/I: German Wartime Society 1939-1945: Politicization, Disintegration, and the Struggle for Survival (Oxford: Oxford University Press, 2008), pp.371-478, pp.402-405.
[379] Gardiner, Wartime: Britain 1939-1945, p.597.

sentenced to five years penal servitude. These were terrible sentences' Churchill said, at a time when the country had _rone too many able-bodied men.' Morrison, with an eye on the press and public opinion, resisted, though promised a review of sentencing for looters.[380] This case illustrates how the practical needs of wartime home front were sometimes in conflict with its heightened morality, in which exploitation of the blackout was a key factor. As in Germany, justice had to be seen to be appropriate to the state of emergency, and what was perceived as just according to the morals, and indeed morale, of the wartime home front.

Conclusion

While it is certainly the case that juvenile rose dramatically as a result of the blackout, it is far from certain whether the blackout contributed to a large scale increase in other kinds of behaviours. The statistics drawn on here, together with more recent analyses of crime trends, give a picture of how the blackout allowed expression of suppressed, anti-social or illegitimate behaviours, and perhaps most importantly the attention paid to those behaviours by the state during the war. While the blackout's link to the dramatic rise in juvenile crime during the war is unequivocal, some caution is needed when trying to discern more general trends attributable to the blackout. While the measures of control are not comparable, concerns over the sexual behaviour of women in both Britain and Germany rested on ideas of _unhealthy' or unproductive sexual desire. In this case, the rhetoric bears some similarity. The blackout, as a feature of the war that enabled such behaviour, formed a destabilising part of the home front. But whether they occurred in any greater number is not certain. It may be that the heightened anxiety of life under the blackout contributed to the morality of the wartime home front, and that this may in turn have exacerbated public and political concerns over sexual activity. This might also be the case with the apprehension of crime amongst women in

---

[380] Cited in Smith, *Britain in the Second World War: a Social History*, pp.87-88.

Britain. High profile reports on their susceptibility to attack during the blackout may have exaggerated their sense of being at risk. Yet while the presence of the blackout made the streets seem unsafe, it was also important in establishing wartime discourses of sacrifice and duty to the community. The blackout's effect on crime during the war was, in this sense, something of a paradox.

Chapter Six – Cultural and Political Reaction

Introduction

Antonia Lant writes that the impact of the blackout on the Britain's wartime community was unequivocal: it addressed _he entire population through the representation of a shared British reality: it signalled national experience and so spoke to its audience as a national group.[381] But the blackout did not actively construct a space with any inherent meaning, the way a public space such as a church or a court of law might do. The blackout could also be filled with meaning by the people who lived under it. Notwithstanding the condition of war itself, the blackout was open to interpretation by everyone. It could excite them, or threaten them. It could symbolise the worst excesses of modern war, or the failure of reason. And by its presence, it could act as a brake on the state's claims for success in fighting the war. This chapter does not assume a coherent cultural or political response to the blackout; apathy was as legitimate a reaction to it as any imaginative one, though it does not provide much for the researcher to write about. Little contemporary analysis of the blackout went beyond statements of whether it bothered people – which of course it did – and an opinion on its dangers and penalties. But there could also be an imaginative, political, or more existential response to the blackout. This chapter argues that the blackout heightened the division between the public and private worlds. While the blackout was generally an aspect of the home front that elevated the community over the individual, and by extension the war-fighting state over the individual citizen, it also left space for people to draw into themselves, away from public life. In the case of Germany in particular, where the possible retreat of individuals into the private sphere, away from the public culture of the Nazi state, threatened to undermine its authority.

---

[381] Lant, *Blackout: Reinventing Women for Wartime British Cinema*, p.114.

This chapter also argues the blackout had an important symbolic function during the war that went beyond its usual practicalities and public function.[382] This chapter also makes clear, however, that the political and cultural response to the blackout was diverse, and needs to be treated separately to the more apparent consequences such as crime, and the blackout's effect on the infrastructures of both countries. This chapter therefore describes some of the ways in which the blackout affected the mind of the nation, as expressed through its culture and its politics. There is a substantial difference in the material available for comparative work here. For histories of administration, Governments have always left papers trails. The material available for cultural comparisons is rather more restricted. Though the war undoubtedly did much to compress the opinions of the British population, the ability to express opinion and associate freely was entirely different to the restrictions of Nazi Germany. There, the nation's culture was in service to the ideals of Nazi ideology, and all public expression had to run with the grain of the state. Because of this, it should be kept in mind that the material from which to draw comparisons is skewed. This chapter does not assume that the more existential associations made with the blackout are explicit and universal across either nation. Rather, it is an attempt to contextualise the meaning of the blackout that is often hinted at in documents of the period but rarely ever analysed in depth.

Light and Reason

Within the Western intellectual tradition, and the Enlightenment in particular, metaphors of light drew on long-standing discourses of divine revelation. Martin Fitzpatrick writes that the Enlightenment project was an attempt to reconcile the ideas of science and

---

[382] The symbolism of ‚darkness' and the turmoil of the war years remains today, and can be seen in Zara Steiner's recent surveys of European history to 1939, titled ‚The Lights that Failed' and the forthcoming ‚Triumph of the Dark'.

theology; of the divine light of revelation and the light of reason symbolised by the march of scientific progress and human understanding.[383] The laws of Newton's *Principia* had revealed a cosmos that operated to a set of rules that could be understood and harnessed by mankind, and philosophers debated the role of God in this cosmos. Newton's friend and colleague John Locke, in his essay *The Reasonableness of Christianity*, made explicit the connection between the 'light of reason' granted by God to mankind, and the legitimacy for understanding God's creation in these terms. Reason, the 'Candle of the Lord', was the principal driving force of the Enlightenment.[384] Yet it was a paradox of the blackout that reason and science could at once lead to mankind's discovery of flight, yet make the blackout necessary. In the week that war began, *The Daily Express'* cartoonist George Strube drew a family of torch-bearing cave dwellers baffled at their modern neighbours in their darkened houses, with a warden yelling 'put that light out!' [see overleaf.]

'Time marches on': George Strube cartoon, taken from *The Daily Express*, 7 September 1939.

Atheist derivations of reason may have removed its divine aspect, but the relationship between light and reason in public discourse remained. In saying that, there is nothing that resembles a crystallization of these ideas in either Britain or Germany; the analogies are often blunt and ambiguous, and to a large extent superficial. The

---

[383] Martin Fitzpatrick, 'Introduction', in Peter Jones Martin Fitzpatrick, Christina Knellwolf, Ian Mccalman (ed.), *The Enlightenment World* (London: Routledge, 2007), pp.159-163, pp.159-161.
[384] John Locke, *The Reasonableness of Christianity: as Delivered in the Scriptures* (London, 1696), pp.255-256.

174

Manichean opposites of light and dark in Western culture have their analogies in other forms; civilized and uncivilized, knowledge and ignorance, sight and blindness. But though they are rather simplistic, this does not mean they do not resonate. Public discourse during war – and of the state in general – tends towards dramatic statement over academic subtlety. The blackout was therefore not only a signifier of the condition of war, but symbolic of a wider malaise of civilization. A few weeks into the war, a researcher for Mass Observation heard two middle-aged men in London discussing the war, and what it meant for them. ‗Science,' said one, ‗is destroying civilisation – the curse of man.‗[385].

Both countries were alive to this in the inter-war years, though in slightly different ways. German discourse on aerial warfare centred on the idea of Germany as under threat from its heavily armed neighbours.[386] In Britain, various fictions written during the inter-war years were influenced by the ideas of Wells' 1908 novel *The War in the Air*, where the catastrophe of bombing would bring about the downfall of civilization. Olaf Stapledon's extraordinary novel *Last and First Men*, published in 1930, imagined the swift destruction of English civilization in a single raid:

> While the London papers were selling out upon the news that war was declared, enemy planes appeared over the city. In a couple of hours a third of London was in ruins, and half her population lay poisoned in the streets. One bomb, falling beside the British Museum, turned the whole of Bloomsbury into a crater, wherein fragments of mummies, statues, and manuscripts were mingled with the contents of shops, and morsels of salesmen and the intelligentsia. Thus in a moment was destroyed a large proportion of England's most precious relics and most fertile brains.[387]

These extravagant predictions, although more prescient of the advent of nuclear weapons than the bombing technology of the period, were common not simply amongst the left wing and pacifists, but across the political spectrum.[388] The language

---

[385] MOA, Folder 1/B, Conversations about the war, 16 September 1939.
[386] For example, see the map reproduced on page XXX of this thesis.
[387] Olaf Stapledon, *Last and First Men* (London: Millennium, 1930), pp.6-7.
[388] On this see Overy, 'Apocalyptic fears: Bombing and Popular Anxiety in Inter-War Britain'.

and imagery invoked was often biblical, with an evident sense of an advancing science that dragged people with it, whether they willed it or not and irrespective of the consequences. When the war began this latent fear would mingle with the rich symbolism of the blackout. As explained in chapters two and three, open development of the blackout in Britain lagged behind Germany amidst a public opinion that was by and large unconvinced and unwilling to accept the necessity of ARP exercises in peacetime. In both countries, trial blackouts elicited in general either an indifferent or else amused reaction from the press and public. The pressures of a rolling blackout were altogether different, and the relationship between the now constant dark of the streets was easily linked with the condition of war and a wider malaise of civilization. In a book on the psychological effect of the war, the Oxford University psychologist K.O. Newman outlined the home front citizen's psychological relationship with darkness.

> [its] importance... can be gathered from the many uses the word finds in trying to describe things or conditions which have nothing to do with real or physical darkness. We speak of _Dark Ages', of _dark hours'... all aim at conveying an impression of fear, uncertainty and death... Nothing in its symbolical application leaves room for hope or joy.[389]

This metaphor was not lost across the Atlantic. On the eve of the war, Roosevelt, in one of his fireside chats broadcast to the American people, called for national unity in the Western hemisphere to prevent a _blackout of peace in the United States.'[390] And Clement Attlee, in a speech to a private conference of Labour MPs in November 1939, advocated the abolition of air forces and the private manufacture and trade in arms. In his words:

> Abolition of national air forces will remove the apprehension of aerial attack, which is to-day driving mankind to the [life] of a cave dweller.[391]

In Germany, the fear of an apocalyptic aerial attack had already been used by the Nazi party to galvanise the nation to arms, and submission to authority. On taking power, the

---

[389] K.O. Newman, _Mind, Sex and War_ (Oxford: The Pelagos Press, 1941), p.71.
[390] Hubert P. Earle, _Blackout: the Human Side of Europe's March to War_ (Philadelphia: J.B. Lippincott Company, 1939), p.211.
[391] 'Attlee Conference Speech', Manchester Evening News, 8 November 1939, p.8.

public sphere was gradually drained not only of competing political viewpoints, but also of anything that might take shape as a political issue. To maintain the public's attention required a diet not of overt political rhetoric, but a more subtle mix that tended towards satisfying, as Ross writes, pleasure and desire'.[392] A constant diet of propaganda would alienate the public, and have the dangerous side-effect of making them more aware of their own circumstances. Draining all criticism from public discourse dampened the ability for any mobilisation of negative associations with any particular feature of wartime. As the discussion of Christmas in wartime Germany will later argue, when the Party sensed its control over the meaning of a public ritual slipping, it chose to avoid engaging with it. Though the British were freer to grumble about the blackout, it is certainly not the case that Germans were any more enamoured of it; amidst the control of meaning and expression exercised by the Party, they simply could not express it in the same way.

The relationship between light and darkness in Germany

It was at Aumont's Cafe in Moscow that Maxim Gorky, on viewing a Lumière Brothers' film, called the world shown by the projector a kingdom of the shadows'.[393] For him the film was little beyond a shallow, if terrifying, representation of the world, mere shadows', as though the wizard Merlin had cast a spell over the entire street, compressing its multi-storied buildings... to minute size', and its people to correspond.[394] If his description was a reaction to cinema's novelty, it nevertheless found its apotheosis in the German cinema of the Weimar years. With the later flight and exile of German film talent in the Nazi years, the symbolism of light and dark articulated in Weimar cinema would later form the creative bedrock of Hollywood film

---

[392] Corey Ross, *Media and the Making of Modern Germany: Mass Communications, Society, and Politics from the Empire to the Third Reich* (Oxford: Oxford University Press, 2008), p.302-340.
[393] Ian Christie Richard Taylor, *The Film Factory: Russian and Soviet Cinema in Documents* (London: Routledge, 1994), pp.25-26.
[394] Ibid.

noir. In the restrictions of the Weimar period, with electricity rationed and with finance and material for mounting productions scarce, producers were forced to creatively build and light their sets. It is the genre of films designed in this manner that is of most interest in considering the blackout, and Chinen Biesen identifies two strands of film-making that were most closely associated with the expressionistic manipulation of light and dark. The first were a set of what can be broadly described as psychological horror movies, spanning such films as *The Cabinet of Dr. Caligari* (1919) to Fritz Lang's *M* (1931). It was in these films that Siegfried Kracauer described what he saw as a strong relationship between the forms of Weimar cinema and the collective psychology of the German population. Kracauer's influential 1947 study of the history of Weimar cinema, *From Caligari to Hitler: a Psychological History of the German Film*, drew on a socio-psychological framework that read Weimar cinema as presaging the advent of a totalitarian Germany. Within the twisted geometry and abstract lighting of German expressionist film, Kracauer saw a body of work that while not unified in genre, author or narrative, nevertheless carried a meta-narrative that reflected, and even prepared, a climate in which totalitarianism could flourish.

Kracauer's study has been resilient, despite its teleological flavour. Side-stepping his assertion that film could programme a society for totalitarianism, his study remains persuasive in determining the regular occurrence of motifs and themes over a long period in German cinema that fore-grounded darkness, chaos and morbidity. As Elsaesser writes, ʻrarely has a body of films exerted such a pull towards verbal paraphrase, in which epithets like ʻdarkʻ and ʻdemonicʻ, ʻtwistedʻ, ʻhauntedʻ and ʻtormentedʻ leap onto the page.ʻ[395] Kracauer posited that these films reflected a desire beneath the surface of the German public's consciousness for order and authoritarian leadership. In his words:

---

[395] Thomas Elsaesser, *Weimar Cinema and After: Germany's Historical Imaginary* (London: Routledge, 2000), p.19.

What films reflect are not so much explicit credos as psychological dispositions – those deep layers of collective mentality which extend more or less below the dimension of consciousness. Of course, popular magazines and broadcasts, bestsellers, ads, fashions in language and other sedimentary products of a people's cultural life also yield valuable information about predominant attitudes, widespread inner tendencies. But the medium of the screen exceeds these sources in inclusiveness.[396]

By the late 1920s Hollywood money was flowing into the resource-starved German film industry. Paramount and MGM established an international distribution arm, influencing the type of films being produced. This led towards what some felt to be an Americanization of German film, perhaps best represented by the *Kammerspielfilme,* pulpy crime films that melded the expressionism of the period with downbeat, realist narratives. These films were the pre-cursors of post war American film noir.[397] It is perhaps no small coincidence that the existential fears of the blackout, of sexual liberation, crime and violence, were thematically mirrored in them.

Nazi use of light before the war worked the familiar Manichean distinctions between chaos and order, ruin and civilization. In an analysis of the conversions' of early Party members, David Redles notes the frequent and familiar allusions to religious and apocalyptic language and imagery. He writes that:

The common conversion metaphors of moving from confusion to clarity, from darkness to light, reflect the psychological process of having a perception of order collapse into disorder and then having that sense of order reconstructed. The sense of order generated by Nazi apocalyptic cosmology was experienced as a revelation of simple but profound truths.[398]

Light was used by the Nazis as representative of order and progress. Expressionism in the use of light had already been seen in German theatre and architecture, but in contrast with film light in these settings held a transformative and redemptive power,

---

[396] Siegfried Kracauer, *From Caligari to Hitler: a Psychological History of the German Film* (New Jersey: Princeton University Press, 2004), p.6.

[397] For a detailed overview see Sheri Chinen Biesen, *Blackout: World War II and the Origins of Film Noir* (Baltimore: John Hopkins University Press, 2005), pp.15-58.

[398] David Redles, *Hitler's Millennial Reich: Apocalyptic Belief and the Search for Salvation* (New York: New York University Press, 2005), p.89.

intimately connected with community. Where Weimar films were arguably troubling dialogues between light and dark, in the world of theatre and architecture it was light itself that was the focus – its power to illuminate was the quality that was most prized, and far preferable to the Nazi ethic than the troubled design and narratives of Weimar cinema. James-Chakraborty writes that light's theatricality was used to

> transcend the country's dangerous social and political polarization. Some of these efforts were benign, wrapping the romance of technological progress around an evening's entertainment... Others were frankly coercive, using militarism on an unprecedentedly sublime scale to annihilate any sense of the individual.[399]

Transcendence and scale were central to Albert Speer's *Lichtdom*, his cathedral of light, which he designed for the Nuremberg rallies. For this hundreds of searchlights were lined along the rally's Zeppelin field, casting beams of light into the sky for 20,000 feet. In 1936 150 lights, eating 4000 kilowatts of energy, cast their beams to a single point in the sky upon Hitler's entrance, effecting what Speer called 'a vast room, with the beams serving as mighty pillars of infinitely light outer walls.'[400] The British Ambassador Neville Henderson admiringly called them 'cathedrals of ice'.[401] Yet the paradox of the searchlights is evident. Though used at rallies to awe the audience sitting under it, these same searchlights would later become a feature of the blacked out landscape of wartime Germany, which in the early days of the war would draw wayward bombers to their targets.[402] The complicated and redemptive power of light in the Nazi worldview found its clearest expression in the war during the Christmas festivities, as the following section will show.

---

[399] Kathleen James-Chakraborty, 'The Drama of Illumination: Visions of Community from Wilhemine to Nazi Germany', in Richard A. Etlin (ed.), *Art, culture and media under the Third Reich* (Chicago: University of Chicago Press, 2002), p.198.
[400] Ibid., p.181.
[401] Joachim Fest, *Speer: the Final Verdict* (London: Weidenfeld and Nicholson, 2001), p.51.
[402] Leonard Cheshire, *Bomber Pilot* (London: Goodall, 1943), p.51.

Lichtglaub

Winter was the time in which the blackout was at its most oppressive. The celebration of Christmas was a marker in people's calendars during the war, and its association with light provided a sharp focus for people and their troubles as the war dragged on. The paradox here was how light was at once venerated at Christmas celebrations, yet at the same time was _the surest bombing target' for enemy aircraft, as citizens were regularly reminded. As discussed in earlier chapters, the domestic world had long been a key focus for the Nazis. The retrenchment of social life outside of the home as a result of the blackout, particularly during the long winter months, meant that domestic life had a renewed importance. Nazi ideology permeated through the control of the public sphere's presence in the home, whether through radio broadcasts and newspapers, or ideas and behaviours learned through state sponsored institutions and organisations outside the home.

Domestic rituals were also a key focus of the Nazi party, and none had greater communal significance than the celebration of Christmas. Initial attempts after 1933 at forming a national church whose ideals were compatible with Nazi ideology foundered. Attempts within the Party to develop a religious component to National Socialism gradually formed into an unsettled and esoteric mix of paganism, Nordic folklore, Indian symbolism and invented rite.[403] The character of this mixture was never unified, nor was it adhered to by all party members. Though Himmler was committed to instilling a quasi-religious order to the SS, with bowls of fire and pagan symbolism at SS wedding ceremonies, Göring and Hitler were themselves less convinced, the latter stating in 1938 that the Party had _no desire to instil in the population a mysticism that lies

---

[403] Richard J. Evans, *The Third Reich in Power* (London: Penguin, 2006), pp.220-260. On the roots of Manichean opposites of light and dark in early German occultism and its links with Nazism see Nicholas Goodrick-Clarke, *Occult Roots of Nazism: Secret Aryan Cults and Their Influence on Nazi Ideology* (New York: New York University Press, 2004).

outside the purpose and goals of our doctrine.'[404] But though attempts at formulating a

Nazi church were ultimately fruitless, the symbolic value of Christmas appears to have

been too important for the state to leave alone. The Christian symbolism of the festival

in Germany was self-evident. Co-opting the festival for the Party's own ends was

necessary, both for its importance in the life of the nation, and for breaking the link in

public discourse between the church and public ritual. Specifically, it was the

importance of light in the celebration of Christmas that formed the key point on which

the Nazis' attempted to claim the festival as their own.

The importance of light was already evident in traditions that had been claimed as part

of the National Socialist ethic. The Winter Solstice in particular had been felt to be most

fitting for Nazism, harking back to a paganism that predated Christianity and bolstered

the Nazis' blood and soil ethic. But the blackout restrictions impacted heavily on the

Solstice's key ritual - the lighting of enormous open-air bonfires.[405] Unable to continue

this celebration, its importance dissipated, and the altogether more private domestic

celebration of Christmas became a target of Nazi propaganda. The war saw a

concerted effort from party officials and propagandists to rebrand Christmas as a

festival of light - a *Lichtglaub*, or belief in light - around which a jumble of associations

of hope, national unity, and fighting spirit, found sharp definition against the blackout

and the dark days of the war. The blackout had a sustained metaphoric resonance

during the war, and amidst the increasing privations of the home front the darkness of

the night time streets provided a vivid visual and spatial symbolism of the state of war

the country was now in. Controlling how light was symbolised amidst this blacked out

landscape had tremendous political importance, and attempts to fix its meaning

permeated throughout. The symbolism of the lit Christmas tree is expressed in the

---

[404] Evans, *The Third Reich in Power*, p.257.
[405] Esther Gajek, 'Christmas under the Third Reich', *Anthropology Today*, 6/4 (1990), p.4. See also Rita Breuer Judith Breuer, *Von wegen Heilige Nacht! Das Weihnachtsfest in der politischen Propaganda* (Mülheim an der Ruhr: Verlag an der Ruhr, 2000), p.93.

following passage, taken from a booklet produced by the Reich's Youth Directorate advising families on how to prepare for Christmas.

> You have known for a long time that our Christmas Tree is more than a child's novelty – and more than an accessory for the Christmas celebrations. Because you know that the lighted, decorated tree is a tradition of our people... You have placed lights on the tree, and you know what the burning candle in the winter's night says: light and glow, warmth and life! And it will quietly bring you to the new year, that has almost arrived – and with it new life and the spring's rising sun.[406]

In fact the tree itself was not beyond martial language: for some commentators it was a participant in the war, a 'Yuletree' in a 'constant fight against the darkness.'[407] This was a metaphor that had wider resonance with the celebrations as a whole. The tranquillity of Christmas at the year's end was a natural point of reflection for the population. The public sphere in Germany was full of messages that were quick to remind Germans of their armies at the front, and readily associated Christmas with the war's progress. These official messages were shot through with associations of light and dark: The people's celebrations were the result of the military's protection; the enemy were 'forces of darkness'; candlelight was variously the coming of spring or rebirth, representing hope or victory, or the memory of fallen heroes.[408] As the war's outcome began to look less certain for Germany, a newspaper editorial in 1943 exhorted the population of Dortmund in these familiar terms, but with a perhaps more desperate tone.

> We understand now far more clearly and soberly, that the true spirit of Christmas time and Light-belief in times of huge and fundamental decisions between light and dark, between life and death, requires a belief in the fight![409]

When in 1941 Christmas candles were rationed there was a wider metaphoric resonance. By 1941, with the German army fighting in the east, candles had become a

---

[406] *Weihnachten: Material für die Kulturarbeit im Kriege* (Berlin: Herausgegben von der Reichsjugendfuehrung, 1940), p.39.
[407] Stadtarchiv Dortmund, Signatur 424-1, wartime scrapbook of city archivist Luise von Winterfeld, newspaper report, 24 December 1941.
[408] Judith Breuer, *Von wegen Heilige Nacht! Das Weihnachtsfest in der politischen Propaganda*, pp.107-163.
[409] Stadtarchiv Dortmund, Signatur 424-1, newspaper report, 23 December 1943.

precious source of light for the armed forces, where the difficulties of the war made for erratic electricity supplies. The war now darkened not only the streets through the blackout, but in homes too. As a newspaper report put it, ̲if fewer lights shine on the Christmas tree this year, it is for the good of our soldiers in the East.'[410] But the enthusiasm of the Party for commandeering the spirit of Christmas seems to have faltered as the war became more difficult. How well the revamped idea of Christmas was accepted is a matter of some conjecture. Perry argues that, rather than being unpopular or unproductive for the state, the ritual and performance of Christmas was one that strengthened it. In his words, ̲The state and its citizens contested the meanings of Christmas, but in sum, the holiday effectively naturalized National Socialist ideology and enlisted popular participation in regime agendas.'[411] But this is underestimating the difficulties the state had in controlling the meaning of Christmas. The attention drawn to it through officials on the radio or in the press could have a negative impact, with each successive Christmas a marker of how many years the war had now been fought, amid the increasing strictures on public life and the domestic economy. The blackout remained, but the Christmas celebrations grew dimmer. As with the rationed candles, the key here is the beginning of the war with Russia. References to Christmas on German radio on the Christmas Eves' of 1940-1942 gradually declined, and an analysis of BBC Monitoring reports from Germany showed a marked switch in tone as well. The second wartime Christmas in 1940 had a wealth of speeches devoted to talking about the festivities, though they were marked by a distinct emphasis on its Germanic rather than Christian roots. Indeed, only Hess in his talk that evening referred to its religious meaning. The declining interest in referring to Christmas, amid increasing deprivation on the home front, indicates some faltering of will of the state to control the manner in which people celebrated Christmas. By 1942,

---

[410] Ibid., newspaper report, 1 December 1941.
[411] Joe Perry, 'Nazifying Christmas: Political Culture and Popular Celebration in the Third Reich', *Central European History,* 38/4 (2005), p.574.

references to what people would have to do without were markedly fewer, against an increase in sentiment of the type venerating the sacrifice of those at the front.[412]

Chart 6.1 - References to Christmas in broadcast news items and front reports, Christmas Eve, 1940-1942[413]

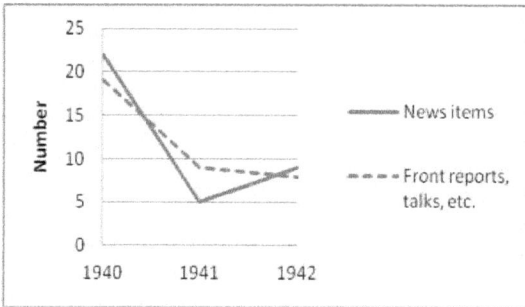

This followed a general pattern in Germany of neutralising discussion on the radio of anything that might engender a political reaction. The increasing privations of Christmas, which in peacetime had been a festival of plenty, became too politically sensitive for the state to contest its symbolism. That the flares marking the RAF's bombing runs over blacked out German cities became known by the population as ‚Christmas Trees' - surely as much an ironic as an aesthetic observation - is a measure of the Nazis' control over the meaning of its Christmas. In fact the enthusiasm for Nazified holidays and traditional ceremonies was never strong before the war, and during it became even less so. An SD report in 1943 wrote that

> [w]hile the church ceremonies are gaining greatly in popularity, the national socialist marriage, christening, and funeral ceremonies, which even in peacetime were few in number, have declined still further... The failure of the national socialist rites of passage to make a deep impression is less the result of superficial flaws and inadequacies and more the consequence of the lack of a religious element.[414]

---

[412] Hans Speier Ernst Kris, *German Radio Propaganda: Report on Home Broadcasts During the War* (London: Oxford University Press, 1944), pp.336-339.
[413] Ibid., p.337.
[414] Cited in Thomas Rohkrämer, *A Single Communal Faith?: the German Right from Conservatism to National Socialism* (Berghahn, 2007), p.222.

It would seem that the lack of interest Goebbels and Hitler had in developing a more

existential philosophy for National Socialism created a vacuum for ritual, which the

more established religions gradually began to fill again.

Goebbels, as the state's chief propagandist, was altogether more comfortable in

envisioning a role for the arts in stimulating the wartime population. According to him:

> We must work from the belief that the darker the streets are, the brighter our
> theatres and cinemas must shine. The darker the times, the brighter art must
> shine over it, as consoler of the human soul.[415]

The blackout had a marked effect on the cultural life of the nation. The organisation

and indeed the availability of a nation's culture was emblematic of its civilization. The

collapse in the nightlife of towns and cities, and in particular in Britain with the rapid

closing down of cinemas, theatres and concert halls at the start of the war, was

disastrous not only for the creative industries themselves, but for morale as well.[416] The

narrator of J.B. Priestley's thriller *The Blackout in Gretley*, published in 1942, was

scathing in his view of it.

> I could just find my way to the exit, but beyond there was a terrific black-out.
> Now I hate the black-out anywhere. It's been one of the mistakes of this war.
> There's something timid, bewildered, Munich-minded about it. If I'd my way, I'd
> take a chance right up to the moment the bombers were overhead rather than
> endure this daily misery of darkened streets and blind walls. There's something
> degrading about it. We never should have allowed those black-hearted outcasts
> to darken half the world. It's a kind of tribute, an acknowledgement, of their
> power. We can almost hear those madmen chuckling as they think of us
> groping in the gloom they wished upon us. We make a darkness to fit the
> darkness deep in their rotten hearts.[417]

If it is not clear from this passage whether the ¸black-hearted outcasts' are the Nazis or

an altogether more nebulous ¸they' – the inventors of the blackout and bombing, or the

---

[415] Hans-Joerg Koch, *Wunschkonzert: Unterhaltungsmusik und Propaganda im Rundfunk des Dritten Reiches* (Graz: Ares Verlag, 2006), p.68.
[416] Lant notes that in the later revival of cinema going in Britain the blacked out streets made a curious intersection with the blacked out interior of the cinemas; ¸a double experience of consuming films and stumbling through the wartime night.' Lant, *Blackout: Reinventing Women for Wartime British Cinema*, p.127.
[417] J.B. Priestley, *The Blackout in Gretley* (London: Heinemann, 1942), p.9.

politicians whose decisions led to it – then perhaps it is deliberate. The pessimism that the blackout engendered in Britain was a threat to any social and political coherency on the home front. The first few months of the war found a severe retraction in night-time entertainment as a result of the restrictions and the threat of bombing, and the audience for plays, for concerts, and for films declined dramatically. Light had made public life in the evenings possible, and because the war began during autumn, the longer nights heightened the anxiety of the war and the impact of the blackout. Londoners saw their entertainment drastically reduced, and the pattern was repeated across the country's towns and cities. The *Manchester Evening News* noted that:

> The black out has done sad things to the dance band world. It has meant practically the end of the golf club, rugger, hockey, and charity dances which are usually held continuously from now until the end of April, and the small bands have had to break up. One saxophonist I know is helping to build aeroplanes, a trombone player is working in a flour mill, and a drummer is working for a joiner.[418]

Unemployed actors and actresses even applied to escort children being evacuated to Canada.[419] As a result of greater numbers of people staying at home, the BBC gained an expanding audience at the expense of public venues across the country. Cinemas in both countries would eventually recover and see record levels of admissions by the war's end, as people grew used to the dark and sought an escape from the war. However, the impact of the blackout on elite arts was too great for the British government to ignore. The impact on what was regarded as high culture was such that the blackout became one of the principal motors for the beginning of state funding of the arts in Britain. Jörn Weingartner's study locates it specifically during the long blacked out winter of 1939-1940 with the establishment of the Committee for the Encouragement of Music and the Arts (CEMA).[420] When the war began, Britain began

---

[418] 'Bands Break Up', *Manchester Evening News*, 9 November 1939.
[419] Robert Hewison, *Under Siege: Literary Life in London 1939-1945* (London: Methuen, 1988), p.23.
[420] See Jörn Weingärtner, *The Arts as a Weapon of War: Britain and the Shaping of the National Morale in the Second World War* (London: Tauris, 2006). CEMA was not established in Northern Ireland until 1943. On this, see Gillian McIntosh, 'CEMA and the National Anthem: The Arts and the State in Postwar Northern Ireland', *New Hibernia Review / Iris Éireannach Nua*, 5/3 (2001).

to formalise the patronage of the arts by the state in a way that other European countries had already been doing since the seventeenth century. Though Keynes had argued in 1936 for state support of the arts, in preference to its exploitation and incidental destruction... by prostituting it for the purposes of financial gain', pre-war attempts at mobilising state support had faltered, with the poor economy contributing to a lack of appetite within government to involve itself. But as the first few months of the war saw a collapse in the nation's cultural life, concern over the morale of the nation as a result of the war's impact acted as an accelerator for state intervention. The character of the art promoted by CEMA ran along the familiar lines of Reith's BBC. The BBC's pre-war preference for high-culture over more popular forms of music hall and variety had been criticized as didactic and patronizing, bringing a defence from Reith that it was Better to overestimate the mentality of the public than to underestimate it.'[421] While the BBC had to rapidly alter its programming policy for the demands of the wartime audience, CEMA's focus on high art – opera, straight drama, classical music – was very much a policy geared towards supporting an elite culture that would have withered without the support of the Treasury. Though CEMA began in January 1940 as a private trust, when Keynes became CEMA's chairman in 1942 it was fully funded by the government.[422] Such was its success that by 1943 Keynes was able to write in *The Times* that:

> The leading symphony orchestras and string orchestras, most of the painters, and a large majority (I think I can now say) of the opera, ballet, and drama companies in the country pursuing a serious artistic purpose are working in occasional or continuous association with us.[423]

Post-war, CEMA would evolve into the now familiar Arts Council. Art and morale also held implications for the nation's security – at least within the minds of the Cabinet. Blacked out trains were now awkward spaces to entertain oneself, a fact which the

---

[421] Cited in Siân Nicholas, 'The People's Radio: the BBC and its Audience 1939-1945', in Nick Hayes & Jeff Hill (ed.), *'Millions Like Us?': British Culture in the Second World War* (London: Liverpool University Press, 1999), pp.62-92, p.65.
[422] James Heilbrun, 'Keynes and the Economics of the Arts', *Journal of Cultural Economics*, 8/2 (1984), pp.38-39.
[423] J.M. Keynes, 'The Arts in War-time', *The Times*, 11 May 1943, p.2.

extravagantly named *Committee on Issue of Warnings Against Discussion of Confidential Matters in Public Places* was quick to realize.

> It occurred to us that the dimly-lit railway carriage on night journeys is a very fertile breeding ground for indiscreet talk with or in the presence of strangers. The suggestion was accordingly made that phosphorescent warnings might be placed in railway carriages, but this proposal was rejected, both on account of the cost, and the fact that people would be tempted, to scratch them off. We feel that the best remedy would be to devise some means of allowing sufficient light to enable people to read rather than to talk. In this connexion, we note that the Ministry of Transport have decided to increase the lighting of railway carriages on long-distance night journeys, and we therefore hope that the Ministry of Home Security may see their way to extending this concession to cover all night train journeys.[424]

Books on rail journeys, particularly the longer ones, served to distract and occupy the mind. In his study of literary life during the war in Britain, Hewison wonders if a book by the very fact it constituted an organised view of the world, might supply a pattern or a sense of harmony missing from uncertain wartime existence.'[425] Being occupied and quiet was better for national security than being bored and talkative, and official concern at the potential for the undirected boredom of the blackout filtered into public life too. For those wanting more structured activities, entertaining oneself through the blackout could also take rather more prosaic turns. Local blackout clubs were formed such the Collyhurst Cheerful Chums', which promised

> something different for all ages and both sexes. Fathers and mothers, husbands and wives, sons and daughters, friends and lovers can all become chums... Mr Len Hutton, the all-England cricketer, and his wife will be there, and the programme will include joyful singing, cheery talks, bright music, happy laughter and bright comradeship.'[426]

For those seeking lonelier pursuits there was now a new opportunity for stargazing. The darkened cities, largely absent of the glow of streetlamps, revealed a night sky more familiar to those who lived in the countryside. Perhaps more pertinently, the phases of the moon became a key consideration in the public's security. Various charts, some of which could be quite elaborate, appeared in newspapers allowing

---

[424] TNA, CAB 67/2/38, minutes of the Committee on Issue of Warnings Against Discussion of Confidential Matters in Public Places, 13 November 1939.
[425] Hewison, *Under Siege: Literary Life in London 1939-1945*, p.94.
[426] 'Collyhurst Cheerful Chums', *The Manchester Evening News*, 4 November 1939, p.3.

people to note the days on which the moon was at its brightest, and so more likely a

night for a bombing raid.

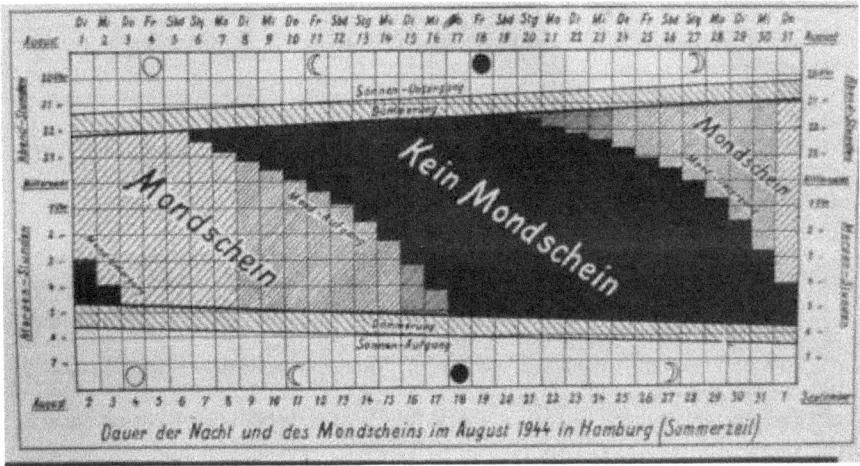

German moonlight chart. Taken from the *Hamburger Fremdenblatt*, 27 July 1944, p.1. 'Mondschein' translates as moonlight.

But when the moon was in shadow and the blackout at its most effective, the stars

again became more visible. Children's blackout activity books guided readers across

the sky, naming the constellations.[427] At the BBC, programmes on astronomy were

quick to take advantage of the rising interest in the night sky. The very first of these

outlined what could be seen from Britain in October, the war having done one good

turn to those of us who live in large towns by giving us back the stars'. An almost full

eclipse of the moon later that month was trailed with the words it'll be something for

air-raid wardens and other night watchers to enjoy, and we'll hope that's *all* there'll be

in the sky for them to see.'[428] The theme of the blackout was also incorporated into

programming. A comedy show from 1940, rather awkwardly titled Blackouts for the

Blackout', promised blackout sketches and a little song or two' and ablackout to black

all the blues out; the censor won't stop us from giving the news out.'[429] Programming of

this kind was part of a response at the BBC to vary its schedule for its expanding

---

[427] Evelyn August, *The Black-Out Book* (London: Osprey, 2009).
[428] BBC Written Archives, T115-116, Home Service script, [undated] October 1939.
[429] BBC Written Archives, Blackouts for the Blackout', 3 December 1940, Home Service

wartime audience, and the radio was peculiarly suited to the construction of some

semblance of a unified public. Through it the listener was transported into an

immaterial world, what Priestley called a _blackout of closed eyes', to find on the other

side a _richwonderland of memory, reflection, imagination.'[430] But the war had caught

the BBC in a dilemma between broadcasting to the nation in serious times while at the

same time maintaining its levity. In wartime Britain, the German *Volksgemeinschaft*'s

principle of the _community before the individual' was one that political and cultural

elites had to quickly establish. Programme policy makers at the BBC discussed how

they could iterate the strength and unity of the nation under wartime conditions, and

early discussions were held on how best to mitigate the class differences that the

blackout had begun to highlight amongst the BBC's audience. With more people at

home, their entertainment had to be found through, amongst other activities, the radio.

As a consequence the BBC's audience mushroomed, and it became increasingly

sensitive to the mood of the nation and its role in the war.[431] A memorandum of 16

September 1939 cautioned against the scheduling of either too many escapist or

highbrow items, now that so much of the population - what one memorandum referred

to as its expanded and more _lowbrow' audience - was forced to listen to radio through

blackout conditions.[432] Further memoranda argued that comfort for the audience could

be found in widening the scope of programming to reflect _life in different parts of the

country.'[433] As another respondent put it, _Wales would like to hear the unaffected

voice, thoughts and good cheer of the Scotsman, the Northcountryman, the Devonian

and the Londoner', and vice-versa.[434] By expanding the BBC's audience, the blackout

formed part of the process by which the nation was represented through its culture, and

discussions at the BBC about constructing something analogous to the idea of the

people's community through its radio programming were part of a wider discourse,

[430] Cited in Patrick Deer, *Culture in Camouflage* (Oxford: Oxford University Press, 2009), p.140.
[431] Nicholas, 'The People's Radio: the BBC and its Audience 1939-1945', pp.68-70.
[432] BBC Written Archives, Box R34/3161, _Programmes', 16 September 1939.
[433] BBC Written Archives, Box R34/3161, _Broadcast Programmes', 27 September 1939.
[434] BBC Written Archives, Box R34/3161, _Broadcast Programmes', 22 September 1939.

propagated by the media and government throughout the war, of a coherent national wartime identity.[435]

As in Britain, radio had a huge impact in how the German state communicated to its wartime population. If the airplane had changed the face of war since its invention, it was no less true of the invention of radio's impact of the German Home Front. In an article published in 1938, Goebbels wrote that:

> It would not have been possible for us to take power or to use it in the ways we have without the radio and the airplane. It is no exaggeration to say that the German revolution, at least in the form it took, would have been impossible without the airplane and the radio.[436]

So firm was the relationship between state propaganda and the radio in Germany, that the most popular model of radio – the *Volksempfänger* or People's Receiver – became colloquially known as *Goebbels' Schnauze*, or Goebbels' Gob. However, the relationship between the Party and the radio audience was by no means straightforward. The Party's preference was for public spectacle, where it could both see, and orchestrate, its propaganda. Public life was where the Party and its myriad officials could be sure it retained control. The domestic pleasures of the radio set were far less certain, and this meant a shift in power from the public to the private - or perhaps rather the domestic - sphere. Surveys conducted at the time noted the effect this had on public discourse.

> Radio takes people out of the public sphere and meets them again in the familial circle. It gives the home a new centre around which to fix. Certainly, there have been any number of attempts to re-establish the old public sphere for the radio. Listening works shops were founded. But they can't change the fact that the natural community for the reception of radio is the family.[437]

---

[435] Rose, *Which People's War? National Identity and Citizenship in Britain, 1939-1945*, pp.1-28.

[436] Joseph Goebbels, "'Der Rundfunk als achte Großmacht," Signale der neuen Zeit', *25 ausgewählte Reden von Dr. Joseph Goebbels* (Munich: Zentralverlag der NSDAP, 1938), pp.197-207.

[437] Peck, cited in Kate Lacey, *Feminine Frequencies: Gender, German Radio, and the Public Sphere, 1923-1945* (Michigan: University of Michigan Press, 1996), pp.99-100.

The blackout's effect of limiting the possibilities for life outside of the home in the evening heightened this, and its impact extended beyond the streets and into the culture and mind of the nation. Recognising the dangers of a housebound home front, propaganda in Germany encouraged the population to leave the house during the evenings and to entertain themselves. The Party paid particular attention to the distractions of the population from the war and overcoming the blackout's effect on night-time entertainment.[438] A comic strip published in early 1940 to demonstrate good wartime family behaviour shows a husband chastised by his wife for buying theatre tickets - Going to the theatre in these serious times? And in the darkness!' - only for his wife to remark in the final frame You were right – sometimes you just have go to the theatre; you start to think of new things.'[439] Yet the importance of radio for securing the morale of the home front gave it paramount importance in Nazi Germany. When the Party took power in 1933, it centralized and purified' control over the airwaves, sacking those who were either racially or politically undesirable. Though broadcasting was nominally independent from the state in 1933, the Party began to dictate the diet of programming which, despite Goebbels's instructions to the contrary, carried a heavy dose of overt political propaganda – fifty speeches by Hitler were broadcast in 1933 alone. Adjustments made over the years to foster an entertaining mix of programming were primarily made to retain the attention of the audience. By 1939 the diet of programming had been re-oriented towards light entertainment.[440] Foreign broadcasters were available to listeners throughout this period, and throughout the war the radio was the one glaring chink through which foreign propaganda could leak through. To mitigate this the most popular set was built with a reduced range for picking up radio signals. Technical solutions were not enough however, and the penalties for listening to foreign broadcasts could be extraordinarily high.[441]

---

[438] *Deutschland-Berichte der Sozialdemokratischen Partei Deutschlands (Sopade) 1934-1940*, p.177.
[439] Ibid., p.175.
[440] Micheal Burleigh, *The Third Reich: a New History* (London: Pan, 2001).
[441] Noakes, *Nazism 1919-1945, Volume 4, The German Home Front in World War II*, pp.124-128.

Entertainment, rather than propaganda, became more than a need for distraction for a population labouring under the strains of war. Ross writes:

> When, in the final months of the war, broadcasters temporarily deviated from the cheery prime-time format, it triggered widespread grumbling that too little light and entertainment music is being broadcast. Instead one hears some –Opus 296" or the like that would be better placed in the late-night slot.[442]

The danger was that dissatisfied listeners would turn their dial and possibly come across one of the foreign broadcasters. Striking the right note for entertaining a radio audience hemmed in by the blackout was a concern for both countries. As with public space, the blackout had a specific impact on the compression of the public sphere; though it expanded their audience, broadcasters had to mitigate the divisive effects of propaganda and class or regional differences in their programming.

The strangeness of the blackout

In Britain, the most notable response from artists to the blackout came from the change it brought to the atmosphere of the streets and landscape of Britain. There was, in this darkened world, a sense of a return to a life not seen since before the industrial revolution, and with it came different ways of seeing modern civilization and the war itself. In Britain, an articulation of the strangeness of the wartime home front was not left to the spiritualists and astrologers. Deer writes that many of the –topnotchers" of the literary world were summoning up ghosts and the uncanny in their writing in order to explore the hallucinatory aspects and psychic disturbances of life in the blackout.[443] As seen in chapter four, the paradox of the blackout was that its role in protecting the safety of the community had profound implications for the sense of personal security. The blacked out public space made people more aware of themselves and their surroundings, and caused them to draw into themselves; the blacked out city was

---

[442] Ross, *Media and the Making of Modern Germany: Mass Communications, Society, and Politics from the Empire to the Third Reich*, p.374.
[443] Deer, *Culture in Camouflage*, p.154.

private as well as public. If the extract from Priestley's book above showed a political response to the blackout, the following case studies are far more ambiguous in their interpretation.[444] What they have in common is a response to the blackout that is more troubling than reassuring, one that complicated the usual discourses of patriotism and community of the people's war. In the case of the following example, the effect was what Brooke describes as a 'working against a narrative of a comprehensible, public world,' instead evoking a 'world of private meaning and desire.'[445]

The writer Elizabeth Bowen engages with this in probably her most famous short story, *Mysterious Kôr*, published in 1944. In it, her protagonist Pepita wanders the streets of a moonlit London, with the relief of light on the darkenened buildings making it seem like 'the moon's capital.' In this half-lit world, Pepita is inspired by a poem to imagine an empty, immutable analogue of London, Kôr, a city without history and whose rhythms are dictated by her own imagination. Asked by her boyfriend why there should be such a place, she says:

> 'Every thing and place had been found and marked on some map; so what wasn't marked on any map couldn't be there at all. So *they* thought: that was why he wrote the poem. "The world is disenchanted," it goes on. That was what set me off hating civilization.'
>
> 'Well, cheer up,' he said; 'there isn't much of it left.'
>
> 'Oh yes, I cheered up some time ago... If you can blow whole places out of existence, you can blow whole places into it... By the time we've come to the end, Kôr may be the one city left: the abiding city. I should laugh.'[446]

Moonlit London becomes a liminal space between what she experiences as reality, and what her imagination can fashion from its blacked out streets. Traffic lights no longer regulate the passing of traffic but count out strange minutes, lit by gases flowing

---

[444] For a wider survey of British films that utilise the blackout in their narrative see Lant, *Blackout: Reinventing Women for Wartime British Cinema*, pp.114-152. For a discussion beyond film see also Deer, *Culture in Camouflage*, pp.106-191.

[445] Stephen Brooke, 'War and the Nude: The Photography of Bill Brandt in the 1940s', *Journal of British Studies*, 45/1 (2006), p.138.

[446] Elizabeth Bowen, 'Mysterious Kôr', in Anne Boston (ed.), *Wave Me Goodbye* (London: Virago, 1999), pp.162-176, p.164.

through them. The sun and moon revolve, but at a frequency entirely of their own

whim. There is a sense of independence from other people, from the laws of society.

Kôr is a desolate city, and London at night is too opppressive for others to venture out.

> The Germans no longer came by the full moon. Something more immaterial
> seemed to threaten, and to be keeping people at home. This day between days,
> this extra tax, was perhaps more than senses and nerves could bear. People
> stayed indoors with a fervour that could be felt: the buildings strained with
> battened-down human life, but not a beam, not a voice, not a note from a radio
> escaped. Now and then under the streets and buildings the earth rumbled: the
> underground sounded loudest at this time.[447]

Bowen's protagonist internalises her own perception of public space, and finds within it

a place to imaginatively express her own thoughts, emotions and desires. This

psychological treatment of the blackout was common across Bowen's output during the

war. Corcoran writes of her work that it is as though, just as the interiors of London are

being opened up by the bombs, human psychology is being opened up to its formative

psycho-sexual patternings or stresses.'[448] In *Mysterious Kôr*, the blackout allows for a

recovery of mystery that civilization had tamed. In this way she was similar to writers

such as Arthur Machen and M. R. James, exploring fiction's possibilities for revealing a

forgotten or imagined past. Here then we can see that the blackout was a liberation;

just as it could be exciting for some people, it could also provide inspiration for a way of

seeing more openly. That this should be so is perhaps not surprising; as discussed in

the previous chapter, the blackout allowed for certain expressions of sexual and

criminal behaviour that was otherwise less possible in peacetime society, as well as a

heightened awareness of them.

Bowen's work in this period was a great influence on the photographer Bill Brandt, and

his photographs of moonlit London mine a similar vein of mystery that Bowen explores

in *Kôr*. Brooke writes that Brandt

---

[447] Ibid., p.162.
[448] Neil Corcoran, *Elizabeth Bowen: the Enforced Return* (Oxford: Oxford University Press, 2004), p.155.

remarked upon the brooding fantasy hidden in [London's] stones' and the surreal vista opened up by the blackout: [quotes Brandt] for a minute or two this street in Bayswater had something of the dream-like atmosphere of an Italian piazza in a Chirico painting.'[449]

Brandt's sense of self is important here. Born in Hamburg, he would later reject his German origins and style himself as an Englishman. Yet for all his attempts to blend in with his adopted homeland, his success as a photographer arguably stemmed from his alien eye. Brandt's early work had explored surrealism, but he built his reputation during the 1930s through a series of projects that cast his outsider's eye over the quirks of English society, and finding again a strangeness within the British landscape. In 1938 he published a set of pictures under the title of *A Night in London,* inspired by Brassai's own photographs of the Parisian night, a project that would prepare him well when he returned to photographing a entirely blacked out London in September 1939.[450] At the beginning of the war Brandt's was a documentary style, and his shots of huddled people sleeping in underground stations during air raids are perhaps the most familiar of his images. Yet these images in themselves are a strange mix of the private and the public. His blackout work allowed him to return to his training in surrealism and explore that strange liminal space used by Bowen in similar ways. Moonlight, the photographer's only source for taking pictures at night during the war, had a bewitching effect for Brandt. In his words:

> Moonlit scenes always have a very peaceful if not desolate atmosphere. The housefronts and rows of buildings in the street may sometimes appear almost eerily ghostlike. This deadness is what an effective moonlight picture tries to catch.[451]

Brandt's pictures are dialogues between shades of grey and black, echoing the dreamy and mysterious world of a dark and desolate London, and the psychology it inspires. This dream state that the blackout inspired was accompanied with intimations of new and different sexual freedom. The themes Brandt covered during the war echoed in his

---

[449] Brooke, 'War and the Nude: The Photography of Bill Brandt in the 1940s'.
[450] See Paul Delany, *Bill Brandt: a Life* (Chicago: Stanford University Press, 2004).
[451] Cited in Ibid., p.166.

post-war work with female nudes; photos that _mapped a dark and often surreal world of sexual and psychological obsession.'[452] By the end of the war Brandt's taste for reportage had diminished, and he was rediscovering the more private interpretations of surrealism. One of his last commissions for *Picture Post* in May 1945, _The Magic Lantern of a Car's Headlights', is his most vivid attempt at capturing strangeness of the blackout, though this time in a rural setting. The interplay between the modern and the dreamlike darkness is vividly played on by the photograph's captions, the car's flying headlights illuminating the mysteries of the passing world of a blacked out and rural Britain; one strange and out of time. One caption reads:

> Signposts they call them. But at night they look more like incantations, secret messages, or warnings of mysterious dangers that lie brooding in the night.

Another:

> The car is almost on them before they are aware. He pulls her near to him for protection. And, when the lights vanish down the land, the darkness is far darker than it was before.[453]

This psycho-sexual quality of the blackout was again prominent in one of Powell and Pressburger's more peculiar wartime films, *A Canterbury Tale*, released in 1944. In it, an American sergeant is waylaid on his journey to Canterbury by disembarking too early at the blacked out village station of Chillingbourne, confused by the dark and the shouts of the station master. Along with a British soldier and a newly arrived landgirl, he makes his way to the village to rest before the next morning's train. But on the way the girl is attacked. A man, under the cover of darkness, throws glue into her hair and runs away. A short chase comes to nothing, but they learn that the girl's misfortune is one of a series in the village; many girls have been attacked by _the glue man'. Their attempts to unmask the glue man form the spine of the film, over which a curious mesh of themes of nostalgia, English history, identity, religion, sexual freedom, thwarted

---

[452] Brooke, 'War and the Nude: The Photography of Bill Brandt in the 1940s', p.119.
[453] Bill Brandt, 'The Magic Lantern of a Car's Headlights', *The Picture Post*, 31 March 1945, p.13-17.

happiness, the war itself, and human's place within the universe, are all a part. It is a fascinating mess.

In contrast with Bowen and Brandt's work this is a less personal representation of the blackout. But its relevance here is that it shares with them the exploration of the blackout as a site of both freedom and threat, and makes an altogether strange use of it. This is most telling in the motivations of the glue man, unmasked as the village magistrate, a gentlemen farmer and amateur historian. Excited at the potential for lecturing the locally billeted soldiery on the area's history, he forms a growing resentment of the distraction the landgirls become for them, to the detriment of the attendance of his lectures. Attacking the girls during the blackout keeps them away from the barracks, and frees up the soldier's time to attend his lectures. A strange conceit for a film certainly, and it was not terribly popular with audiences; an indifferent review in The Times called it ̲incompletely successful'[454]. Peter von Bagh notes that more than other films of the period, A Canterbury Tale is almost ̲reaching for another reality'.[455] The blackout in this film becomes, amidst the hotch-potch of ideas on offer, a contested site of personal liberty and sexual morality versus a more existential appreciation of humanity's - and indeed England's - place in the world. The film positions the viewer to admire the history of the country, and to reflect on what has been lost. Indeed, it begins with a sequence following pilgrims marching to Canterbury in the 14th century, that quickly jumps to the present day, with armoured vehicles careening along the same hills. The bachelor figure of the glue man, whose signature act may be read for what it is or else as representing a repressed sexual violence against women, is custodian of this history. By the film's conclusion the viewer is never certain if they are to pity him or in some way approve of him.

---

[454] 'A Canterbury Tale: a Chaucerian Romance', The Times, 10 May 1944, p.6.
[455] Peter von Bagh, 2006, A Tribute: A Canterbury Tale, criterion.com,
[http://www.criterion.com/current/posts/432-a-tribute-a-canterbury-tale], last accessed 20 July 2010. See also Tison Pugh, 'Perverse Pastoralism and Medieval Melancholia in Powell and Pressburger's 'A Canterbury Tale", Arthurania, 19/3 (2009).

Though the three examples given here by no means offer a comprehensive or unified interpretation of the blackout, when read against the popular memory of the blackout as a banal intrusion in daily life this is precisely what makes them interesting. What they do share is a representation of the blackout that reorients its public, community focus towards one that recognises its impact on private worlds, and private passions. Six years of near total darkness in the cities, towns and villages of Britain left a space for dreaming, and for an imaginative response to the darkness that has been hidden from its dominant narrative.

Conclusion

The cultural effect of the blackout was diverse and ambiguous. As was also the case in previous chapters, this chapter has argued that the blackout's effect on cultural and political life of both countries could both reify the wartime consensus, and yet also challenge it. In Germany in particular, there was a tension between private responses to the blackout, and a public culture that sought to control the meanings ascribed to light and darkness. This tension between the private and public worlds was something that the blackout exacerbated, as it could act as an inhibitor of public life, causing individuals to withdraw into themselves. Both countries attempted to mitigate the potential effect of the blackout on home front morale through the control and financing of public culture. While the blackout had a constitutive role in the for the wartime community through the system of obligations it imposed on individuals, it could also provide a space for introspection and privacy. For a war which popular memory had emphasised inclusivity and community, this is perhaps an aspect of the blackout that has been ignored.

Chapter Seven – Industry, Labour and Transport

The final part of this study is concerned with the blackout's impact on the wartime economies of Britain and Germany. Because both countries had such comprehensive blackouts, nearly every aspect of the war economy and industry was directly affected by the restrictions. These extended from the shop fronts of streets to the traffic driving along them, to the shipping and transport that delivered their goods over land and sea and waterway, to the factories producing those goods through wartime night shifts. This chapter argues that poor lighting and ventilation through blackout measures was a real problem for wartime productivity. Again, these problems were not restricted to Britain alone, where industry had been unwilling to invest in blackout preparations during peacetime. Despite earlier efforts to raise awareness of blackout measures in Germany, little benefit appears to have been gained, and similar problems to those seen in Britain were encountered in German industry too. The chapter also explains that war productivity was the only real area in which compromise on the blackout restrictions could be negotiated. The restrictions for industry were always more fluid and susceptible to review than those for civilians. Only in the traffic systems of both countries was the safety of civilians a major consideration. In Britain especially, which had higher numbers of cars, the dramatic increase in road accidents at the start of the war provided the greatest test of the blackout's legitimacy during the war.

Industry

If there was a marked difference in planning between Germany and Britain, it lay in the level of preparations undertaken by industry before the war. As outlined in previous chapters, German business groups were involved in blackout and ARP preparation early on, with the first meeting of the ARP committee of the RDI and the Ministry of the Interior as early as 1932.[456] In contrast, preparation within British ARP would not begin in earnest until the Munich crisis. A 1938 report by the Ministry of Works found many businesses to be under the impression that, in the event of war, they would be able to carry on largely as before, albeit with the knowledge that lights would be extinguished on an alarm.[457] The scope of the alterations that would have to be made in peacetime had neither been communicated by government nor planned for by businesses, who were already bridling at the potential expense and impact of the restrictions on their work. For industry in both countries, blacking out a factory or installation was significantly more complex than blacking out a house, and it impacted directly on working conditions, productivity and energy consumption. Preparations were not restricted to the usual system of light locks on doors and blinds over windows, though these were enough of a problem in themselves where tens or hundreds of workers had to pass through. Some factory roofs consisted almost entirely of glass, whose reflective surface would also have to be obscured to avoid the bright glint of moonlight. The more elaborate the design for letting in light during the day, the more elaborate - and expensive – the system had to be for keeping it in at night. Taken overall, the measures required to blackout industry had significant implications for the war economy. This aspect of the blackout has only had little consideration in existing literature on the war, but it is one that is fundamental to understanding the change in working conditions in both countries. The problems encountered by industry in both countries were more often than not identical; factories were built and had to be blacked out in largely the same way, whether they were British or German. There is evidence to support the conclusion that, while German preparations in industry may have had greater prominence during the inter-war, they were nevertheless insufficient when tested in a rolling blackout. This mirrors behaviour amongst the population as a whole. To reprise the argument of preceding chapters, the true difference between the two

---

[456] See BA Berlin, RS36/2715, documents relating to industrial ARP from Deutscher Gemeindestag.
[457] TNA, HO 45/18188, log of conversation with Office of Works, 19 August 1938.

countries lay in the way the existential threat was communicated before the war. This in itself was no guarantee of action, even within a totalitarian society. Asking industry to plan their preparations for potential bombardment was less difficult in Germany when couched in terms of national defence and faith in the National Socialist community. However, diverting actual resources, manpower and time at the factories themselves was a different matter entirely. As will be seen, extensive talk about preparations in Germany did not make for a smoother transition to blackout.

One of the main problems in securing the blackout in premises was the need to let light in during the day. Because relatively few businesses had prepared their buildings before the war, cheap and quick solutions were preferred; it was common to use paint to black out windows. Of course, this was at the expense of being able to regulate the flow of light into and out of premises, and there were several undesirable side-effects to this. Having the windows permanently shut made for poor circulation of air, and workers spent whole days under artificial lighting. In the depths of winter, where the effects of the blackout were more acute, it was possible to arrive at and leave work without having seen sunlight all day. This impacted directly on worker's productivity; not only did artificial light depress them, it was less efficient as a means of lighting production, and led to decreased rates of productivity on the lines. There was also a corresponding impact on the use of electric lighting during the day. With factories permanently blacked out around the clock artificial lighting became necessary for day shifts, which led to a large increase in electrical energy demand and consumption. This was soon recognised as being extremely wasteful for a wartime economy that needed to conserve its sources of coal and gas. In Britain, though changes to the way factories were blacked out were eventually forthcoming, it was still the case in 1944 that many places of work were poorly lit and ventilated, owing to the blackout restrictions. An article in the journal *Public Health* noted that

Some windows are still permanently obscured, others carry mourning borders'
which cut down by about one-half the light which they should give, and the
usual natural ventilation is often cut off, especially at night, with unfortunate
consequences for those working on night shifts.[458]

Alongside this was concern at the drag the blackout would have on industrial

productivity. The inter-war work of the Industrial Health Research Board had already

looked into how labour productivity was affected by environmental pressures such as

temperature, noise, humidity and, most particularly, light. During the winter months,

when the use of artificial light was far higher, the board found a reduction in productivity

when compared with working under natural light.[459] By late 1941, a British lobby group

composed of manufacturers of blinds and shutters set out a case for the restoration of

daylight in factories. Their intent can be interpreted in two ways. Certainly it was made

with no small amount of genuine interest in improving conditions, and the group allied

its case to the government's fuel economy drive and highlighted the improved health

and productivity of the workforce under daylight. But the memoranda of the group again

underscore the inadequacy of pre-war planning in industry, and indeed amongst their

own members, as the following extract illustrates.

> It is perhaps useful to consider why there has been any prejudice against
> shutters and why total obscuration has been recommended for existing
> factories and especially why it is still being recommended in the building of new
> factories... Owing to the urgency of the work firms carried out on factories
> installations which were no more than experiments. There was no time to do the
> usual try out' and preliminary research work, with the result that various types
> though sound in principle failed in practice... In the factories themselves
> shutters were often not given a fair trial... Instances are known where one
> labourer was given the task of opening or closing many ranges of shutters
> perhaps covering thousands of square feet. In those installations which were
> hand operated, this constituted considerable hard work with the result that the
> labourer did everything he could to have as few shutters working as possible.
> He left a proportion closed and the management left it at that and reported to
> the ministry that the shutters were no good.[460]

As a remedy, the note suggests the installation of fully electric mechanisms for closing

blinds and the educating' of managers in their use. It forms a blend of griping at a

---

[458] 'Lighting and ventilation', *Public Health,* 57 (1944).
[459] A.J. McIvor, 'Manual Work, Technology, and Industrial Health, 1918-39', *Medical History,*
31/2 (1987), p.167.
[460] NAS, File GD326/956, Minutes of the Committee for Advocating Daylight in Factories', circa
1942.

stifling bureaucracy, a noble wish to improve wartime productivity, and a thoroughly self-interested one to make money. But the subtext of the note makes clear that there simply wasn't commercial space before the war to market expensive solutions to a problem that, as yet, did not exist – or at least was not popularly acknowledged as such. The effect of this was that manufacturers were neither prepared for the blackout, nor had they developed their systems well enough to cope with it when it began.[461] The commercial exploitation of ARP before the war had generated some less than savoury language in an attempt to create demand, as the following advert for Costain air raid shelters illustrates.

> The bombing of military objectives' – the supposedly unwritten law – gives the enemy bomber pilots all the excuse they require for blasting out of existence any premises, anywhere, which might be suspected' (from a height of thousands of feet!) of housing troops, war departments, arms, ammunition, stores, or factory machinery for making warlike material. Every office block, every big building or group of buildings – even schools – seen from the bombers' altitude may be deemed a target for their devastating rain of destruction and death.[462]

Given the generally ambivalent attitude of the public towards ARP, such language could be unproductive at generating demand in Britain. The militarization of commerce was as likely to be resisted as it was to generate the fear required to invest in a private shelter. However, notwithstanding the commercial opportunities for installing blinds, the case for reintroducing daylight in entirely blacked out factories was taken up by others with an interest in economic productivity once the war began. An article in *Aircraft Engineering* argued for a blend of artificial and natural light where possible, and where not a cheerful' form of high intensity lighting.

---

[461] By 1940 the advantages of designing fully blacked out factories for war production were self evident, and the Douglas Company in California commissioned the building of their Long Beach –Blackout" factory which, amongst other aircraft, built the Boeing B-17 bomber. Entirely windowless, it was the world's first fully air conditioned factory, lit with rigs of 14,000 low power and glare free vapour and fluorescent lights. At peak production the factory was turning out one aircraft every hour. See The Douglas Aircraft Co. ...Building Up for War', Boeing.com, [http://www.boeing.com/history/narrative/n026dou.html], (last accessed 20 September 2010) and Gerrie Schipske, *Rosie the Riveter in Long Beach* (San Francisco: Arcadia Publishing, 2008), pp.9-30.
[462] MOA, Box 23/4/E, Costain Air Raid Shelters, circa 1939.

It appears that no matter how effective the artificial lighting system may be, there is an adverse subconscious effect upon workers who operate entirely under its influence during daylight hours. While it is not feasible to exclude the psychological value of daylight itself, there is every reason to believe that the prime requirements for welfare are bright or cheerful surroundings... fatigue on the part of the worker in a permanently blacked out building is probably largely induced by the knowledge that daylight is present outside, and this fact will obviously be accentuated in situations wherever lighting is notably artificial.[463]

The following table illustrates the levels of production of fine detail work under two different systems of lighting; the first under an old system of lamps, and another under a system using new lamps that dissipated light and heat that was more comfortable for workers, and of a colour more true to daylight.

Table 7.1 – Productive value of better lighting on industrial processes[464]

Process	Foot-candles		Increase of Production
	Old System	New System	
Typesetting by hand	1.3	20	24
Foundry	2.5	7	7.5
Tile Pressing	1	3	6
Silk Weaving	50	100	21
Lathe Work	12	20	12
Post Office (sorting)	3	6	20
Wire Drawing	3	9	17
Roller Bearing Manufacture	5	20	12.5

Adequate lighting was key to maintaining good working conditions and high levels of production. At some factories in Britain medical officers tested new workers' eyesight, and some were prescribed spectacles for fine detailed work, which in certain cases required 100 times more light than for ordinary processes.[465] The will of workers to get behind the war effort was not taken for granted, and in 1940 this was already proving a vexing issue for the government. In particular, Communist party agitation had focussed

---

[463] 'Factory Lighting in War-time', Aircraft Engineering and Aerospace Technology, 12/11 (1940).
[464] Ibid. Note that foot-candle is a non-SI unit for measuring luminance, and is now largely out of use. 1 foot-candle is generally rounded to 10 lux.
[465] N.M.D., 'Review: Ventilation and Heating: Lighting and Seeing', British Journal of Industrial Medicine, 1/2 (1944).

on the poor preparations by government within industrial ARP.[466] A Ministry of Supply

survey of working conditions taken at the beginning of the war identified the increased

psychological strain of working in blacked out factories.

> Heavy engineering shops are not prepossessing places under normal
> conditions but with all the daylight shut out and only purely local artificial light
> the effect was, with one or two exceptions, depressing in the extreme. The
> managements of the various concerns were unanimous that the men were not
> working with their usual energy... Another question is that of getting to and from
> work. As the days shorten this is going to interfere more and more with the
> movements of the workers and the winter-time drop in output is likely to be
> greatly increased. I have discussed it with other industrialists and they feel that
> there might be a gradual reduction in the intensity of the black-out.[467]

Thomas Ling, medical director at the Roffey Park Rehabilitation Centre and an early

pioneer in dealing with stress in industry, argued that while some factories' working

conditions were excellent, the majority are mediocre and the minority leave much to be

desired'.[468] In a review of psychiatric cases referred by the Ministry of Labour to the

outpatient department of Mill Hill hospital, Ling found eight women classed as suffering

from a fatigue state' not seen under peace-time conditions, and somewhat analogous

to the flying stress' of RAF crew.[469] Their number was increasing and noted by GPs.

Ling wrote that it was characterised by irritability, loss of appetite, and the accentuation

of minor difficulties into major wrongs, with some associated anxiety. Disturbance in

gastro-intestinal functions and loss of appetite are common features.' Its occurrence

was precipitated by fatigue under the wartime conditions of factory work, with

Excessive noise, continual blackout and badly organised canteens... that will light up

an underlying psychological disturbance or physical disability.' This was coupled with

the domestic demands of working women:

> The psychiatric history reveals a well-balanced person who is carrying more
> than a fair share of work and responsibility. Many women are working overtime
> in the factory, have substantial journeys to and from work, and then have to do
> domestic work in the evenings and on Sundays. Shopping presents its special

---

[466] Jones, *British Civilians in the Front Line: Air Raids, Productivity and Wartime Culture, 1939-45*, p.47.
[467] TNA, AVIA 22/5, briefing written by Bennett, 27 October 1939.
[468] T.M. Ling, 'Industrial Neuroses', *The Lancet*, 243/6304 (1944), p.830.
[469] On this see Martin Francis, *The Flyer: British Culture and the Royal Air Force, 1939-1945* (Oxford: Oxford University Press, 2008), pp.106-130.

difficulties to those working in the daytime, while husbands still expect a cooked dinner and the family mending done.[470]

The blackout could not be said to be the sole cause of workplace ailments. Early reports of ‚blackout anaemia', with doctors reporting symptoms similar to those mentioned above of ‚pallor, indigestion and lassitude', were likely to have come from a mixture of general anxiety about the war and domestic pressures, which were then compounded by the poor conditions of blacked out factories.[471] But it did nevertheless place huge pressures on the workforce and strained labour relations. This was as true outside of the workplace as within it. In 1940 the Trades Unions Congress made representations to the Home Office complaining of Exeter City Council's refusal to upgrade the city's lighting, in contrast with its neighbour Bristol.[472] The revision of the lighting restrictions to a brighter standard was, as previously discussed, entirely voluntary and at the discretion of local authorities. Though initial complaints blamed the city's Chief Constable for rejecting the new lighting standard, it was later revealed to have been the decision of the council itself to reject it, on the grounds of cost.[473] These costs were not insubstantial. In 1941, when Bristol City Council discussed the desirability of returning to the improved lighting system after the Luftwaffe's raids on the city, it was estimated that the cost of running it would be £13,000 annually, when including the costs of gas and electricity and maintenance of street-lighting - roughly £500,000 in today's money. These considerations had to take account not only of the monetary cost, but the cost of using valuable energy resources. And while these considerations were of course important, some felt that restrictions on public lighting was parsimonious and debilitating. The journal Public Health, in reviewing the Medical Research Council's Industrial Health Research Board's pamphlet on ventilation and lighting, wrote that:

---

[470] Ling, 'Industrial Neuroses', p.831.
[471] 'Industrial Diseases and Accidents in 1939', The Lancet, 237/6133 (1941), p.357.
[472] After the war's first winter in Britain, a new system of lighting was quickly developed to help minimise the blackout's impact on town and city centres. Its adoption, however, was left at the discretion of Local Authorities, and not all cities chose to adopt this system.
[473] Exeter Records Office, ECA ARP Box 19/220, letters circulated between the Home Office, Trades Union Congress and Exeter Town Council, dated May 1940, May 1941.

The Board has not conditioned its tune, so far as lighting is concerned, to excessive demands for fuel economy. Some of the examples of light saving which one finds in public places strike one as being, not economy, but wild extravagance. They save a few pence on lighting at the cost of pounds in the shape of loss of alertness, vigor, and cheerfulness of the people, not to speak of peril to life and limb.[474]

The availability of light during the war was intimately tied to authority, and its presence or absence was a visible marker of that authority's priorities. But this authority was not necessarily that of the management or council or government against the worker. For example, in 1941 at a colliery village near Durham, the miner's lodge asked that the village be blacked out entirely via its main switch on receipt of an air raid warning, much to the inconvenience of villagers.[475] Rather, it was that while the blackout was a universal restriction for civilians, it was a different matter for industry, where a sliding scale of importance determined how severely the blackout had to be applied. Those areas of economic and social life that could be expected to suffer the blackout with no drastic effect on the prosecution of the war, such as the ordinary civilian trade in goods and services, were generally left to deal with the blackout as it was. But where the infrastructure of the war economy demanded it, relaxation of the blackout restrictions was forthcoming; maintaining war production was the overriding concern. The rhetoric of home front mobilisation that had featured so prominently in German was also now peppering the British public sphere, as the following extract from a Ministry of Information leaflet from 1940 illustrates.

The Armed Forces are protecting our homes at very great risk to themselves. They are entitled to the maximum production of arms, equipment and ammunition in order to carry out their duties effectively. The Government will do all in their power to protect the civil population, but *everyone* is in the front line this time. And everyone must be prepared, as a citizen duty, to take a risk.[476]

Lobbying for relaxations in Britain came from all quarters, from trade unions to Ministries themselves, asking the Home Office and Ministry of Aviation for more light to increase productivity and improve safety. Reducing the impact of air raid warnings and

---

[474] 'Lighting and Ventilation', *Public Health*, /57 (1944).
[475] Hansard, Rathbone to Morrison, HC Deb 01 May 1941 vol 371 c554.
[476] TNA, HO 186/2942, 'The air raid warning system: what it is, and how it is operated', circa 1940.

the blackout on production was the main reason for introducing a new air raid message, the ‚purple' or the ‚lights warning', in July 1940. This was not a public signal; rather it was sent by telephone to exempted establishments with external lights or glare in the flight path of enemy aircraft. As a preparatory warning, and to minimise disruption, it was specifically restricted to those responsible for extinguishing lights, and could not be passed on to other workers or districts.

While much work occurred in closed areas, operations such as shipbuilding, shunting yards, mining, quarrying and especially plants with furnaces, such as iron and steel mills, required some measure of flexibility in how the restrictions were applied. These large establishments, which generated intense heat and light, were profoundly useful for enemy pilots flying at night. A report by the Air Ministry in 1940 stated that ‚The industrial undertakings in the Ruhr show up so well that they may be classified as self-illuminated targets.'[477] Between 1938 and the beginning of the war, these trades were aware of the impact the lighting restrictions would have on their work, and clarification of any potential limitations was sought, with a particular concern being the potential bar on night work.[478] Schemes for exemption were conditional on being able to extinguish lights within a minute of an air raid warning, and approval was at the discretion of local Police Chiefs under section 12 of the Police War Instructions.[479] After the Munich Crisis, some premises were beginning to take the initiative to screen their plants in advance of war. Amongst its plans for baffles and screens for its blast furnace, a plant in Cardiff had ordered an experimental ‚mud gun' for covering the glare of molten metal on receipt of an alarm.[480] Yet the extent to which the lighting restrictions were addressed within these larger industries was not uniform before the war, and again

---

[477] TNA, HO 186/1395, ‚Notes on flying conditions at night...', 3 February 1940.
[478] On this see papers contained in TNA, Box BT 64/74, file Lighting Restrictions, and TNA, Box SUPP 3/4, file Lighting Restrictions and Industrial Glare.
[479] TNA, Box SUPP 3/4, ‚Lighting Restrictions and Industrial Glare', ARP Department Circular 194/1939, 26 August 1939.
[480] TNA, Box BT 64/74, ‚Lighting Restrictions', letter from Fennelly to Johnston, 11 November 1938.

much work had to be done to screen them adequately at short notice after war was declared. By 1941 the issue was still being taken up by the British Iron and Steel Federation, arguing for survey flights from the RAF so its members could avoid incurring heavy expenditure, amounting to possibly hundreds of thousands of pounds, over the whole country, quite unnecessarily' if their measures were already sufficient.[481]

Though industrial ARP in Germany well planned in comparison, at least on paper, it is not entirely clear from the records how well it was actually carried out on the ground. Hampe's study is rather vague on the blackout's success in industry, though he does note the familiar difficulties of permanent versus removable blackouts, and how restrictions hampered production.[482] Some measure of its success can be found in reminders sent by government and local officials to businesses, which continued well into the war. By the end of its first month businesses in Hamburg were being reminded to blackout their storage areas; forgivable perhaps, given the slow progress of the war so far, but certainly showing a lack of forethought given the strategic importance of the city.[483] By 1942, however, the police chief was still reminding businesses to blackout correctly, noting that it was not enough to simply black out the lights that fell onto the street - ostensibly those visible to patrols - but that all sides of a building, as well as any outbuildings, must be darkened as well.[484] This particular trick of only blacking out areas that were visible for easy inspection was common throughout the war, and reminders invariably referred to the obligation to protect surrounding neighbourhoods. More indicative of the indifferent success of pre-war preparations is another circular sent by Hamburg's Police Chief to local businesses in March 1943, only a few months before the RAF's devastating Gomorrah raids. The letter stated that given the need to conserve electricity, the permanent blacking out of factory windows with paint was

---

[481] Ibid., Larke to Hodge, 20 October 1941.
[482] Hampe, *Der Zivile Luftschutz im Zweiten Weltkrieg*, p.460.
[483] Stadtarchiv Hamburg, 731-06 I 16, circular from Police Chief, 28 September 1939.
[484] Ibid., circular from Police Chief, 14 April 1942.

undesirable. That this was only identified so far into the war is perhaps a little peculiar.[485] Given these reminders sent out within one city alone, it is evident that the blackout was not executed as thoroughly as it had been planned. The constraints on businesses, which had to divert money, labour and energy to ARP preparations, were the same as those in Britain, and were only tenable where there was funding for it. There were of course instances in both countries where the blackout was either too expensive or impractical to undertake thoroughly. In Germany, a November 1939 employment tribunal in Berlin stated that workers at a factory whose roof was made entirely of glass, and was too expensive to blackout immediately, were not entitled to receive compensation for loss of wages as a result of no longer being able to work nightshifts.[486] This was in common with general practice during the war; when the air raid alarm sounded and workers had to make for the shelter, their pay was stopped until they could work again.[487] Thrifty blackout solutions were also liable to be a false economy. For instance, some shops in Germany had chosen to paint their large display windows black, rather than go to the trouble and expense of arranging a removable screen. The consequence of this was that where lights from inside the shop struck the window they would heat it up, with the dark paint absorbing the light's energy and shattering the pane of glass. With glass a valuable commodity in the wartime economy, such accidents had to be avoided.[488] This sort of clumsiness in implementing the lighting restrictions was not exceptional, and they have a curious place in Nazi society. Few aspects of the war were as tied to the survival of the state as ARP, but poor implementation of it cannot be tied to the forms of dissent or greed normally found in studies of transgression in Nazi Germany. Instead, they share in common with similar cases in Britain the rather more banal reasons of tiredness, ill-consideration or else plain fecklessness. Whether institutional or personal, such cases were common across societies that were forced to do something that impeded their day's work. The extent to

---

[485] Ibid., circular from Police Chief, 3 March 1943.
[486] BA MA, RL41/1, Reports of the RLB, 22 November 1939.
[487] TNA, HO 186/2046, Intelligence memorandum on German ARP, 4 April 1943.
[488] BA MA, RL41/2, Reports of the RLB, 27 March 1940.

which this endangered production in Germany is illustrated in the following excerpt from a 1940 circular of the RLB, which again demonstrates the link made between the prosecution of the war and ARP.

> The prevention of accidents during the war is one the most important tasks of civil defence. Effective preventive measures secures the working environment and ensures higher productivity. From the statements of representatives of commercial trade associations, particular attention must be paid to safety when working in the blackout. They advise:
>
> Be careful when working in the blackout!
>
> Ensure good organisation at your workplace!
>
> Keep areas of traffic clear!
>
> Cover or mark pits, ditches, etc.!
>
> Allow eyes to adjust when moving from bright rooms to darkened areas![489]

As in Britain, maintaining productivity as the frequency of bombing raids increased meant altering the restrictions for industry. By 1943, the movement of goods at railways stations and at factories was no longer interrupted by air raids, and the blackout itself was less restrictive.[490] Though this preference for the rights of the state and the community over individual safety was far from a new thing, it became more evident as the bombing war intensified. Indeed the rights of the community in ARP led to some confusion over the right of private persons to patent inventions that contributed to the blackout. Though the German authorities stated that whoever invented a device or material for the blackout had a right to patent it, this right did not extend to withholding it; improving the blackout system superseded commercial interest. This was, the RLB said, especially true of those persons who for whatever reason have not properly patented their invention and through fear of it being copied keep it secret, and only make it available [privately] for good money.'[491]

---

[489] Ibid., 4 December 1940.
[490] TNA, HO 186/2046, Intelligence memorandum on German ARP, 4 April 1943.
[491] BA MA RL41/, Reports of the RLB, 19 June 1940.

It is difficult to discern how much freedom there was to criticise the industrial blackout and its administration. Certainly the principle itself was not questioned publicly. But given that any improvement made to the blackout must necessarily come from critical appraisal we must assume that it did take place, though certainly not in the form it did in Britain. What is clear is that though the planning of ARP schemes was well in advance of what British industry had undertaken, the general tenor of official worries over blackout adherence during the war in Germany does not indicate that it was any more successful in instilling complete adherence.

Though both countries had problems in implementing their blackout systems in industry, it should not be assumed that they were not to a large degree successful. Strategies for countering the blackout had to be developed by both sides, and these were not limited to the lighting of cities through flare bombs from pathfinder aircraft. Photo reconnaissance provided some of the most valuable intelligence for both sides during the war, and was used variously for gaining an overview of static sites and objectives, enemy movement, damage assessment and support for land operations.[492] But with the blackout obscuring the details of the land at night, aerial reconnaissance photography was initially restricted to daylight operations, with the window for taking photographs changing with the seasons. It was only in 1943 that the RAF and USAAF had begun to put in place night-time reconnaissance photo operations, using Mosquito aircraft equipped with powerful cameras and timed flash bombs to illuminate the landscape. These flights provided vital flight and bombing run data for subsequent bombing operations.[493] However, the flash bombs used to light the ground were unwieldy; highly explosive and therefore dangerous to crews, they were also limited to detonate at set altitudes that were fixed in their fuses. In the cause of developing their

---

[492] For an overview of Allied operations see Robert C. Ehrhart Alexander S. Cochran Jr., John F. Kreis, 'The Tools of Air Intelligence: ULTRA, MAGIC, Photographic Assessment, and the Y-service', in John F. Kreis (ed.), *Piercing the Fog: Intelligence and Army Air Forces Operations in World War II* (Darby: DIANE Publishing, 1996), pp.80-94.
[493] Martin W. Bowman, *Mosquito Photo-reconnaissance Units of World War 2* (Oxford: Osprey, 1999), pp.40-43.

capability in night-time photography beyond this system the American army's photographic laboratory drafted MIT's Harold Edgerton at the beginning of the war. Edgerton was already a pioneer of stroboscopic photography; the art of lighting and photographing brief snatches of movement. Over the course of the war, Edgerton developed a system of electronic photography using strobe mounted aircraft, providing a flexible alternative to flash bombs where low cloud cover prevented their use. Edgerton's trials in England produced remarkable images from a trial of the strobe system over Stonehenge, whose effect seems to light the henge from within.

Lighting experiments conducted over Stonehenge, circa 1943. Taken from MIT's Edgerton Digital Collections, accessed 14 August 2010, [URL: http://edgerton-digital-collections.org/galleries/iconic/observations#hee-nc-44001]

As well as this, both sides had begun to develop early forms of infra-red sighting systems. Already in 1940 a night-fighter variant of the Dornier Do17 became the first aircraft to be equipped with the *Spanner* passive IR system, though the system was not a great success.[494] Primitive IR systems were already being developed for various applications across the Allied and Axis forces, but it was not until 1942 in Germany that it was realized that the *Spanner* system could render the blackout entirely obsolete. The fear was that if Germany had invented an IR system capable of seeing through the blackout, then the Allies may have too. The development was therefore kept secret to maintain public order, and blackout materials, which had to be approved by the state, were afterwards mixed with a chemical additive to reduce light leakage.[495] Yet the

---

[494] Chris Bishop, *The Encyclopedia of Weapons of WWII* (New York: Metrobooks, 2002), p.354.
[495] Hampe, *Der Zivile Luftschutz im Zweiten Weltkrieg*, p.557.

panic was all for nothing; no similar discovery appears to have been made in Britain. Lighting cities by marking runs and fire-bombing was, in all probability, far more efficient than these early IR systems.

Notes on blue light

Blue lights returned to blacked out Europe, though for the most part in Britain they were not as ubiquitous as they were in the First World War. Strolling around London on the first night of the war, an official from the Home Office found some drivers reverting to old habits, incorrectly screening their headlamps with blue filters – though this was marginally better than those driving with no lights on at all.[496] In fact, white light was now the standard for external lighting; blue lights were mainly restricted to the interiors of public transport. Their effect is captured in the following extract from *The Glasgow Herald* from the second week of the war.

> Now that the blue lights in tramcars prevent passengers reading after dusk, now, too, that there is no point in looking out of the windows, travellers, particularly those who have any distance to go, will have to develop a new method of entertainment. Sleeping may be tempting, but it is dangerous, though no more dangerous than merely sitting and brooding on the follies of mankind. There remains only conversation, which has its perils but may be mildly rewarding. But it must be said that the pantomime ghostly tinge that the blue lights give to even the well favoured is no encouragement to make the first remark to the stranger planted at one's side.[497]

But why was blue light favoured? To explain this requires a brief explanation of how the eye perceives light itself. Essentially, the eye's perception of colour alters as the level of illumination reduces. This is a result of how the eye's photoreceptors are structured, which are formed of two sets; cones, which govern colour vision, and rods, which govern night vision. Rods are insensitive to long-wavelength light – reds and yellows – and are coated with the extremely light sensitive pigment rhodopsin, also known as visual purple, which can only appreciate short-wavelength light – that in the blue to

---

[496] TNA, HO 186/200, report of blackout inspection, 2 September 1939.
[497] 'Under the Blue Lights', *The Glasgow Herald*, 12 September 1939, p.6.

violet end of the spectrum. This is why, as night approaches, the eye perceives colours towards this end of spectrum more easily, and why working by red-light does not affect night vision.[498] Hence the prevalence of blue light in blacked out societies, and blue street lamps in the First World War; low levels of blue light are easier for the eye to appreciate. But there were problems with using it. The most significant was that it was rather inefficient in terms of energy used relative to its output. A study of aids for street lighting in 1941 noted that 'The general use of pure blue light involves considerable absorption, and is therefore uneconomical.'[499] Indeed, Hampe notes that the absorption of light by blue filters was as much as 80%.[500] The study also found that 'for some purposes [blue light] is considered inexpedient owing to certain loss in sharpness of outline of objects illuminated when viewed from some little distance away.'[501] This latter problem was caused by the parts of the eye dealing with low-light vision being placed away from the eye's point of focus. Finally, the fact that the eye could perceive blue at lower levels of illumination than longer-wavelength yellow or red light went against the principle of the blackout – low levels of blue light would be more visible to enemy pilots. As Hampe explains, it is one of the curiosities of the war that though blue lights in Germany were initially restricted, by 1940 they were reinstituted in most public spaces. That this happened is not the result of poor research on the part of German scientists, but instead meddling from Hitler's office for short-sighted political and economic ends. When the war began the use of blue light was already frowned upon by officials. Directions sent from the Luftfahrt Ministerium in October 1939 had already sought to correct the use of blue light amongst the public, advising they use screens of grey or black instead.[502] The reversion to a system of blue-lights a year later came directly from Hitler's office, bypassing the advice of technical specialists. The wording

---

[498] Steven Bleicher, *Contemporary Colour Theory and Use* (New York: Thomson Delmar Learning, 2005), pp.7-9.
[499] 'War-time Street Lighting and Aids to Movement in Streets', *British Journal of Ophthalmology*, 25/3 (1941), p.127.
[500] Hampe, *Der Zivile Luftschutz im Zweiten Weltkrieg*, p.555.
[501] 'War-time Street Lighting and Aids to Movement in Streets', p.127.
[502] BA Berlin, R4602/09, circular memorandum from Reichsminister der Luftfahrt, 25 October 1939.

of the original instruction is clear; the new blue light system was on the Führer's orders, and its intent was to lighten the burden of the blackout.[503] The areas where blue lights were now allowed were mainly public spaces; areas of human and vehicle traffic such as roads, entrances for buildings, and public transportation. It also made a concession for the opening of blacked out windows and doors where rooms were lit with a blue light – the examples given being hospitals and bedrooms. Hitler's interference in matters of the blackout shows that he was alive to its effect on the morale of the nation, if not its efficient operation, and he may also have thought the new system a benefit to the movement of goods and night-time working in the blackout. The following year the German Air Ministry issued another memorandum reminding officials and departments of the new blue lights system, the result of Hitler seeing building sites and roads in Berlin still lit with red lights rather than blue.[504] The irony here of course is that red light was less visible from a distance than blue light. The new system was also introduced just as factories were getting to grips with and installing adequate blackout systems under the old regulations. While adapting to it may have brought some relief for the workers, the capital and energy invested over the previous year could not be returned. But perhaps more than this, the poor efficiency of blue lights, seen in the context of the needs of the war economy to be as energy efficient as possible, made the system questionable from a long-term perspective.

Energy efficiency was, in fact, a useful side effect of the blackout. Certainly in Germany, the blackout's effect of dampening energy demand was helpful in making efficient use of limited resources. Even in the eastern reaches of the Reich, which because of their distance from Allied bombers were not subject to as rigorous policing of the blackout as in the west, the blackout restrictions were nevertheless used in some

---

[503] BA MA, R43/II/1298a, circular memorandum from Milch, 22 October 1940.
[504] Ibid., circular memorandum, 6 February 1941.

areas as an energy saving measure.[505] British data on electricity supply during the war shows the extent to which the majority of the country's generating capacity was used for industry. The table below shows that during the period 1940-1943, over which the blackout lasted a full year under generally unchanged regulations, the increase of electricity sent to domestic and commercial premises rose by 8% and 2% respectively, relatively stable and in line with general trends throughout the 1930s. In industry it rose by 48%; a substantial increase. Rises in the amount sent to domestic and commercial premises in 1944, as well as in public lighting, may be attributable to the relaxation of the blackout as the dim-out standards came into force towards the end of year.

Table 7.2 - Electricity consumption in Britain, 1937-1947 (Units given in Terawatt hours)[506]

Year	Domestic and farm premises	Shops, offices and commercial premises	Factories and industrial premises	Public lighting	Traction	Total
1937	4.69	2.94	10.02	0.339	1.180	19.17
1938	5.36	3.11	10.32	0.367	1.249	20.40
1939	5.94	3.12	11.67	0.248	1.261	22.23
1940	6.23	3.00	13.87	0.017	1.147	24.26
1941	6.64	3.27	16.24	0.018	1.143	27.31
1942	6.72	3.26	19.14	0.020	1.148	30.29
1943	6.71	3.06	20.52	0.020	1.142	31.45
1944	7.84	3.51	19.98	0.029	1.169	32.52
1945	8.81	3.48	17.68	0.161	1.236	31.36
1946	11.66	3.89	17.63	0.242	1.369	34.80
1947	12.73	3.97	17.61	0.190	1.361	35.86

While there was no great dip in the overall amount used - with the exception of street lighting, as seen in the chart below - the blackout worked as a brake on the pre-war increase in electricity consumption amongst the population, to the benefit of the war economy. Certainly not every kilowatt in industry went into lighting, but under the extended working hours and blacked out premises, lighting constituted a large part of it.

---

[505] Hampe, *Der Zivile Luftschutz im Zweiten Weltkrieg*, p.558.
[506] BERR, *Electricity supply, availability and consumption 1920-2007*, www.berr.gov.uk/files/file40593.xls, [Last accessed 22 January 2009].

Chart 7.3 - Electricty consumption of public lighting, 1937-1947

The significant fall in energy devoted to external public lighting is indicative of a general fall in external lighting at all exposed industrial sites. By 1943, Churchill was concerned at the extent to which the blackout's effect on the external lighting of factories was hampering production. Given the ‗comparative impotence of enemy bombing', he asked for a review to allow for more external lighting and ‗an assurance that the Air Ministry is not insisting on any restrictions... which hamper production.'[507] The Air Ministry's response was that the Luftwaffe's bomber force was comparatively impotent because it was ‗not thoroughly trained', and so ‗cannot find its way about the country, especially on moonless nights.' It was the Ministry's opinion that allowing for more external lighting at industrial sites would markedly increase the chance of bombers navigating the landscape and finding their targets.[508] The scale on which external lighting had been dampened as a consequence of the blackout restrictions had a limited but useful side-effect in moderating energy usage. It was certainly enough for the Ministry of Fuel and Power to worry in 1945 that the restoration of gas street-lighting, which was more prevalent same parts in Britain than electric lighting, would

---

[507] TNA, PREM 3/93/6, Churchill to Sinclair, 5 July 1943.
[508] Ibid., Air Ministry to Churchill, 8 July 1943.

consume an additional 750,000 tonnes of gas coal at a time when stocks for industry

and domestic use were already extremely low as a result of the war.[509]

Driving and lighting restrictions

The mechanization of society could not only be seen through the spectre of bombing.

From the turn of the century to the start of the war, British and German citizens

witnessed how the use of technology brought changes to all facets of civilization; from

the development of mass communication, to the construction of ever larger ships, the

development of these modern wonders' was a marked feature of the pre-war world.[510]

Within the context of the blackout, the two most important developments were flight

and motor vehicles. Both made a significant impact on how civil society related to its

increasingly mechanized civilization, and how public space was organized and

apprehended by the public. Traffic systems were, in the same way that ARP and

airmindedness were, evolving systems of civil discipline. The increased use of motor

vehicles of all types involved a redefinition of the relationship between the pedestrian

and road traffic, and the place of the pedestrian in the urban infrastructure. In Britain

and Germany, it was the motor vehicle that was privileged in this arrangement. The

traffic regulations brought in under the Nazis in 1934 codified a preference for the

motor vehicle over the rights of the pedestrian.[511] Later in the war, as the bombs left

huge swathes of German cities in ruins, Albert Speer saw an opportunity for urban

renewal, and to manage the expected increase in traffic after the war. In a

memorandum to Hitler, Speer wrote that bombing provided a unique opportunity to

make our cities, after the war, again viable from the traffic viewpoint.'[512] Traffic

management and air raid protection were to be main points on which future German

---

[509] TNA, PREM 4/37/12, Street Lighting', 20 June 1945.
[510] On this see Rieger, *Technology and the Culture of Modernity in Britain and Germany 1890-1945*, pp.21-50.
[511] On this and regulation of behaviour in urban spaces more generally see Elfi Bendikat, 'The Public Urban Space in the Modern Age: Technical Functionality and Regulation', *German Journal of Urban Studies* (41, 2002).
[512] Blank, 'Wartime Daily Life and the Air War on the Home Front', p.446.

cities and architecture would be planned. Within Britain, debates on road safety in the

early years of the war resembled heightened forms of what had been increasingly

discussed throughout the 1930s, as the death toll on the roads climbed. As Luckin

writes:

> It was now claimed by government, the motoring organizations and _moderate‘
> road safety activists that it was naive pedestrian fallibility rather than bad driving
> which frequently determined the severity of road traffic accidents... According to
> this interpretation, motorists must make every effort to adjust to the demands of
> war and the _comprehensive‘ black-out. But even more crucial was the role of
> pedestrians and their readiness to adapt to the disciplines of a fully and
> irreversibly _mechanized‘ civilization.[513]

As in Germany, a pedestrian‘s use of urban and traffic spaces was contingent on them

adapting their behaviour to fit. For Luckin, this implied _nothing less than an emergency

programme in social re-education.‘[514] For as much as people had grown accustomed to

the steady increase in traffic on roads, their safety at night was always contingent on

the availability of light for guiding pedestrians and traffic. Safe passage through cities

meant that pedestrians – who would always come off worse in any accident – would

have to manage their own safety; they were not accorded any special privileges under

the blackout. The status of the pedestrian is therefore an intriguing point of comparison,

and analogies of war were common – in Britain at least – with defenceless pedestrians

pitted against merciless vehicle traffic. It is no exaggeration to say that the lighting

restrictions on traffic and street lighting were lethal, and immediately contentious. The

vagaries of pre-war blackout practices have already been documented, but it is worth

restating again how much was learnt during the first few months of the war when

compared with the preceding years of ARP preparation. This extended from civilian

authorities and the systems written on paper, and marked on tarmac and kerbstone,

through to the behaviour of the public. Fixing the blackout within the home was

bothersome, as was entertaining oneself through it. But in the absence of bombing, few

---

[513] Bill Luckin, 'War on the Roads: Traffic Accidents and Social Tension in Britain, 1939-1945', in Roger Cooter and Bill Luckin (ed.), *Accidents in History: Injuries, Fatalities and Social Relations* (Atlanta: Clio Medica, 1997), pp.234-254, p.236.
[514] Ibid., p.237.

of the criminal dangers of the blackout compared with the enormous death toll it caused in the first dark and wintry months of the war. In writing this section, the discrepancies between sources should be made clear. The uproar generated by traffic accidents in the blackout in Britain is not to be found in Germany. So high was the casualty rate and its potential impact on the morale of the nation that it placed huge pressure on the government's handling of the war and ARP, and difficult questions were asked as to its use in the absence of any threat. While it is certain that the dangers for German pedestrians were no less than they were in Britain, public discussion of the threat from traffic, given the restrictions on opinion and information, is difficult to find, and complicated by an apparent absence of comprehensive traffic death figures in the 41/42 edition of the Reich's statistical yearbook.[515] It may also have been the case that, given lower levels of vehicle ownership in Germany in comparison with Britain, as well as the severe restrictions on petrol use, the traffic was simply not as heavy.[516]

The road accident figures were a severe political problem for the British government. Though the blackout was intended as an instrument of national security, its direct impact on road safety was a glaring paradox that the government had to fix if the blackout was to be kept in place. Questioned in parliament on the level of road accidents in October 1939, the transport minister Euan Wallace's reply that total road deaths had doubled in September 1939 to 1130 from its previous level in 1938 of 554 was met with a ˌgasp of dismay' from the House.[517] A note to the Home Office the following day advised them to undertake consultations with motoring and pedestrians' groups as soon as possible, citing Bonar Law's advice to Asquith that ˌIn war time it is

---

[515] *Statistisches Jahrbuch für das Deutsche Reich* (Berlin: Statistischen Reichsamt, 1942).
[516] Richard Overy, 'Cars, Roads, and Economic Recovery in Germany, 1932-8', *The Economic History Review*, 28/3 (1975), p.470.
[517] HC Deb 18 October 1939 vol. 352 cc851-3; TNA, HO 186/200, memorandum RB to Minister, 19 October 1939.

not merely necessary to be active, you have to seem active as well.'[518] The result was a meeting held by Anderson and Wallace at the Home Office on 6 November with the AA, the RAC, two pedestrians' rights groups - the Safety First Association and the Pedestrians Association - and two groups representing cyclists and motorcyclists. This was a meeting of essentially private road users, and conspicuous by their absence were representatives of commercial transport. This did not go unnoticed. Two days after the meeting a letter from the London Passenger Transport Board arrived at the Home Office complaining that they had not been consulted, especially since they found themselves _with considerable conflicts of view with the private car associations, cyclists associations and people of that sort.'[519] Their omission is indeed curious, given the number of accidents between pedestrians and public transport, and because the stresses of working in blackout conditions for drivers of public transport were considerable, as the following exchange captured by a Mass Observation researcher illustrates.

> A big tough trolley bus driver came in today and said loudly _What dyer think of the blackout?' _Oh' I said _not bad.' _Well' he said _I'm fed up. Do you know at 12 o'clock last night you couldn't see two yards. There'll be an accident - - a bad accident afore long and every few yards there [sic] a great flash as the trolley crosses the points. The police stopped us gannen' but our manager said -go on." Now who's the boss?' He went away fuming. The blackout means too much to his nerves. He'd rather be in the army.[520]

The accident figures formed a base from which to question the very idea of the blackout. An editorial in *The Star* asked why the French system was, in contrast to Britain, so liberal:

> That there is ample room for discussion is shown by the report we have published from the _Autocar' to the effect that in Paris streets are lighted, traffic can travel at normal speeds, and motorists are only compelled to put a blue wash over their lamps. The practice there is based on the confidence that in an air raid nobody but a lunatic would leave lights on, and lunatics could be dealt with... France is as earnest about the war as we are, and the question should

---

[518] Ibid.
[519] TNA, HO 186/200, Pick to Eady, 9 November 1939.
[520] MOA, Folder 1/D, Blackouts, circa September 1939.

be decided, not merely from a mechanical and official point of view, but as one which affects the life and efficiency and war zeal of the public.[521]

Though the rate of accidents declined as the public began to grow used to the blackout, action was still needed to make the streets safer, and a 20 mph speed limit for urban areas was amongst the most prominent. At a press conference, one of the suggested solutions for adapting to the new law was for drivers to acquaint themselves with the ‗feel‘ of driving at 20 mph – an ambiguous measure at best. Speedometers in cars tended not to be permanently lit owing to the blackout restrictions. Light was instead cast from a dashboard switch, which the driver controlled. Checking speed therefore involved the eyes briefly adjusting to light in the car, then readjusting to the darkness on the road. Given the greater disparity between the two on blacked out roads, the potential for the driver temporarily dazzling themselves was increased. Tory MP Sir William Brass, in a debate on blackout restrictions and road accidents in January 1940, argued that the new restriction would

> not be a public benefit but a public menace and danger. If he is going to keep to the 20-mile limit, as he suggests, he will have to have his speedometer light on in order to see that he is keeping to the 20 miles an hour. When one drives at night, as I do very often, I always have my dash-lamp out because when the light is on I cannot see ahead. If I have to look at the speedometer, in future I shall not be able to see the road. But I shall not do that; I shall drive as I do to-day.[522]

This was still early in the war, and the debates on the blackout at this time were suffused with irritation at its effect on the nation‘s life. Indeed, that debate veered from its intended subject of road accidents to a more general discussion of the blackout, already by then a regular pattern, with the Home Secretary Sir John Anderson stepping in to the debate‘s later stages in order to defend the blackout. The very fact of the war was still remote, and Brass, himself a former pilot in the RAF, could not imagine anything like a bombardment sufficient to justify the restrictions as they were; ‗you cannot bomb accurately at night. If bombing takes place at night, it will be

---

[521] ‗London in the Dark‘, *The Star*, p.4, 24 October 1939.
[522] See Hansard, HC Deb 23 January 1940 vol 356 cc473-548.

225

indiscriminate, in order to create chaos and affect the morale of the people, and I do not believe that is going to happen.'[523] When this did indeed happen, public dissent lessened, and the focus shifted to coping with the restrictions. One of the principal campaigns run to improve pedestrian safety during the war was to promote the wearing of white clothing, or else carrying something white. Yet the public's indifference to carrying around gas masks was mirrored in their disdain for wearing white. After the first campaign over the winter of 1940-41, a Mass Observation study concluded that a figure of just 7% of people heeding the advice was likely to be the national average.

Table 7.4 - Carrying white items in the blackout, London, MO survey 1941[524]

TYPE OF WHITE	of Male %	of Female %	of Both Sexes %
Newspaper	4	2	3
Armband	0	1	0
Clothing	1	2	2
Other things	1	3	2
TOTAL	6	8	7

This is perhaps surprising, given that the Luftwaffe's bombing campaign against Britain had begun in earnest. The report concluded that the advertising campaign had failed, and questioned whether the figures were in fact any different to that for people wearing white in the daytime - though rather frustratingly failed to follow up this idea.[525] Such high indifference was not sustained, though, and the following year saw a ten percent increase in people wearing white. The continued level of bombing alongside a propaganda campaign are the likely factors for this rise – certainly there were no changes in the regulations for the blackout. Again though, this figure indicates an indifference amongst the majority of the population towards their own protection, which to some extent mirrored the carelessness exemplified by the early absence of gas masks in Britain, and of air raid discipline in general.

---

[523] Ibid.
[524] MOA, Box 23/11/P, Wearing white in the blackout, 12 January 1942
[525] MOA, Box 618, Five weeks of white in blackout count, 27 March 1941.

Table 7.5 – Carrying white items in the blackout, London, MO survey 1942[526]

TYPE OF WHITE	of Male %	of Female %	of Both Sexes %
Newspaper	14	7	11
Armband	1	0	0
Clothing	6	6	6
Other things	2	1	1
TOTAL	23	14	18

As the British population grew used to the blackout restrictions during the war, and the amount of vehicle traffic reduced, the level of traffic accidents in the blackout decreased. Indeed, accidents on the roads in London, when measured over the course of the year, actually decreased overall between 1938-1943. The following table is adapted from a report on traffic accidents trends in the blackout, from the records of the Metropolitan Police. It breaks down the level of accidents measured across a whole year rather than just the winter months, and compares the rates of deaths and accidents against a base level drawn from peacetime figures in 1938-1939.[527]

Table 7.6 – Traffic deaths and injuries in Metropolitan Police District in September-August 1939-1943, expressed as a percentage of the number in 1938-1939[528]

Year	Day			Night			Total		
	Deaths	Injuries	Total	Deaths	Injuries	Total	Deaths	Injuries	Total
1938-1939	100.0	100.0	100.0	100.0	100.0	100.0	100.0	100.0	100.0
1939-1940	83.6	66.4	66.7	146.2	83.5	85.0	110.3	72.0	72.5
1940-1941	116.4	71.3	71.9	123.0	58.0	59.5	119.2	67.0	67.9
1941-1942	81.4	51.8	52.2	62.1	42.3	42.7	73.2	48.7	49.2
1942-1943	59.7	43.7	44.0	51.6	29.3	29.8	56.3	39.1	39.4

What the data appears to show is a general decline in accidents over the period. Taken in isolation, deaths on the road rose markedly for the first two winters of the war – the

---

[526] MOA, Box 23/11/P, Wearing white in the blackout, 12 January 1942
[527] Frustratingly, the file from which this data is adapted does not give the numerical values of accidents, only percentage values.
[528] TNA, MEPO 2/6709, 'Road Accidents in the Blackout', est. winter 1943.

latter's daytime increase attributed to Blitz conditions – and then trending downwards

for the third and fourth war winters.

Chart 7.7 - Deaths on roads in Metropolitan Police District, 1938-1943, expressed as percentage of peace-time levels

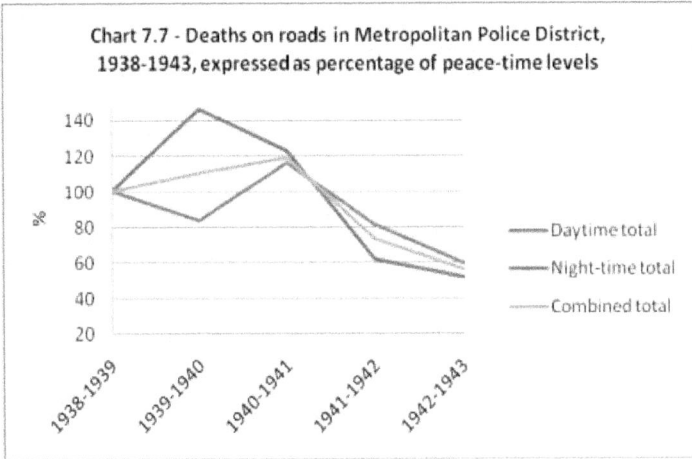

When totalled together, accidents and deaths appear to show a general decline over

the course of the war.

Chart 7.8 - Accidents on roads in Metropolitan Police District, 1938-1943, expressed as percentage of peace-time levels

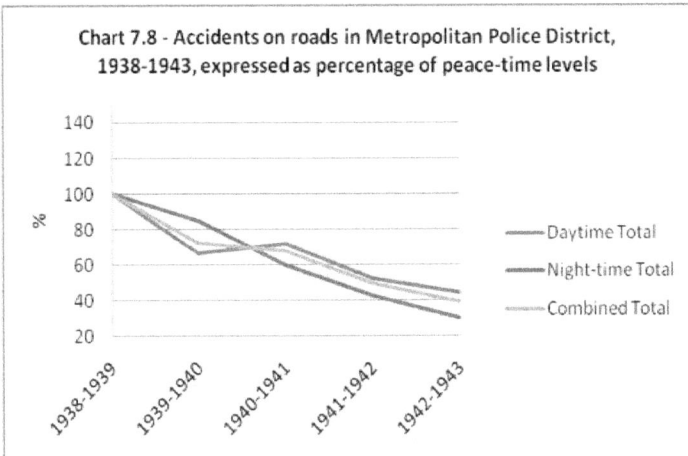

As a result, concern over the level of blackout accidents was downplayed in the report

from which these statistics were taken; they were, according to the report's authors,

‗nothing remarkable' when set in context with overall rates of peacetime accidents. Yet

the figures do mask the extent to which overall traffic decreased over this period, and

no attempt is made to calculate the death toll or rate of accidents according to traffic density. It is not possible to do this retrospectively, as the figures for an adequate analysis are not available. However, a traffic census in London from 1937 and 1942 gives some indication of the large drop in traffic.

Table 7.9 – Traffic census from the Metropolitan Police District, 1937 and 1942[529]

	July 1937	August 1942
Motor Vehicles	605527	307904
Pedal Cycles	177629	100430
All Vehicles	783156	408334

The census registers that traffic density in London was 51% of its level in 1937, a marked decline which is masked in the charts given above. Adjusting the figures to take account of overall traffic density would give a more nuanced picture of overall road safety, and while it seems reasonable to say that the level of accidents did not rise as dramatically as it did during the first blackout winter, their level may indeed have been far higher than is illustrated by simply adding up the accident figures.

In Germany, an SD mood report from 15 December 1939 noted the continuing extraordinary rate of traffic accidents. Assessments of large cities in North Rhein Westphalia indicated that 70-100% of accidents occurred in darkness, with 50-80% attributable to pedestrian fault.[530] Newspapers ran stories throughout the war of repeated incidences of accidents, though any criticism of the blackout itself was absent. Its necessity, so thoroughly incorporated into the Nazi social ethic, was unquestioned by the media. But this did not prevent the usual griping. In November 1941, SD mood reports noted that drivers were still complaining over the restrictions. Permanent use of screens on headlamps made it near impossible to see even in good weather, and there was a wish for the easing of restrictions in certain areas or up to a

---

[529] TNA, MEPO 2/6709, 'Road Accidents in the Blackout', est. winter 1943.
[530] BA Berlin, R58/146, SD Mood report, 15 December 1939.

certain time - 10pm is suggested in the report.[531] The weight of the restrictions was intended to fall equally across all citizens, no matter what their status, and even the frustrations of high ranking party members were sometimes ignored by police officials. A case found within the Bavarian State archives illustrates the complex relationship between the authority of the party and the authority of the police here.

On the night of 2 October 1939, SS brigadier Hans Saupert and his driver were cautioned for insufficiently blacking out the vehicle they were travelling in. What might have passed as an ordinary telling off was instead made far worse by the behaviour of the brigadier. In the initial report filed the incident went as follows. The officer, on seeing an insufficiently darkened car driving along Hans-Mielich-Straße in the centre of Munich, stopped the vehicle and spoke to the driver about correcting it. At this, a passenger emerged from the vehicle and asked the officer, in a heightened tone of voice, to take his seat and examine from inside the car whether it was indeed possible to drive with less light. When the officer declined, he was told 'If you knew who I was you wouldn't question me.' When the officer asked for the car's papers, he was told 'The papers are none of your business. You can write down the licence number.' Only on a second request were the papers shown by the driver, which indicated that the car was being used by the Nazi party. The report was subsequently sent on to the party by the police with the intention of advising the driver and his passenger to keep to the blackout regulations.[532] Subsequent representations made by the brigadier to the police were indignant, angry at both the tone of the officer and rejecting the idea that he threatened the officer with his position in the party. In his words:

> I tried again to explain to the officer that driving in almost total darkness
> extremely dangerous firstly for pedestrians, and secondly for the occupants of

---

[531] BA Berlin, R58/166, SD Mood report, 10 November 1941.
[532] BayHStA, Minn 87016, memorandum from Polizeipräsidium München to Reichsleitung NSDAP, 4 October 1939.

the vehicle. The officer said that it was nothing to do with him, and that the car had to be, like he had said, blacked out.[533]

In fact, he said, the car had no more than a minute before been checked by another officer who had not commented on the car's blackout. This was not entirely true, for though the car had indeed been stopped by another officer – in that instance for speeding at 40 km/h in a 15 km/h zone – the officer who had stopped them had remarked on the headlamp's mask to the driver, which was beginning to pull away and show more light. This was not fixed immediately, and hence at the next stop – little over 700m away – the second officer stopped the car again. Some understanding also seemed to exist over the kind of light being shown. Under the vehicle lighting scheme, motor vehicles were allowed to use full beam outside areas designated under the German traffic regulations as ‚geschlossene ortschaften', a term that generally refers to areas of the road system distant from housing. As the car was in the centre of the city, this was not allowed, and such was the light cast from the headlamps that the officer assumed the driver to have switched on his headlamps at full beam. Though this was discounted in the final report on the matter from the Ministry of the Interior, it did not negate the failure of the driver and passenger, both equally liable for securing the car's blackout, to do so properly. The brigadier's sniffy rejoinder that he resented being lectured on driving regulations by men who probably had no car or licence to drive was answered with confirmation that the officer who had cautioned him had been qualified since 1927.[534] This case perfectly illustrates the extent to which the aggravations of the blackout were levelled across all points of authority, and all groups of citizens. Poorly blacked out vehicles were as contentious as poorly blacked out buildings, and where these were used by people of authority even more so. As seen in earlier chapters, equality in adherence to the blackout regulations was important to its legitimacy. However, in Britain, as with the altered restrictions for industry, alternate schemes existed for non-civilian traffic. Restrictions on the type of lighting allowed by road

---

[533] Ibid. Letter from Saupert to Eberstien, 17 October 1939.
[534] Ibid., letter from Munich Police Headquarters to Bavarian Ministry of the Interior, 4 December 1939.

vehicles were therefore not always consistent, and could lead to accidents. Military vehicles were assigned a separate scheme of lighting, designed for lighting convoys during exercises and manoeuvres. The following case illustrates the consequences this could have.

On the evening of 12 November 1941, a lorry was being driven through southwest London by a soldier in the Scots Guards. It was, the record notes, 'a dark night with a mist'. As the lorry reached the top of a hill its engine failed, and when the driver could not restart the engine he let it coast down in attempt to get a rolling start. This also failed, and the lorry came to a stop. The driver left the vehicle parked close to the kerb, and walked to a telephone box to call for assistance. By the time he returned, two accidents, one fatal, had been caused by the stationary lorry. The first accident involved a motorcyclist, who later died of his injuries. The second accident occurred within ten minutes of the first, when a cyclist collided with the vehicle. When the matter came to court arguments centred on how well the lorry had been lit from its rear lights. When police surveyed the scene after both accidents, they found that the lorry did have its rear light on, though it was visible only from a distance of about 30 yards. Both accidents had been caused by the driver of the vehicle not seeing the stationary lorry until it was too late. In court, it was argued that the lorry had not been using the regulation aperture of one inch, and the defence acknowledged that this was the case, with the rear lights instead using a 3/8 aperture to obscure the light. Here the matter became more complicated. The defence contended that vehicles in military service were not bound to the civilian regulations laid down in the Lighting (Restrictions) Order 1940, but instead were subject to the regulations issued by the Army council, which stipulated a smaller aperture. And this was true; service vehicles at the time were carrying reduced lighting in comparison with civilian vehicles due to a separate system of light restriction. The law had been interpreted to give an exemption to service vehicles from civilian standards, despite their using public roads. When the case was put forward on appeal to the Law Officers, they were asked whether this was in fact legal. Their reply was ambivalent, advising only that it could not be assumed that the lighting restrictions, though clearly intended to exempt military vehicles, actually did so according to how it was written. The Law Officers also commented on the fact that the Army Council restrictions were designated as not to be published.' In effect, this meant that civilian drivers were not aware that there was traffic on the road carrying a different lighting standard. Were service vehicles to show more light under their own regulations, this would not have been a problem. But where the lighting was less, it was the opinion of the law officers that this was undesirable.[535] What this case shows is that despite the militarisation of public life there remained a discrepancy between the military infrastructure and the civilian, which in this particular instance contributed to the danger on the roads. Why the Army decided upon an even more restricted lighting scheme is not entirely clear from the records, but exemptions issued in September 1930 and December 1940 under the Road Transport Lighting Act 1927 may provide an answer. The wording of the exemptions states that army vehicles are exempted while being used on manoeuvres' and while meeting invasion or anticipated invasion or on special exercises', respectively. While neither was deemed to cover the lorry in this case, their intent seems to imply that the Army required a different standard to reduce their appearance not only from the air, but from the ground as well.

Maintaining this balance gave the authorities some difficulties. A happy medium had to be found between the secrecy necessary for the military to organise and conceal itself, while allowing military traffic to mix with civilian road users and potentially causing a hazard, as demonstrated in this case. By the end of the war, when the threat of invasion had long disappeared and Allied forces were marching further into occupied Europe, the restrictions were becoming a hindrance to the movement of military traffic. Most particularly, it was the American forces who were arguing for its removal. On 19

---

[535] TNA, LO 3/1295, account of Crook vs. Luther, 18 March 1943.

December 1944, the War Cabinet considered a request from American Headquarters for the complete relaxation on headlight restrictions over the winter period. Their arrival in the country had already generated complaints over the amount of light showed by their vehicles. Removing the restrictions on vehicle lighting was, they argued, of immediate operational necessity. Reinforcements from Britain to the European theatre were prepared and despatched to the continent according to a tight timetable. The lighting restrictions, coupled with the conditions of winter, which always exacerbated the blackout's effects, were causing delays in supplying reinforcements at the front, and compromising the war effort. Their request was supported by the War Office, who had similar difficulties. But this was not a cut and dried case, and the war cabinet again had to balance military necessity against the impact the lessening of restrictions would have on civilian traffic. Though the Air Ministry and the Admiralty were not happy at the prospect of vehicles casting more light, their objections were held in check by the need to move men and materials through the country and on to the continent at a greater pace. But running different standards of lighting had the potential for causing more accidents, not least from dazzled drivers and pedestrians on unlit roads. The lighting restrictions impinged on the British end of the war effort, and it was already assumed that any relaxation afforded would be requested and granted to British departments pursuing vital war work. And were American forces to be allowed special favour, it was feared it would exacerbate the existing public discontent at the lights already shown by American vehicles, and which had already drawn questions within the Commons.[536]

So when the relaxations were made – announced on 27 December 1944 – it was extended towards all vehicles, civilian or military, British or American. When relayed through the press, the announcement was made with the following caveat: _The relaxations should not be taken as implying that all risk of assisting the enemy by the use of all full headlamps has disappeared, but the risk is outweighed by the operational

[536] TNA, PREM 4/37/12, War Cabinet memorandum _Motor Vehicle Lighting', 19 December 1944.

need.'[537] Though the AA and the RAC were both arguing for an improvement in vehicle lighting at this time, it was the progress of the war itself that provided the impetus for the gradual relaxation of the blackout on the streets and, eventually, homes.[538]

Conclusion

The blackout acted as a brake on the wartime economies of Britain and Germany. Because of this, while in the civilian sphere the blackout was indeed total, the restrictions for industry and transport were graded according to the needs of wartime production. The domestic life of both populations was secondary to wartime production, and this preference underscored the coerciveness of the blackout system. The blackout also made working conditions far more difficult, turning poorly prepared industrial premises into light-locked but stuffy, poorly ventilated and sometimes more dangerous places to work. The restrictions of the blackout were far more flexible for industry than they were for civilians, and the permissions for industry served to underscore the coerciveness of the civilian system. The needs of the war economy to provide material for the front over-rode the universal restrictions; operational necessity' was the key to what had to stay dark, and what could afford to be lit more brightly. The differences in how the systems were implemented in Britain and Germany show again that though the German system of planning before the war was more thorough on paper, it nevertheless suffered the same teething problems and systemic flaws over the course of the war as those seen in Britain. Both countries were fortunate in having the months of the Phoney War to fix their specifications and cajole industry into securing their property for the blackout. Even then, installing systems that were easy to use for large premises on a daily basis was expensive and time-consuming. The drag on production that poorly installed blackout systems had, whether in how navigable premises were in darkness, or whether they were well ventilated and lit, was a

---

[537] 'Headlamps on Motor-vehicles', The Times, 27 December 1944, p.8.
[538] 'Motorists and Street Lighting', The Times, 19 December 1944, p.2.

substantial problem that has hitherto received little attention in the literature of the home fronts of either country.

Chapter Eight - Conclusion

This thesis has explored the blackout in Britain and Germany during the Second World War. While the blackout has always been present in histories of the home front and bombing, its limited presence in those studies was at odds with the extent to which the blackout affected civil society during the war years. The blackout showed how the technology of war could alter the relationship between the state and the citizen, and it formed one of the most visible manifestations of the totality of modern war. The blackout's social obligations were intrusive and coercive, and embedded within both countries a system of behaviour that could reify the construction of a unified home front through its focus on community obligation over the individual, and also undermine the wartime community by opening up new wartime spaces of transgression, danger, and tension. It is therefore the contention of this thesis that the blackout requires greater consideration in histories of the home front than previous work on the home front has generally allowed for. This research demonstrates that the blackout was more than simply a persistent inconvenience for the public, but an aspect of the war that had a significant impact on British and German home fronts.

Post-war blackouts, and the implications of this research

Seven years after the Second World War had finished, in the period between the invention of the atomic bomb and inter-continental missile technology, the chiefs of staff in Britain recommended a blackout policy in the event of nuclear war. This, though, would be one that was nominally less restrictive than that of the previous war, effecting a disruption of the pattern of light rather than total obscuration. Their report makes for an interesting post-war analysis of the blackout's effectiveness. Claims that radar guidance made the blackout obsolete were, at this stage at least, unfounded. Blind-bombing through radar guidance – the H2S system – was estimated to deliver an accuracy of about one mile. Visual targeting, by contrast, was estimated to deliver an accuracy of between a quarter and half a mile. With the effectiveness of early nuclear bombs dependent on the proximity to their target – the report estimates 100% destruction with a direct hit, 5% destruction at a mile's distance – the blackout's usefulness was evident. The report concluded, rather ominously, that:

> If the enemy is prepared to use atom bombs in large numbers the influence of these considerations would be less important. But while the number available to the enemy is limited, or if (as may well be the case) a war will be won by the side which can resist atom bomb attack the longer, then it is important to take every measure which can reduce the effectiveness of the attack. We consider that black-out is such a measure.[539]

There was swift recognition that planning had to be arranged quickly. Trial flights were arranged over cities whose external lighting would be distorted to disrupt visual recognition. Though it was assumed that any trial would happen without the public really noticing, the Home Secretary nevertheless notified his intention to make the trials public.[540] This shows a recognition of past mistakes. Indeed, the report itself begins with the words that Britain at the start of World War Two was _dangerously unprepared', and that _a blackout cannot be introduced at short notice'.[541] The press reported on the ongoing development of civil defence. *The Times* reported in 1951 that blackout curtains would be fireproofed against heat flash from the bombs.[542] But planning for the blackout dissipated over the course of the fifties. No substantive reference to blackout planning appears after this period; it may be that the increasing size of nuclear weaponry, coupled with the development of ballistic missile technology, finally made the blackout redundant for civil defence planning. The Sandys Defence White Paper of

---

[539] TNA, PREM 11/367, Chiefs of Staff memorandum on blackout policy, 16 April 1952.
[540] TNA, PREM 11/367, RJS to Oates, 24 November 1953.
[541] TNA, PREM 11/367, Chiefs of Staff memorandum on blackout policy, 16 April 1952.
[542] 'Role of Civil Defence: II - Future Needs and Present Plans', *The Times*, 24 August 1951, p.5.

1957 committed Britain to a system of nuclear deterrence, though had little to say on how the country would defend itself in the event of an attack.[543]

In his survey of post war Europe, Tony Judt claimed that, over the period from 1953 to 1963, war was for most West Europeans ‚unthinkable', and that ‚in contrast with the fraught debates over disarmament if the 1920s and early ‚30s, the nuclear question in Europe did not move people much. It was too abstract.'[544] The signing of the Test Ban Treaty in 1963 neutered the Campaign for Nuclear Disarmament and its allied movements in Europe, with anxiety over the bomb not resurfacing until the tension of 1979-1985, when once again the spectre of nuclear war became greater. Behind this brief narrative summary lies a wealth of detail with great potential for incorporation into a study of the social aspect of civil defence over the period. The bombs dropped on Hiroshima and Nagasaki announced the beginning of a new kind of bombing that really could put Western society in jeopardy. The apocalyptic fantasies of the inter-war period were now, more than ever, approaching prophecy. Bombing in the manner of the Second World War's European theatre would not be seen again - though Cambodia would later suffer under tonnages even exceeding what Europe saw. However, the threat from the air in Europe is a narrative that begins with the advent of flight, and ends with the collapse of the Soviet Union. Throughout this period, the citizens of Europe were conscious that the sovereignty of their airspace was compromised, and lived with the threat of catastrophic bombardment. As the century wore on, this threat was modified and made more certain by the advent of nuclear bomb and missile technology. The threat may have altered its form, but the existential fear remained the same. A history that traced how this manifested itself over the course of the 20th century in Europe would be a fruitful avenue along which to develop the research in this thesis.

---

[543] On this see Matthew Grant, 'Home Defence and the Sandys Defence White Paper, 1957', *Journal of Strategic Studies*, 31/6 (2008).
[544] Tony Judt, *Postwar* (London: William Heinemann, 2005), pp.255-256.

But though this may have been the case in Britain, blackouts remained a feature of war until very recently. The last use of the blackout as understood in this research appears to have been in the Iran-Iraq war – certainly the 20th century's last true conventional war – where nightly blackouts against raids by enemy aircraft again provided some small measure of protection. The civilian experience bears similarities to those of European cities forty years earlier; the Iranian poet Ghaysar Aminpour wrote of the raids during the war:

> The siren never ends its moaning
> Over corpses that didn't finish their night's sleep,
> Where bat-like jets which hate the light
> Bomb the cracks in our blind blackout curtains...
> We can't even trust the stars in case they are spies,
> We wouldn't be surprised if the moon blows up...[545]

More recently, with the advancing technology of aerial ordnance, the denial of light has become a war aim rather than a measure of defence. Graphite bombs released through remotely targeted missiles were used during the first Gulf War and the NATO campaign in Serbia to disrupt electricity supplies. At one point in the Serbian war 85% of the country was without power. Commenting on this, a NATO spokesman stated that The fact that the lights went across 70 percent of the country, I think, shows that NATO has its finger on the light switch in Yugoslavia now, and we can turn the power off whenever we need to and whenever we want to.'[546] Technology has now made the blackout redundant; augmented vision and the advanced spatial mapping of modern warfare makes it very unlikely therefore that any return to the blackouts Europe experienced during the war will be seen again.

---

[545] Robert Fisk, *The Great War for Civilization* (London: Harper Perennial, 2006), p.353.
[546] William M. Arkin, 'Operation Allied Force: "The Most Precise Application of Air Power in History"', in A. J. Bacevich & Eliot A. Cohen (ed.), *War Over Kosovo: Politics and Strategy in a Global Age* (New York: Columbia University Press, 2001), pp.1-37, p.18.

This research has provided far more detail on the blackout where previous research has in general failed to give it more than momentary or superficial attention. Indeed, there are aspects of the blackout which have until now gone almost entirely unnoticed in histories of the Second World War. The impact of the blackout on the economy is, in particular, a strange omission, and it suggests that there is room for a fuller examination of the practical effects air warfare and civil defence had on industrial mobilization in both countries. This study has also debunked some of the myths of the blackout which continue to circulate, most particularly over its actual usefulness. Michael Foot, in his entry on the European blackout in the *Oxford Companion to World War II*, states that 'no one seems to have consulted the air authorities about whether the blackout was really necessary.'[547] This study shows that this is clearly false. Indeed, it was *because* of the advice of the Air Ministry that the blackout in Britain lasted throughout the entire war largely unaltered. Foot's error is symptomatic of the general lack of attention given to the blackout in the existing literature.

There is also perhaps a sense that comparing two very different countries in this period is rather like the apple and orange problem; are they not, in the end, entirely different? What can be learned by comparing either that could not be learned in greater detail, and with perhaps more proximity to the sources, through a study based in one nation alone? This is where this thesis is most ambitious. It has attempted to describe the effect of the blackout over two separate nations by describing the development of airmindedness within each as a consequence of the invention of powered flight, and as a corollary to both nation's approaching the high modernity of the technologic state. This transnational process, with its roots across many developed nations at the turn of the century, forms the discursive context within which civil defence is explained and understood for the civilian population. This research has contributed to the study of the

---

[547] Michael Foot Ian Dear, *The Oxford Companion to World War II* (Oxford: Oxford University Press, 2001), p.105.

social history of the home front and the social, political and economic effects of the blackout. In doing so, it has fore-grounded the *civil* in civil defence. It has highlighted that there is an aspect to organising national defence that must involve society and more importantly, have a degree of legitimacy conferred by it. The blackout, as the most social' form of civil defence, is one of the most appropriate aspects of national defence to examine this by, in that it involved drastic alterations of private and public space, and of behaviour.

Both Germany and Britain were bound together as nations at the forefront of modernity. What is perhaps most interesting is the similarity of the language these two states mobilised in support of the blackout, and of ARP in general, though certainly its pitch was heightened in Germany. Robert Mackay, responding to a review of his book *Half the Battle. Civilian Morale in Britain during the Second World War,* noted that a comparative approach to examining the character of the British and German home fronts might produce an explanation owing more to reflections on the nature of *homo sapiens* than on *homo Britannicus* or *homo Germanicus.*'[548] To a great extent, this is borne out in this study, and provides a necessary corrective to accounts that assume a more inward looking exceptionalism.

Indeed, there may in fact be a case that the blackout's effectiveness has more to do with the character of Britain and Germany's development as modern nations. Ulrich Beck, one of the leading thinkers on risk and modernity, examines in his work:

> the risks and consequences of modernization, which are realized in the irreversible endangering of human, plant and animal life. Unlike operational and professional risks in the 19th and the first half of the 20th centuries, these risks of modernization cannot be limited locally or in terms of their group specificities. Rather they represent a globalizing tendency, which encroaches on the spheres of production and reproduction while also crossing national boundaries. These

---

[548] R. Mackay, Response to Review no. 332, *Reviews in History,*
http://www.history.ac.uk/reviews/review/332/response [accessed 10 October 2010]

risks and dangers pose a potential global threat which is supra-national and not class-specific.[549]

This research poses interesting questions about the ability of the state to mobilise itself in preparation for existential threats. Current debates on the impact of climate change on western and global civilization have a surprising resonance with the debates on the blackout and civil defence. There are of course differences; while the sometimes all-or-nothing apocalyptic language of climate change is no less shrill than the pre-war speculation on bombing, the debate itself is rather more ambiguous. No one argued over the existence of bombs and their effects. If there is a fault within the apparent discontinuity of research on risk in post-war society, it is in the generally ignored threads of technologic modernity that begin in the early half of the 20th century, and which to a certain extent pre-empt the concerns of the post-war decades. As an example of the state's interference in the life of the nation the blackout has had few parallels in this regard, either during the war or in our present time. This research therefore identifies a potential bridge in the impact of technology on the politics of space. Responses to risk are engendered through frameworks of state administration and discourses of risk associated with the features of modernity. By extension, the blackout also formed a framework of home front life that was arguably as important as government propaganda in constructing a unified home front, and a relatively high level of adherence. This was formed both directly and indirectly. The focus on the blackout's universality in both countries was as much a political as well as practical consideration. The general *practical* principle of the blackout had to be adhered to in order to secure the nation from night-time bombing raids. But the *political* principle of universality formed a tight thread that bound the people under the blackout to each other, and the state to the people. Thus the only reasons for relaxing the blackout were economic, attached to the prosecution of the war.

---

[549] Ulrich Beck, 'On The Way To The Industrial Risk-Society? Outline Of An Argument', *Thesis Eleven*, 23/1 (1989), p.88.

Civil defence against the threat from bombing in Europe provides a wealth of material with which to reconsider the literature on risk and modernity. It is perhaps a general feature of modernity that what is rationally good for the individual and the community, is sometimes deferred in preference for what is most immediately convenient. It is startling that even at the height of the bombing campaign in Britain, some people would still watch it from the streets, and that the majority of British pedestrians, when exhorted to simply wear something white in the blackout for the benefit of traffic and their own safety, comfortably chose not to bother. To return to Beck's argument, aviation was perhaps the first of the supra-national vectors of modernization, bringing with it behaviours associated with the risk society of high modernity.[550] The aerial threat is an ideal topic for reintegrating the modernity of the first half of the 20th century with the post-war world.

The fact that the blackout was most comprehensively achieved in Britain and Germany speaks to both the intensity of the bombing in these countries, their technologically advanced infrastructure and economies, and the traditions of authority and administration already existing in them. The Italian blackout was by contrast far less well attended to by the population, despite the severity of the American and British air raids.[551] A fascist system of government was no guarantee of a good blackout. Baldoli and Fincardi write that:

> From the very first bombing operations in Italy, RAF planes crossing the Alps were welcomed by the sight of Milan and Genoa fully illuminated. Non-compliance with the blackout is evident not only from the prefects' letters, but also from many newspaper articles and from the reports in the files of the interior ministry and the air ministry citing problems of public order. In September 1941, Il Popolo d'Italia complained about the indiscipline of most citizens in Milan in ignoring the blackout. Similar news came from other newspapers; for example, Il Resto del Carlino denounced the fact that in

---

[550] Ulrich Beck, *Risk Society: Towards a New Modernity* (London: Sage, 1992), p.76.
[551] The death of Italian civilians that died as a result of the British and American bombing campaign is estimated at 60,000, comparable with British civilian losses.

Bologna houses were brightly lit and cars and bicycles drove with full lights. The reason for such disregard, the journalist thought, was a misplaced optimism.[552]

We might wonder at what optimism could be found amidst the drone of enemy bombers. What is clear is that the Italian state lacked what had been well mobilised in Britain and Germany; a discourse that engendered adherence, coupled to an administrative system that maintained it.

---

[552] Claudia Baldoli, 'Italian Society under Anglo-American bombs: Propaganda, Experience, and Legend, 1940-1945', p.1026.

www.ingramcontent.com/pod-product-compliance
Ingram Content Group UK Ltd.
Pitfield, Milton Keynes, MK11 3LW, UK
UKHW021436080825
7302UKWH00026B/638

9 787237 143120